Their Manners Noted

"Wand'ring from clime to clime, observant strayed,
Their manners noted, and their states surveyed."

Homer, Odyssey Bk.i, l.5. (Pope tr.)

Their Manners Noted

Michael Arnold

HERONHILL BOOKS
PETERSFIELD HAMPSHIRE

HERONHILL BOOKS
1, MONTAGUE GARDENS,
PETERSFIELD
HAMPSHIRE GU31 4DT

This edition published in the UK in 2005

ISBN 10 : 0-9548232-1-4

ISBN 13 : 978-095482321-4

Printed and bound in Great Britain by RPM PRINT & DESIGN

Produced and printed by members of
THE GUILD OF MASTER CRAFTSMEN

Book design and setting by Cecil Smith
Typeset in Caxton

RPM PRINT & DESIGN
2 - 3 Spur Road, Quarry Lane, Chichester, West Sussex PO19 8PR
Telephone: 01243 787 077   Fax: 01243 780 012
e-mail: sales@rpm-repro.co.uk   website: www.rpm-repro.co.uk

For my
beloved wife Wendy,
to whom I owe
fifty years of
happiness

Also by Michael Arnold:

A Game with Dice

www.heronhillbooks.com

Contents

Introduction

The office door burst open and slammed against the wall. Startled, I looked up from my desk, to see Paloma, my diminutive secretary, being thrust aside by a burly forearm as Don Pablo stormed in, purple with rage. He was waving a large revolver, which he clutched in his right hand.

In 1970, Honduras, in Central America, was as close to being the Wild West as was possible in that century. I was General Manager of the Shell Company there, and had adapted, mostly, to the very different culture and customs, coming, as I did, from two years in the Sudan.

One of the main characteristics of my latest home was that everyone had at least one gun and usually more than one. I had three: one at home, one in the car and one in the office. These were not unnecessary toys; they were there for protection.

Don Pablo advanced towards my desk, with Paloma, vainly clinging to his left arm, fluttering behind him like an agitated flag. He pointed the revolver at me.

"I am going to kill you," he announced in a hoarse voice. "I am going to kill you right now!"

Don Pablo was well known to me. He owned a large petrol station in the rugged, extreme north-east of Honduras, near the border with Nicaragua. It was a difficult place to get to, given the inadequacy of the so-called roads, but I had sometimes flown there in a small airplane, to visit and make sure all was in order. His station was supplied from our depot in San Pedro Sula, the industrial capital of the country near the north west coast of the Atlantic, where I lived.

I was now standing up and trying to calm him. "Sit down, sit down, Don Pablo," I said soothingly. "Sit down and have a cup of coffee; you will feel better."

"I feel fine," he growled, "but I will feel better when you are dead."

I racked my brains. Why this sudden irruption and fury? What had happened? I could think of nothing.

"You have dishonored my name and made me look a fool," he growled again. "You have made me a laughing stock! You have ruined my business!" He took another step as I motioned for Paloma to let him go. She did so and I indicated with my head that she should leave us.

"What are you talking about?" I asked, as calmly as I could. "How have I done all these things?"

He glared at me with eyes that were now bloodshot and glittering with rage. "You have stopped my supplies and everyone in Lempira is laughing at me."

Now I understood. One of Don Pablo's well known characteristics was his disinclination to pay his bills. The trip by road tanker to replenish his station was a long one, taking several days over rugged and hazardous terrain. He had recently had three loads of mixed products and had not paid for any. I was somewhat irritated by this and, in spite of my Sales Manager's attempts to dissuade me, had instructed the Operations Department not to deliver any more until payment was made.

Don Pablo had, presumably, run dry and this was the cause of his wrath. He must have been assailed by his customers, not least the fishing boats he supplied.

My visitor continued to wave his revolver and make threatening noises. I sat down and looked at him then, very slowly and deliberately, opened the top drawer of my desk. I paused, and took out my own pistol, a 9mm Beretta automatic. This I deliberately and gently laid on the desk in front of me.

Don Pablo stopped growling and looked at it. He then leaned forward and examined it more closely, then looked at his revolver. His eyebrows rose.

"What is that?" he enquired, in a belligerent tone. "What is the caliber?"

"It is a 9mm," I replied. "A Beretta."

"Mine is a .32," he said, looking at it. "Yours is bigger." I nodded.

He sighed and also nodded his head. He then sat down opposite me and laid his own revolver on the table. "What did you say about coffee?" he asked, in a mollified tone.

I got up and went to the door. "Doña Paloma," I said. "Would you be so kind as to bring us two cups of coffee, please?" She looked at me in astonishment. "You don't want me to call the police?" she asked. "He looked mad."

"No, thank you," I said. "It was all a big misunderstanding. Everything is just fine."

I went back and sat down again. Don Pablo had picked up my pistol and was examining it closely. "Is it any good?" he asked.

We then had a longish conversation about the relative merits of revolvers and automatic pistols, calibers and so forth. We drank our coffee in friendly camaraderie and he relaxed completely.

"Now then, Don Pablo," I finally said. "What about it?"

He sighed deeply. "No more credit?" he asked piteously. He was a very wealthy man.

"No," I said firmly. "No cash, no product."

He sighed again and tilted his sombrero back on his head. "Ah well," he said. "You are a hard man, Don Miguel." He paused and looked at the weapons again. He scratched his chin, bristly with a two day stubble. "Mmmmm," he mused, "9mm against .32." He paused again, then reached into the back pocket of his dirty jeans, stretched tight over his burly frame, and produced a rather grubby cheque book. He filled in the required amount for the full sum owing and gave me the cheque. I thanked him, and quietly put my pistol back in the drawer, while he tucked his revolver into his straining waistband.

We parted amicably, as the friends we were, and I never again had any trouble in getting him to pay his bills promptly. I decided that guns had their uses, not necessarily lethal.

But that was how business was done, in those days, in Honduras.

CHAPTER ONE

Cambridge

The engine spluttered, shuddered and died. I sat astride my
motorcycle at the entrance to Jesus College, Cambridge as the
cold rain fell from a grey sky. I had arrived. It was late 1952 and
I was twenty years old.

It had been a long road: childhood in Poland, school in
Baghdad, Egypt and finally in England. Learning languages,
changing names and nationality. Now here I was, ready to take
up my County Scholarship at Jesus, after twenty months in the
Army. I felt grown-up – not nervous but excited.

The College is well set back from the street, some 60 yards.
The massive front doors are at the end of a long narrow passage
with high walls on each side. It is called the Chimney.

I left my motorcycle at the kerb, together with my guitar case
and military kitbag which contained all my worldly possessions,
and went up the Chimney. One could leave things on the street
in those days.

The Chimney was cluttered with dozens of bicycles leaning
against the walls. They were all identical, battered, with a
basket on the front, and a number, preceded by the letter J on the
mudguard. These were, I was to find out, almost the only means
of undergraduate locomotion throughout the town.

Just beyond the small wicket gate in the huge, ancient doors,
was the room occupied by the College porters, the guards,
friends and disciplinarians of the College.The Head Porter, a
dignified and beautifully dressed person was there. I

remembered him from my brief visits two years previously, to sit the scholarship exams. His name, I recalled, was Captain Austin.

He leaned out of his little window and looked at me. I was dressed in my fur-lined leather flying jacket and trousers, with fur-lined flying boots and leather gauntlets. I had purchased them from an Army friend, some months earlier, for the princely sum of four pounds. They made winter riding much more comfortable.

"Hello, Mr. Arnold," said the Captain, raising his eyebrows. "Just flown in for the start of Term, have we?" I was astonished; he remembered me. I found out later that he remembered everybody, from years and years back.

"Oh no, Captain Austin," I replied, "I have come on my motorcycle and it is almost winter, you know..."

"Well, you are in good time. Here is your envelope, which will tell you all you need to know. Hall is at 6.30pm and you are expected to attend." He handed me a bulging envelope. I moved back, since others were beginning to gather.

The envelope contained many papers: notes about College functions, rules, lodgings, societies to join, events to attend, and a sheet with appointments for the next day with my two College Tutors, one a Director of Studies who would supervise academic work and discuss any problems related to study for the degree. The other was the Domestic Tutor who was responsible for personal matters, discipline, lodgings and my general well-being as a student.

A Cambridge College was like a family. At the time, Jesus had about 250 students and we all more or less knew each other, meeting almost every day in Hall for our supper. We also got to know the Fellows, many of them eminent scholars, and the staff in general. The system, with its intense chauvinism *vis-à-vis* other Colleges, bonded us together and made our lives very much more comfortable than I imagine they are in Universities with a campus involving literally thousands of students.

One of the papers instructed me to go to my appointed lodgings for my first year. This was in a house in Jesus Lane, opposite the College, which owned a long terrace of Victorian double-fronted dwellings.

I crossed the road, with my kitbag and guitar, to 50 Jesus Lane. I knocked and after a short time the door was opened by a large, grizzled lady in her sixties, in an apron, with her grey hair bound up in a flowery kerchief.

"Yes?" she said, looking me up and down with fierce blue eyes.

"My name is Arnold. I am told that this is to be my lodging this year."

"Oh yes," she said and stood back. "Come in. I was told you would be arriving. Put your things on the floor and I will show you your room and tell you the rules. You have to follow them, you know, or I have to report you to the College." She turned and went into a room on the left of a gloomy corridor. I followed.

The room was quite large and contained some dingy furniture, including a battered desk. The window onto the street was covered with grubby net curtains and there was a gas fire, with a box for coins to pay for the gas and an attached small gas-ring. This, together with a little, chilly bedroom in the eaves (which contained a narrow bed, a chest of drawers and a small table with a basin and ewer of cold water), would be my home for the next nine months.

The landlady, Miss Germany by name, then expounded to me on the many sins and shortcomings of undergraduates and gave me a set of rules. These included the injunctions to be in by 10 pm, not to entertain girls without notice, not to cook – with the possible exception of toasting bread or   crumpets in front of the gas fire (a toasting fork had helpfully been left by a former inhabitant) or a small pan of baked beans on the ring – and to hand in the laundry on Fridays. Also, to leave the sole bathroom as I found it.

I soon organised my meagre possessions and sat down in the elderly armchair, to read the papers in my envelope.

These introduced me to Cambridge life. There were official documents listing College rules, meal times and when it was mandatory to wear the undergraduate gown: principally for Hall meals, lectures and supervisions, and outdoors after dusk. There was a message from my Director of Studies, Dr. Rossiter (a famous Shakespeare scholar whom I had met on my Scholarship attempt visit to Jesus) telling me who would be my Supervisor. This personage, a post-graduate student, I would visit every week with some two or three other students to discuss the weekly essays we had to write for him.

There was a time-table of lectures for my English Tripos. These, for Arts degrees, were wholly voluntary and no check was kept on how many one attended. In Science degrees it was rather different and more disciplined. As it was, the student decided which lectures (and, more importantly, lecturers) were of interest and value, and attended those.

There were many leaflets from innumerable student organisations and clubs, covering every subject under the sun, offering various inducements to new recruits.

All in all there was a great deal to digest.

Between Army and Cambridge, I had been able briefly to visit my Mother and Stepfather, who were in England for a time, between contracts in China and New York. My Stepfather Ronnie Arnold was a senior executive in BP (or the Anglo-Iranian Oil Company as it was then known) and my parents lived mostly abroad.

In Chipstead, Surrey, where they had a house, we had a Discussion. My Stepfather always had such Discussions when something important had to be considered. He had a degree from King's College, in Cambridge, in the twenties, and wished to give me his views on what should be my proper behaviour and conduct at the University, though he regarded Jesus as a somewhat inferior college.

"I suggest you don't try for a First," he said, to my astonishment. Since he had always emphasised high achievement, this was a staggering statement. "You must realise that your time at Cambridge will probably be the only time in your life when you will be surrounded by exceptional people and also have the leisure to learn from them and form lasting friendships."

He paused and paced up and down, frowning. Mother sat in a corner and looked at him adoringly.

"You must take full advantage of your opportunities. A good Second will be quite satisfactory. Develop your interests and do some sport, but not in a way which will limit your other activities. Of course, you will not have much money, so you must be careful." He paced up and down some more. "Your fees, food and living essentials will be paid by your Scholarship. Your Mother and I, with the responsibilities we have towards my first wife and the two other children, cannot afford to give you very much extra. But you shall have eight pounds a term, that is a pound a week, to spend as you please. Naturally, this will have to cover your clothes, transport and amusements. I am sure you will manage."

I blinked. This was rather less than I had been earning in the Army and I had no other income. The future began to look somewhat bleak.

Back at 50 Jesus Lane, there was a slamming of doors and a rushing noise. My door banged open and a red-haired youth poked his head into my room.

"I am Campbell," the face said in a strong Scots accent. "I am next door. Very busy. Talk later. Third year. Engineering."

The face vanished.

I found out later that Scotty Campbell, one of the two undergraduates who shared my 'digs' that year, was a sort of invisible man. His interests and activities were wholly limited to studying, eating, sleeping and movement between them. He disliked social contacts and our communications were limited to borrowing some matches, a little milk and occasionally a crumpet.

The other occupant was quite at the other end of the spectrum. He was a junior scion of an obscure Lord and was thus the Honourable Ewart Fortescue-Sinclair. His interests in Cambridge were almost wholly social: he was a member of the Pitt Club (an exclusive clique of moneyed, fashionable offspring of the County Set and blue blood high society). They dressed in identical clothes, spoke with a drawl, gambled, played merry pranks on each other, 'studied' Estate Management and did no work at all.

Ewart – or Wart, as he was known – was charming, kind, generous and brainless. He was always good for a loan of five shillings or a lift in the rain in his Lagonda and pathetically grateful for a cup of tea and a biscuit late at night. But he was elusive, spending his time at the Pitt, or dashing around the country, usually accompanied by a thin, neighing girl in a headscarf. I liked him very much. He was also in his final year and confided in me that "Pater is awfully pleased that I have lasted the full three years..."

My first year was one of settling in, sorting out my priorities, learning to manage on a tight pittance and trying things out. Also, in making friends.

There was one interesting thing I noticed. During the era of National Service, one had the choice of going on to University straight from school, or postponing entry until after two years' service. I had chosen the latter, since I wanted to have a clean break between school and university and a period of independence when I could earn my living and, perhaps, grow up a little. What was interesting was the clear difference between the two sorts of students. Those straight up from school treated the university as a sort of extension of the sixth form; similar attitudes and behaviour; expecting to be taught, rather than learn; to accept, rather than to query; to obey rather than to question.

Those who had done their Service (sometimes in Malaya, Korea and other hotspots) were much more mature and self-confident. They realised that now they were studying for themselves, for the success of their future and to satisfy an intellectual curiosity rather than just to please Mummy and Daddy.

A couple of days after I moved in, there was a knock at the door. It then opened slowly and a young man walked tentatively in. He was of medium height, slim with dark hair and an apologetic manner. I later discovered that he was the most apologetic person I had ever met.

"Er, my name is Colin Arnold," he said. "Are you A. M. Arnold?"

"Yes, I am. But I am known as Mick," I replied. "Come in and sit down."

"I am sorry to break in on you like this," he apologised, "but we have the same sort of name and I thought if we are going to read each other's love letters and bills and things, we may as well know each other." He smiled charmingly, and handed me a letter, addressed to me, from a school friend, which had been delivered to him.

He sat down and I gave him a cup of tea, having borrowed some sugar from Scotty.

I was not to know that Colin would become my best friend, even after more than fifty years, and would be Best Man at my wedding. We were to have many adventures during our three years at Jesus and after.

My first attendance at Hall was a memorable experience. Dressed in my tattered gown (new gowns were despised, as I quickly discovered, so I exchanged mine for a suitably ragged one I found on the next peg to mine) and a jacket and tie, I entered Hall punctually at 6.30. Hall was an enormously long and high panelled chamber, with three parallel rows of tables, end to end, down its length and another large table, on a raised dais, forming a T-bar at the top. The room was full of chatter as undergraduates crowded in and took their places, haphazardly, at the tables.

The new ones, like me, tended to find their own grouping, since most of the second and third years knew each other. The tables, highly polished, were laid with glass and silver and there were College servants darting about.

Suddenly, everyone rose and there was silence. From a door in the far corner there filed in a procession of gowned figures with satin hoods down their backs, the Senior members of the College, who stood behind their chairs at the High Table. We all stood too, as one of the dons walked to an ornate lectern and began to intone a Latin grace. This took what seemed a very long time, but I found out later that it was only used on special occasions and normally a brief, ten word affair would suffice.

The College servants then served us a very acceptable three-course meal (much better than the Army) and I made a number of new acquaintances, many of whom became friends.

Colin was also reading English, so we went to our first lecture together. We cycled, in our disreputable gowns, with notebooks wrapped in a newspaper in the baskets of our bicycles, to the lecture halls. It was bitterly cold, wet and windy. Inside it was damp and cold as well, and since everything seemed to be painted in the familiar institutional brown, rather depressing. The lecture was, I think, on Middle English and very boring. The lecture room was packed.

We discovered fairly quickly that Lecturers in English tended to repeat their lectures year after year and that they had mostly published books on their subjects, which were more comprehensive that their live presentations.

Thus, it was clear that it was better to sit in one's rooms in front of the fire, eating hot crumpets and discussing the books we had bought, than to cycle at an unearthly hour through rain and wind, to a draughty lecture hall, to acquire the same knowledge (as well as having to take notes). Accordingly, with a few exceptions, I did not attend any lectures for all my three years. Nobody checked to see who did.

As far as sport was concerned, there were multiple choices, all voluntary. At this time, Jesus was a major force in rowing, using a unique and individual style called Fairbairn. We were Head of the River. The First Eight were heroes. They sat at a separate table in Hall, got special nourishing food and were much admired. They trained and trained and did virtually nothing else; got up far too early, were on the river in all weathers, and were discouraged from having late nights or too much alcohol. Most were reading for degrees which were not too onerous. I had never rowed and, though mildly interested, was not immediately tempted to try.

My best sport was swimming. This was a very minor affair at Cambridge in those days and only merited a half-Blue, in races against Oxford. Out of curiosity I went to the swimming pool on a reconnaissance and found the familiar steamy, chlorine-laden atmosphere, with a number of very keen undergraduates busy exercising and training. I also found out that my recorded times would undoubtedly get me a half-Blue but at the expense of total immersion in the sport. Effectively, I would be able to do nothing else. So I did not join the enthusiasts.

Rugby football seemed to be a better diversion. Naturally, to take it really seriously and try for a Blue had all the handicaps of the other sports. Besides, it seemed necessary to be more than six feet tall and weigh hundreds of pounds. I had captained the First XV at school and also played some fairly serious rugger in the Army, but time was too precious to commit to playing at a high level. So I signed for the College Second XV, more to soothe my conscience than anything.

Then I was faced with the problem of my motorcycle. Strictly speaking, undergraduates were not permitted to have a motor vehicle while at College. This was only possible with a special dispensation.

As was the habit of all Jesuans with a problem, I went to see the Head Porter, Captain Austin. He was lurking at the back of the Porters' Lodge, but came forward when I coughed loudly at the little window inside the gate.

"Mr. Arnold," he said with a faint smile. "How are you settling in, then?"

"Well, thank you, Captain," I replied. "But I have a small difficulty and I wonder whether you may be able to help me with it..."

He leaned out of his window. "Ah, I see. Is it legal or illegal? If it is illegal you should speak to one of the Under-Porters who will be able to help you."

"No, no," I said hurriedly, "it is perfectly legal. It is about my motorcycle, you see. How can I get permission to have it here and park it in the College at night?"

The Captain rubbed his chin for a moment. "You are interested in sailing," he said. This was a statement, not a question. I held my peace.

"I seem to recall that the Cambridge University Cruising Club keeps its sailing boats on the river at Ely, some distance from Cambridge." He paused. "Naturally, Club members have to be able to get there somehow so usually dispensation is made for them to keep a vehicle." He grinned. "Try it."

So I did. I rode, with Colin as a rather nervous passenger on the pillion, to Ely and signed up as a member at the clubhouse (a wooden hut) buying a club tie for a shilling as a mark of goodwill. There was no difficulty with the permission and the problem was solved. I am ashamed to say that I only visited Ely on two or three occasions, but dutifully paid my annual dues.

Academically, life was not particularly demanding. Since Ronnie (my stepfather) had said to me that I should not exert myself to try for a First, but should savour the opportunities that Cambridge life had to offer, I took him at his word.

Teaching I found was more guidance than information. Apart from lectures (or their equivalent) and a very occasional session with Dr. Rossiter, my main work was guided by and submitted to my Supervisor. This post-graduate student in my subject supplemented his income by overseeing the work of under-graduates, while pursuing his own studies.

We met once a week, in twos or sometimes threes, presented our essays on the subject set and argued our viewpoints while attacking the others.

At the time, it was fashionable and desirable, in essay and discussion, to support all points of view expressed with quotations. This was a chore, since finding apt quotations was time-consuming and difficult. The problem caused me to create the Reverend Dr. William Stallworthy, Rector of a small village in Lincolnshire during the reign of Queen Victoria. This divine, apart from guiding his flock, was a noted authority on English literature, and had written learned commentaries on the subject. I said I had been fortunate enough to find a manuscript of his work mouldering in a cardboard box in a second-hand bookshop in Charing Cross Road and had purchased it for ninepence.

This accomplishment enabled me to invent and use my own 'quotations' and I was occasionally complimented on their aptness and relevance. When eventually, in my final year, Dr. Rossiter asked to see the manuscript, I was distressed to have to tell him that it had been stolen from the basket on my bicycle. But it had served me and my friends well over the years.

I made some good friends in Jesus. They were a very mixed bunch, covering the whole spectrum from pure sporting activities to full academic.

Axel Ohlsson was a Boer from Capetown. He was a huge, blond, good-natured companion, his full attention focused on rowing, and his aim somehow to scrape a degree so that he could go back to his school in South Africa and teach, as well as coach the rowing eights. Axel was fun to know. He had told me of a language which was spoken around Capetown, called 'Xhosa, which included a large number of various clicks made with the tongue. I tried to learn a few words, but my mouth just could not make the right noises.

He was in the Jesus First rowing eight and was a happy, social and beer-drinking friend throughout my time in Cambridge. He first introduced me to *biltong*, sun-dried meat of some wild animal sent to him from home, which one chipped at with a penknife and chewed on – it had the consistency of a piece of wood, but had a nice gamy flavour.

Other friends much preferred philosophical discussions long into the night over endless cups of coffee to sporting activity. Mike Zander, intense, sparklingly intelligent, was fascinated by his studies of law, and became Emmeritus Professor of Law at the London School of Economics; Sam (later Sir Samuel) Brittan, laid back, witty and erudite was an economist and destined to be an Associate Editor of the *Financial Times*. They were always good for a cup of coffee and, in spite of their concentration on academic matters, were interesting, humorous and good companions.

My first term passed smoothly and Christmas came. Exceptionally, my mother and stepfather Ronnie were briefly home from abroad and were ensconced in a hotel in St. James's. I spent some fifteen days with them, in comfortable luxury, though with no special seasonal celebrations. Regrettably my clothes did not match the elegance of my surroundings.

My total wardrobe at the time consisted of one suit, a pair of flannel trousers, with a hole in the seat; two shirts (one shiny one of nylon, which was easy to wash); a very worn tweed jacket with leather on the elbows and cuffs; a threadbare pullover and a pair of brown shoes which the cobbler had finally refused to re-sole on the grounds there was not enough to which to attach a sole. I had sold my leather motorcycling outfit to raise a little money for basic supplies.

Ronnie took a horrified look at me when I arrived at the hotel and charitably took me in hand to outfit me in a manner worthy of his adopted son.

My new clothes were a mixed blessing. He found me a pair of indestructible trousers made out of a hellish hairy material called 'thornproof'. This had clearly been developed for country people who were obliged to walk through thorn hedges and other obstacles, and required some form of protection. It was the toughest material available and guaranteed to last. However, it meant walking about with a feeling that one's nether regions were encased in barbed wire.

He also bought me a pair of 'veldtschoen'. These were huge and thick shoes, made I believe of buffalo hide, which workers on the South African veldt used to wear. They were guaranteed for ten years and made walking a physical effort though they did make me an inch and a half taller. When Axel saw me wearing them, it took some time for him to stop laughing.

Finally, I was given a thick, woollen blazer and two new shirts. I was thus fully equipped, with only minor additions, for the next three years.

I felt like an old-timer when I returned to Cambridge on a freezing January day. It felt like coming home; I had my friends, familiar surroundings and knew, more or less, how things worked.

Shortly after my return, Miss Germany came into my room.

"A parcel came for you last week," she said. "It got wet in the rain and after a day I couldn't stand the smell any more, so it is in the garden shed. You better have a look." She sniffed. "I think there is something dead in it."

I went out to the shed and, sure enough, there was a brown paper parcel with lots of stamps and string. The address and the sender's details had run in the rain and were unreadable. As Miss Germany had said, there was a strange indescribable odour coming from it.

I opened it carefully. There was a sort of furry thing inside and a letter. I opened the letter; it was from my beloved Uncle Max, in Baghdad.

"My dearest Nephew, Greetings!

It has been reported that you are cold in Cambridge and with many expenses. So I am sending you a small gift to make you warm. A warm body is most important medically.

*Also it is important for health to eat much. I try to help
because you are my Nephew which I love.*
*Your Aunt is same as always. Hussein and Entah send
Greetings. One palm tree in the garden is dead.*

Your Uncle and friend,
Dr. Max Makowski Pasha"

My Uncle, who lived in Baghdad, was Royal doctor to the King
of Iraq and his family, and a sort of medical Robin Hood,
overcharging his rich patients so as to finance a free clinic he
established for indigent people, who had no other means of
getting medical help. He had done so for more than thirty years
and was much loved by the poor of Baghdad. He could not speak
any language properly, but could make himself more or less
understood in a dozen. He and I had a close relationship, united
against the discipline of Aunt and Mother, when I lived in Iraq
during World War II. He was a wise, warm, generous and loving
person and my very best relative of all.

I also, to my delight, found a £5 note in the envelope. A
fortune.

I then cautiously examined the furry object. It turned out to be
a thick embroidered leather waistcoat, furry side inside, made of
goatskin. I think it came from Afghanistan. It had been
amateurishly and incompletely cured. This meant that it had a
rather strong smell. I later found that, in the rain, the smell
multiplied considerably, and when I wore it – which was almost
all the time – my friends and people in general did not wish to
be too close to me. I always found a place in buses and trains,
though strangers looked at me in a peculiar way. Hippies did not
yet exist, and respectable young males dressed in sports jacket,
grey flannel trousers and a tie.

I wrote immediately to thank Uncle Max, though I did not
mention the £5 note since, by long standing convention, we took
precautions in case Aunt saw the letter. She would not have
approved.

This term, out of curiosity, I became involved in rowing. I was
allocated to the 'engine room' (number 6) of the Rugger Boat,

which was actually the Jesus Fourth. I trained very hard, going for an early morning run in the frost, then undergoing total immersion in an ice-cold bath (with the cox making sure I did this). The boat possessed little skill but a lot of muscle, and in the four day Lent races, we on three days bumped the boat ahead of us. Had we bumped on the fourth day as well, we would have been allowed to keep our oars.

It was, I thought, a somewhat pointless exercise, with huge expenditure of energy. We were glued to our sliding seats with a sticky black substance and encouraged to produce 'bell notes' with our blades. This was a 'plop' as the blade created a vacuum and water rushed to fill it. Our coach, on a bicycle, pedalled furiously and dangerously down the towpath, with a megaphone, yelling instructions and bad words.

I remember rowing past a notice on the bank, on a short pole, which said only "Do Not Moor Boats To This Notice". I thought about this, but it made no sense.

This was also the term during which I celebrated my twenty-first birthday. I was given £5 by my parents and further surreptitious £5 arrived from Uncle Max. I was therefore able, with this sudden wealth and after bribing Miss Germany with a bottle of brown ale, which she favoured, to invite my friends to a party in my room.

I purchased a kilderkin of beer, a large number of buns and biscuits, with fish-paste and other delicacies, and invited my Jesus friends – all seven of them – to come. We caroused, rather loudly, until midnight, when Miss Germany, who had already stretched a point, threw my friends out. All were somewhat merry but comparatively well behaved.

This was also the term when I became involved in theatre. Although I played the guitar, there was no place for me in the Footlights, the satirical theatrical revue group.

Dan Massey (son of thirties film star Raymond Massey) was a leading light of the Arts Theatre, which was a more serious enterprise. He had heard me play and asked if I would come and act with him in "The Madwoman of Chaillot". I had to stroll across the stage, playing and singing and being picturesque while people acted and declaimed all round me. I enjoyed myself enormously, and Dan became a friend.

Sometimes Colin and I escaped illegally from the college after dark, climbing over the wall, and often narrowly missing being stopped by the Proctor and his Bulldogs. This was the Don who paraded the Cambridge streets nightly after college gates were locked, wearing mortar board and flowing robes and accompanied by two burly gentlemen in bowler hats who stopped any young gentleman not wearing a gown (but looking like a student) to enquire "Excuse me sir, are you a member of this University?"

Easter holidays passed quickly. I was lucky enough to be invited to stay with the Pattinsons. Mr. Pat (as he was known) was deputy Chairman of BP. He had also been to Jesus where he had won a tennis Blue and was an old friend of Ronnie. He and Mrs. Pat were parents of Mike, who was a friend and contemporary at Jesus. They lived in a splendid house in West Byfleet.

Mrs. Pat had known Ronnie when he was still married to his first wife, who was her friend. I believe she thought of my mother as a blonde, Polish hussy who had seduced Ronnie from his true path. Certainly my mother was, by no stretch of imagination, a tweeds and golf Englishwoman.

Nevertheless, Mrs. Pat was extremely kind to me. She was a warm, generous, motherly woman, a good foil for her shy, retiring but charming husband. I enjoyed my holiday and renewed my brief acquaintance with a breakfast of silver side dishes offering multiple choices and games of croquet on the lawn; I had discussions on psychology deep into the night with Chris, Mike's elder brother, who was studying medicine.

Also, in spite of my best efforts, I was very jealous of Mike, who on his twenty-first birthday some weeks after mine, had been given a brand new MG TF, in green. Envy is an unpleasant feeling and I disliked myself for it.

Summer term started. It was normally the best, with punting on the river, warm sunny days, girls in summer frocks and men in summer blazers and straw boaters with their College ribbon round the crown. A time of relaxation and enjoyment, though with the cloud of end of term exams beginning to loom.

Girls were a problem. The student ratio was more than twenty to one in favour of men, as all the men's colleges at that time were single sex, and there were only two colleges for women. Competition would have been keen, except that the men were rather wary of the academic girls, and the pretty ones usually had to deny they had any connection with the University if they wanted to be invited out. Many of the girls anyway were more interested in study than companionship. The local Cambridge "Town girls," as they were known, had seen it all, done it all and were only interested in ruthless exploitation of the richer students.

This left me in limbo. I had always found difficulty in interesting girls in me. Perhaps it was lack of skill and polish; perhaps I was not handsome enough; but I now believe I frightened them away.

I had never, after the age of seven, had a proper home. My time was spent in boarding schools, other people's houses, and even in Ronnie's and Mother's house I was a guest. I did not have my own room but slept in the spare room. I had few possessions, so this was not a difficulty.

Subconsciously, I must have been seeking roots and a home of my own. Thus I looked at every girl I went out with, flirted with or, indeed, spent any time with, as a prospective bride with whom I could establish my own base and family. I remember proposing to some very varied girls, but happily for me none of them accepted. But I think anyway they were put off by my serious attitude. It may well have been this attitude, however well concealed, which made any relationship with a girl problematic and brief.

The most exciting event of the term was my meeting with Teddy Harper. The background was guitar playing.

One day, there was a knock at my door. I opened it and there stood an elegant figure, carefully dressed, with gleaming, barbered black hair and lacquered fingernails. I noticed that those on his right hand were longer than on his left.

"I am Teddy Harper," said the figure. "I saw you in the play at the Arts and heard your singing and playing the guitar." He looked down modestly. "I am also quite good and interested in playing, so I thought we could talk."

Teddy was also at Jesus, also in his first year. I found out that he had six Christian names, (George Edward Antoine Clifford Louis Christophe), spoke Spanish and French, and had a mysterious past. I could never get him to say anything about his parents, his origins or anything that might shed light on his life before Cambridge, though he tended to hint at mysterious aristocratic connections. He was a devout Roman Catholic – more in the telling than in the performance – and an acute diabetic. He told me that he was the most successful seducer of young girls that Cambridge had ever known. I thought him something of a mixed-up person.

We sat and talked for several hours. He ate all my crumpets and drank many cups of my tea. He played me some flamenco, very badly, on my guitar – which he pronounced to be execrable – and sang folk songs in his three languages.

At that time in the early fifties, the guitar was not very well known in Britain. Its use was mostly confined to the rhythm section of traditional jazz bands and to a group of mainly American folk singers such as Burl Ives. Pop and all its derivatives were unknown and yet to come.

"Perhaps we should try to sing together," he said. "I can take the lead and you would support me and sing the harmony."

"We could always try it and see what it sounds like," I said tentatively. Did I really want to be bound to this gilded butterfly, who would outshine me at every turn? I could not, at the time, even speak Spanish let alone play flamenco.

Cautiously I got to know him, and we met in his room fairly frequently to sing and play. In time we sounded quite good: Teddy had a fairly competent tenor and I was more of a bass/baritone. Colin and my other friends approved, with reservations. Teddy seemed to have no other friends, only girls, who changed regularly every three weeks or so.

The end of term approached, and with it the exams and also the problem of what to do in the summer vacation. My parents would be away all summer, I had to fend for myself, and I needed to find a job.

At the time, due largely to the fact that my Polish father, now dead, had been a journalist, I was seriously thinking of having a career as a journalist. I could see myself, in a raincoat and hat, rushing into the newsroom shouting "Stop the presses!" I dreamed of being an ace reporter, much sought after by editors of the great National dailies.

I wrote to a number of papers, offering my services for the duration of the summer holiday, stating I was studying English and keen to work creatively.

The only answer I received was from what was then called the *Manchester Guardian*. They told me to come to Manchester for an interview and sent me a postal order for thirty shillings. I was delighted and proudly showed the letter to all my friends.

At the *Guardian* office, I was interviewed by the News Editor, who quickly saw I was wholly inexperienced and would not do. However, he was a kind man and directed me to see the Features Editor.

This gentleman, in his shirtsleeves and in a cluttered, paper-strewn office, offered me a cigar and cross-examined me as to my past.

"Hmm," he said at the end, plucking at his right eyebrow. This was a nervous habit and resulted in a huge, bushy left eyebrow, while the right consisted of only a few miserable hairs. It gave his face a curiously lopsided look.

"I think we may use you to write some fourth leaders and an occasional feature," he said. "Of course, you won't be getting union rates, but there will be enough for you to live on." He grinned. "If you're careful, of course."

The exam results came through and I had done reasonably well, a great relief. These first year ones did not count towards my final degree, but were just an indication of how I was doing so far.

I enjoyed my time at the *Guardian*. I found a very cheap lodging on the outskirts of the city – just one room – and settled in. My bed was a convertible sofa which had the painful and sporadic habit of snapping shut like a mouse trap if I moved too much in my sleep.

The paper was a leading intellectual broadsheet and had many well-known writers on the staff. I met Alistair Cooke, on his frequent visits from the States. He had also been at Jesus, so befriended me, took me out for cups of coffee and gave me a lot of good advice about foolproof ways to get in and out of college at night. He urged me to join the Roosters, a Jesuan Society with interestingly quirky rituals, of which he had been an enthusiastic member.

My duties as a journalist were not onerous: I wrote light pieces on all subjects, some travel features and book reviews, and felt like a seasoned professional.

I also enjoyed riding my motorcycle here and there, particularly at weekends. The summer countryside round Manchester can be very beautiful.

I then met the Hellcat. This was a vehicle owned by Jerry, a reporter friend, with which I immediately and hopelessly fell in love at first sight.

The car had a home-made crude aluminium body of riveted panels and huge Marchal headlamps. There was a windscreen and two fairly rudimentary seats. It was open to the elements, had no hood, boot, doors or any amenities at all and a giant four-inch exhaust, which ran just under the elbow of the passenger sitting in the second seat. There were holes drilled in the steel floor to let the rain drain out. Your passenger got into it by vaulting carefully over the red-hot exhaust pipes. It was gorgeous.

Jerry took me for a run and told me the story. Hellcat had been built by an RAF fighter pilot from bits and pieces. The engine was a huge Standard six-cylinder monster, the gearbox had no synchromesh and the brakes were not very reliable. It sounded like a motorboat. Instead of an ignition key, there was a panel from a Messerschmidt 109 the pilot had shot down, with a row of eight switches marked, in German: machine-guns, magneto, navlights and so on. These switches had to be arranged in the right combination for the engine to start. Hellcat was fast, loud and beautiful.

Jerry's wife was not, as he put it, an understanding woman and he was under orders to get rid of it. I had no money, so I offered without much hope my Triumph in exchange. He accepted and I will never forget the unutterable joy of roaring to my lodging in my new car.

The summer wore on and I spent every spare moment in cleaning and driving Hellcat. As I drove, I noticed girls eyeing me and I made a number of transitory friendships, which, however, succumbed to the curse of my being too serious. But while each lasted, I drove the current girl about, preening myself, and revving the engine frequently. It was not quite as much fun when it rained.

There was never very much excitement at the *Guardian*, but it gave me some insight into how a newspaper worked. I got to know the functions of sub-editors, photographers and layout people. But the most fun was down in the printing room, with a smell of hot lead, clattering Linotype machines and wonderful shouts of: "Where are the formes?", "How many 'em's?", "40 point Pica!" and so on, barely audible above the roar of the presses.

The holiday passed quickly and it was time to return to Cambridge. Now I could go there in Hellcat, in great style if not comfort, ready to dazzle everyone with my new acquisition. After checking with my friend, Captain Austin about parking (he said it would be acceptable if I parked neatly and even came out to admire Hellcat which he pronounced 'unusual and striking'), I put it round the back of the College, among the dons' boring vehicles.

Captain Austin told me that my second year would be the one I had in College and said my rooms would be Set 3 on Staircase D in Chapel Court.

He also gave me my key and told me that my bedder would help sort me out. I did not know what a bedder was.

I found the staircase, and identified my room. It had an outer door, which was open, and an inner door which was closed. I opened it and went in. My rooms were palatial: a small, neat sitting room with a gas fire, decently furnished with chairs, a desk and a bookcase; a separate bedroom with a washbasin, bed and chest of drawers and a minuscule kitchen, with a gas ring, a small table and a sink. I had never had so much space just for myself in my life and I felt I would be living in the lap of luxury.

There was a knock at the door and, after a pause, an elderly man poked his head into the room.

"Hullo, sir," he said cheerfully. "I am Dawkins, your bedder and I thought we should get acquainted."

I asked him in and invited him to sit down, but he said he preferred to stand.

"I look after all the young gentlemen on this staircase," he said. "You know, do the beds and the cleaning and the washing up." He grinned and tapped his nose in a conspiratorial way. "And I know a lot of secrets, too. You can't help it after twenty-seven years on the job."

He then explained to me that the baths were in the basement of the building, some hundred yards away, across two courtyards, that I could cook anything I liked so long as it didn't smell offensive and that I could close the outer door whenever I pleased (this was known as 'sporting the oak') and that this meant that I wished to be undisturbed and no one would so much as knock on it.

"Anything I can do to help, all you need to do is ask me." He gave a small smile. "What goes on here behind the oak is nobody's business, as long as she is out of College by 10 pm, when the gates close. Howsomever, there are ways of exiting and entering the College after dark, too. You know," he grinned, "in Oxford we are known as 'scouts'. Would you believe it? I wonder if they wear khaki shorts?" He burst into a peal of laughter.

We were to become good friends and he saved me from many a predicament during my year in College.

This was one of Colin's years out of College, but Teddy Harper like me was in college. I made the acquaintance of the other five denizens of Staircase D. They were an interesting bunch, ranging from a homosexual actor to an enormous boxing Blue, a 6'7" painfully thin budding Anglican priest to the titled heir to thousands of acres in Wiltshire. They were reading a variety of subjects and there were many nights we spent, in different combinations, drinking coffee, smoking and arguing hotly about The Meaning of Life, the Value of Morality, Was There a God and other similarly esoteric subjects. Such activities were very much a part of Cambridge life. It was considered not gentlemanly to discuss the detail of one's amorous adventures and most people were reticent about their families and backgrounds. The fifth denizen was very quiet, very studious, and usually invisible.

One of my activities during the year was to join the Roosters, as Alistair Cooke had suggested to me. This old Jesus club met in the College rooms of an eminent don, Dr Frederick Brittain, known by all as ffreddie. He was an unusual man, who entered fully into the life and entertainment of undergraduates, while maintaining his serious academic side. He was also treasurer of the Footlights, which presented its satirical entertainment at smoking concerts, and featured Jonathan Miller among other future stars. At one of these concerts I met Tony Westcott, a gifted pianist and singer, who was to become a good friend and the cause of my going to Chile.

The Roosters (and later their senior branch, the Red Herrings) were fun. The name came from the three roosters on the College crest, which was taken from the arms granted to John Alcock, founder of Jesus College in 1541. The meetings were run according to an elaborate ritual, with titles, forms of address, speeches and jokes, very much prophetic of the Monty Python style of humour – a mystery to outsiders.

Sometimes Colin and I decided to sneak up to London for a party. Dawkins always managed to cover for me, which was just as well, since there was great danger in absenting oneself overnight during Term, without an official *exeat*. In order to be awarded a degree, a rigid rule demanded that a specific number of nights be spent in Cambridge for all nine terms. There was no leeway and a missed, unauthorised night could mean an additional complete term in residence. This was extremely difficult to obtain, thus one's degree depended on not being caught.

Since I was interested in journalism, I joined *Varsity*, the undergraduate weekly tabloid newspaper; this was staffed entirely by undergraduates and professionally printed at Bury St. Edmonds. But all the editorial and layout work was done by us.

We had a great deal of fun. The contents were supposed to be supervised by a senior member of the University, but I do not remember ever meeting him. The only prohibitions were blasphemy, libel and nude pictures. Opinions, however extreme were welcome, as were news items, gossip and particularly critical appraisal of current books, films and theatrical events.

On my second day at the *Varsity* office, I saw a cheerful, black-haired young man who was busy writing a criticism of a film I had just seen. I introduced myself.

He looked up. "Hullo," he said. "I'm Michael Winner – this is what I like doing."

Since it was lunchtime, I suggested we should go and get a half-pint of bitter and a cheese roll at a nearby pub. This was my usual modest lunch.

"No, no," exclaimed Mike with horror. "Let's grab a bite at the Arts Restaurant. Much better for you." The Arts was a proper restaurant, moderately priced, lunch was 4/6 (22.5p) while my pub lunch was 1/- (5p) – and close to the office. I had very little money, so I hesitated.

Mike's black eyes sparkled and crinkled up with laughter. He was exceptionally sensitive to other people. "This is the first time," he said, "It's on me. I've just been lucky," he added mysteriously.

Over lunch, we exchanged bits of information about ourselves. He was interested to hear that I was a Pole. "My mother is Polish and my father Russian," he remarked. "Fortunately, the family is wealthy and so you shouldn't worry about the bill when we eat or drink." He was nothing if not straightforward. As we became friends, however, I insisted on paying my way from time to time. I liked him, he was a very interesting person, but it was difficult to keep him off the subject of the cinema.

"My whole life is in films," he remarked. "I am only doing law as something to do. But you mark my words; I shall direct famous films and have celebrated stars working for me." And so he did.

The other main friend I made at *Varsity* was Gavin Lyall. He reminded me of Nidge, my school friend, in his love of aviation – he had done his National Service in the RAF – and in his open and cheerful friendliness. He wrote pieces for *Varsity* on all matters even remotely connected with airplanes and was also a gifted cartoonist. Gavin and I frequently had lunch together in a local pub, (usually a cheese roll and pint of beer – he was as hard up as I was) and exchanged anecdotes of our National Service life. We found we had the same sense of humour and the same ambitions. He was truly an expert on old aircraft and interested in arms, despite having been brought up in a Quaker family. His aim was to be a journalist and author, and he went on to write excellent thrillers.

My own activities largely involved general reporting, with an emphasis on motor racing and interviews. The Cambridge Union (a famous debating society) was a rich hunting ground for visiting celebrities who had been invited to speak. The interview I remember best was with Billy Graham, the American evangelist, on his first visit to England. I had an hour with him and was quite overcome by his charisma and personality. I wrote a long article on him, with photographs, and felt well on the way to being a professional journalist.

Colin also dabbled in journalism. By some mysterious stroke of luck or genius, he monopolised the job of reviewing music hall presentations at the New Theatre for *Varsity*. This inevitably entailed 'human angle' stories, on which he insisted, and meant that he had extensive interviews with scantily clad *artistes* back-stage. He sometimes managed to get an extra complimentary ticket for me. I remember those evenings with nostalgia.

One evening, Teddy appeared at my door; he had his rooms on the next staircase in Chapel Court. He was carrying his guitar.

After pausing for a moment at the small mirror on the back of my door – he could never pass a mirror without checking that the image he presented had not deteriorated since the previous inspection – he sat down. I was desperately trying to write an essay for the next day's supervision, but he said it was urgent.

"Listen," he said. "I have fixed up a deal at the Fairbairn Ball next month." He smoothed his hair. "I said we would do a half-hour cabaret act in exchange for free tickets."

"What do you mean?" I asked. Cabaret act?

"Well, we can sing and I can do a bit of patter (I can be quite funny, you know) and you can back me up. All the girls will love it and anyway, we can't afford to go to Balls any other way!"

This was true. There were several Balls in every Term, of all kinds: Club, Society, College May Balls, Sports Victory Balls and others. The tickets were certainly beyond my means and I had not been to any.

"We have to make a Dramatic Impact," he announced in capitals, standing up and walking up and down. "I am probably all right, but we have to do something about you." He looked at me critically.

"I know," he said, snapping his fingers. "We will be Spanish – a Spanish Duo..."

"But I can't speak Spanish," I said. "What about a French Duo or an English Folk Duo or something."

"No, no," he said. "It's got to be Spanish; guitars and so on. Anyway, I can teach you a couple of Spanish songs and you can learn them – you don't have to know what they mean." He paused. "Now then, the Impact. Hmmm..."

"Yes! I've got it. We will dress in black shirts and tie a scarlet kerchief around our throats. That will be a splendid Impact." He adopted a Spanish Attitude. "I don't think we need hats. Let's get the stuff tomorrow."

I pondered. I had just received a sudden £5 note, a lifesaver, from my Uncle Max in Baghdad, but I needed it to eat in the latter part of term. Well, perhaps this would be fun.

"All right," I said. "We can try, anyway." So we got down to it and began to put together a half-hour show, using songs from several languages, though mainly French, English and Spanish. We argued and practised for hours. As a result, I had to stay up all night to write my essay, fuelled by cups of coffee. At my supervision the next day I was jittery and fidgety on a large overdose of caffeine. But my supervisor did not notice and the hour with him passed without incident other than an accusation of "living it up a bit, old chap?"

The weather was bitterly cold. No one who has not wintered in Cambridge can possibly appreciate just how biting the icy wind, laden with moisture, howling in from the North Sea across the Fens, can be. I was happy and cosy in my College rooms and looked forward with dread to my final year, again to be spent in draughty, damp and primitive digs. I felt sorry for footballers and rowers.

I had already acquired a pair of worn and rather shiny black trousers. I went out and bought a black shirt, for our performances. I found that it required washing only infrequently and therefore wore it quite often, with my goat-skin waistcoat. We both bought matching scarlet kerchiefs and I felt very romantic and gallant. Of course, I was no match in looks for Teddy, though I slightly re-arranged my hair in what I thought was a more dashing style. It did not help very much.

We did a free (for drinks only) try-out at a private party, given by a rich young man from the Pitt Club. There were some dapper gentry and neighing, angular girls, who talked while we sang, but seemed to like our act, since they clapped loudly when we finished. As the level sank in the bottles, the applause rose and we did some ad-libbing. I discovered that by memorising rhyming couplets of certain words, I could compose *risqué* calypso verses as we played and invited the audience to shout out names. This proved a great success and led to much merriment. We finally escaped, somewhat unsteadily, at midnight and had to climb surreptitiously into College, a difficult proceeding especially when encumbered with guitars.

The time approached for the Fairbairn Ball. I became more and more nervous and twitchy; this was to be a public performance and dim memories stirred of my disgrace at a school concert in Egypt and the fiasco of my appearance, as a Triballian God, in 'The Birds' of Aristophanes, at Berkhamsted School.

Teddy was very cheerful about it, and practised hard with me. I was more concerned with the songs and music; he constantly demanded my opinion on which profile to present, whether he should have one foot up on a stool, if he should introduce us in Spanish and so on. I had learned, parrot-like, a couple of songs in Spanish. I did not know quite what they meant but made a passable go at singing them, under Teddy's correction. Colin, when he heard us, tended to snigger.

So the great day finally arrived – I did not know that it would prove to be one of the most important days of my life.

The Ball was a formal one, held in a ballroom in town. We made our way there through the drizzling rain, carrying our guitars in their cases. We were shown into a little room behind the ballroom, next to the kitchen. It had a large mirror, some coat hooks on the wall and a couple of chairs.

Teddy immediately sat down in front of the mirror, with his comb and a bottle of some sort of lotion. I suggested a quick run through, but he said he wanted to be quite sure that we would make our Impact.

The Ball organiser, an undergraduate, put his head round the door and told us that we could do our act about half way through the Ball. He suggested we stayed out of the way until then and promised us a pint of beer. He said: "After you've performed, you can mix with the guests, but don't intrude where they don't want you."

We were clearly inferior to the paying customers and were expected to know our place. I was not very concerned, but Teddy was most indignant: "We are the stars," he spluttered. "We are the ones they should be thrilled to talk to!" He went on mumbling for quite a long time, even after our beers arrived.

We were finally called and, after a quick look in the mirror, we went out to the ballroom. This was a very large room, with a polished dance floor in the middle and many tables all round it. These were populated by dinner-jacketed men and girls in evening dresses, six or eight to a table, most of which had champagne bottles and glasses on them. The small dance band was filing out of another door at the back.

We took our place in the middle of the dance floor. Teddy announced us: "Ladies and gentlemen. We are the Spanish Duo and we are here to entertain you." He had put on the faintest Spanish accent. "Naturally, we shall also sing songs of many other lands." The conversations gradually died away and we started, as agreed, with our signature tune, 'Lulu's Back in Town'; a rousing jazz song, designed to grab and hold the attention of the audience.

We followed this, after pausing for some polite applause, with a French song, a couple of American folk songs and a Spanish one, which Teddy finished with a great flourish of his hand, throwing his head back in a Spanish sort of way. I noticed that the applause grew warmer and warmer as we progressed.

We paused for some minutes, to regain our breaths and a kind, anonymous person sent us two glasses of champagne. This was welcome and we drank it with pleasure.

While singing, I had noticed a very pretty girl at one of the tables fairly close to us, paying great attention to our singing. Her eyes seemed focused on our guitars, instead of looking at our faces, as most of the audience was doing. Her hand beat time on the table in front of her. I smiled at her but she did not notice, since she was talking, with great animation, to her companions.

The second half of our performance was even better received, especially my Calypso routine. Fortunately, the names shouted out were fairly popular, and it was easy to fit my pre-determined lines and rhymes to them. We finally finished with '*Malagueña*', a Mexican *huapango*, which had some tricky falsetto bits, successfully negotiated. Then, after a couple of encores, we were finished.

Teddy turned to me and said: "There, you see, we made an Impact." Conversations had resumed and the small band was coming to the podium to play music for the dancing.

As we walked towards our back room, the girl I had noticed came up to us. She was very attractive, slim and in a *décolleté* evening dress. Her blue eyes were sparkling. She spoke to Teddy, who stopped and turned to face her. I also stopped.

"I just wanted to tell you how much I enjoyed your performance," she said. Teddy preened, assuming the 'your' was singular. "I am very interested in the guitar and am determined to learn to play it." Her voice was pleasant and she radiated a great air of energy and liveliness. "I wonder if you could give me a few pointers?"

"Of course, of course," he purred. "I can do more than give you a few pointers – I can teach you to play." He smoothed his hair. I could see that he was assuming another easy conquest.

I stepped closer. "I'm Mick Arnold," I said to the girl. She turned towards me and smiled; my heart gave a flip. "Hullo," she said. "I'm Wendy Joyce." She turned back to Teddy. The band was playing and the floor filling up with dancing couples.

"Come and see me tomorrow," said Teddy. "I am in Jesus," he

gave her his staircase and room details. "Can you manage ten o'clock? I'm rather busy."

"I'll be there," she said. As she walked back to her table, she gave me another smile, but I did not feel anything special in it.

We were both tired and did not stay long. Several people beckoned us over to their tables to give us a drink and ask various questions about our songs. They were fairly complimentary and I was glad we had done our first real act.

On the way back to Jesus in the drizzle – there was no hurry, since we had managed to obtain an *exeat* until 1am – we discussed the evening.

"Well, what do you think of her?" asked Teddy. "I bet I can do it."

I thought this idea of betting was not at all that of an English gentleman.

Wendy, the girl at the Ball, was rather special. While not worrying too much about Teddy's many liaisons, I instinctively felt worried and troubled at the thought of Teddy's cynical, practised and persuasive charm overcoming her. I determined to try to prevent this.

Accordingly, the following morning at about a quarter to ten, I strolled nonchalantly into Teddy's rooms. He was quite dazzling – he called it his seduction outfit. His black hair was perfectly combed and glossy, with one careful strand straying onto his forehead. He wore a maroon silk dressing gown over a white shirt and had a foulard cravat round his neck. His socks were of silk and his shoes highly polished as were his fingernails, which he was busy buffing.

"How do I look," he enquired. "The first private meeting is very important." He glanced in the mirror. "She'll be along in a moment, but I think I am ready."

He glanced at me. I was wearing my uncomfortable thornproof trousers and my black shirt with the goatskin waistcoat. My shoes were not very clean.

"You better go," said Teddy. "This is a private meeting – you're not invited."

"But there is a couple of things I want to talk about," I said disarmingly. "The bit in 'The Big Rock Candy Mountain'…." There was a knock at the door.

"Go, go now," said Teddy desperately. "It is her...she...the girl...Go away." But it was too late. "Come in," I said engagingly. Teddy shook his fist at me and Wendy Joyce walked in.

Teddy swept towards her. "How very nice to see you," he purred. "What a pleasure. You make me very happy. Do sit down, have a cup of coffee. Mick was just leaving..."

While this was going on, Wendy came into the room. She was dressed in a black polo neck sweater and black corduroy trousers, quite daringly bohemian for that time. I thought she looked wonderful. As I remembered from the previous night at the Ball, she radiated an exciting, sparkling liveliness. I just stood there.

She looked Teddy up and down and I am almost sure I saw the hint of a smile on her lips.

She turned towards me and smiled properly. "Do you really have to go?" she asked. I could see Teddy frowning and mouthing: "Go, go." "Yes," she continued, "a cup of coffee would be lovely."

So I said that I could stay for a while, and sat down on a chair. Wendy made herself comfortable on the sofa and Teddy went to the little kitchen to make the coffee.

Wendy and I made desultory conversation for a few minutes. She said she was in her first year at Girton College (two miles up a steepish hill from the centre of Cambridge) but that she spent most of her time in the town. She was also reading English. Her greatest interest seemed to lie in the theatre and she loved music, travel and literature. There was no time for any more, since Teddy returned with two cups of coffee – I was not offered any.

Wendy stayed for a while, and Teddy showed her certain simple chord forms on his guitar, and spent some time trying to show her how to hold it. But she gracefully avoided his obvious attentions and, anyway, I am glad to say he was constrained by my presence.

I was in a slight daze; was this truly the perfection I had been seeking? There was something indefinable in the air; my insides were churning and every time she glanced in my direction, I felt odd. In my past encounters with girls, I had felt attraction, admiration and lust. This was quite different – not so much in intensity as in kind. It was a new feeling that everything was right, that everything fitted, that the sky was clear and blue.

I could see, to my delight, that Teddy's tactics were not working and that she saw through his stratagems. Much relieved, I said goodbye and left.

I was sitting in my rooms a while later, when Teddy came storming in. "Swine," he shouted, "you did that on purpose. You've ruined everything!"

"I am delighted," I answered coolly. "You can't have them all. There are plenty of others, as you well know. Just stay away from her."

He looked at me in amazement. "Can't be," he muttered. "Surely not..." A broad grin appeared on his face. "You're in love," he said. "Mick is in love, ha, ha, ha!"

I felt myself flushing. "Nonsense," I growled. "Whatever makes you think such a ridiculous thing!"

"Yes, yes," Teddy danced round the room, right hand on chest and left arm stretched out. "It's love. Ha, ha. Mick the cool, the disapproving, the sober, ha, ha, is in love."

"Get lost!" I said crossly.

"Well, since you are a friend and we sing together, you can have her," Teddy said magnanimously. "I'll keep away and you can teach her to play." He paused. "Otherwise you wouldn't have a chance, you know."

"Get stuffed," I said irritably. "You're stupid. Go away."

Teddy pirouetted out of the room, humming: "Falling in love with love..."

I sat for a while, thinking things over. This was altogether a new thing. All my past relationships had been different. I simply had to see her again. But how could one be so sure so soon? Would she want to see me?

Time passed. Every day I wondered if I could pluck up the courage to seek her out and every time my courage failed me. I sought consolation in my Hellcat and drove around the countryside alone, in the rain, for something to do. I knew that no one could advise me or suggest a course of action. This was private, it was mine and it was up to me to sort out.

Colin got worried and cornered me in my room.

"What's wrong with you, for heavens' sake?" he asked. "You're behaving like a mooncalf. What is going on?"

I relented, and told him my problem; he was much more experienced in these matters than I but not cynical, like Teddy.

He laughed. "Come on, old chap," he said. "You are not the first and will not be the last in the world. Everybody goes through it. Best thing is to get to know her and see how you get on. How can you possibly think sensibly with nothing to base it on?" Of course, he was right.

"Besides," he added, "Judith and Penelope, those girls we met in London, are coming up in a couple of days and you can see how that affects everything. Always wise to compare."

Teddy still sniggered and giggled sporadically when we rehearsed, and also kept winking at me whenever we played in public.

Study went by the board and I only just managed to keep up with my weekly essay and supervision, and avoided censure from my Tutor. It was, after all, only the first term of my second year and I could catch up later. I continued to write for *Varsity* and saw friends from time to time.

Judith and Penelope arrived. Colin and I entertained them as best we could, but we were both impecunious and it was difficult, since walks in the biting wind and cold rain were hardly pleasant. We took them to Dorothy's Café, where there was an inexpensive tea-dance, and sat around in our rooms, drinking tea and eating crumpets.

They were pleasant enough girls and quite good company but were really only interested in their own social set. They kept talking about people I had never met. When the weekend had passed I could see that there was really no contest – even based on the short and superficial contact I had had with Wendy. I told Colin.

"The trouble is," I said, "I'm thinking about her all the time. Even when we were all sitting together in my rooms, and talking to the girls, I was thinking about her. There must be something..."

Colin laughed. "You really have it badly. If you want my opinion, it is get to know her. Spend time with her. See how it goes. It will either get stronger or peter out. But it certainly is in your system and you are being a bore about it all."

So I gritted my teeth, drove up to Girton, and left a note for Wendy at the Porter's Lodge. The note invited her to tea the following day in my rooms, at 4 o'clock. I slept very badly that night.

I spent some time the following day in careful shopping, choosing with much thought jasmine tea, which my mother always used, some biscuits and a small chocolate cake. I also tidied, dusted, cleaned, organised and polished everything – I knew how to do this from my Army days. My bedder was astonished. "Somebody special, hey?" he said. "Anything I can do?" I thanked him and said there was nothing, but he did bring me a jar with some flowers in it at lunchtime. It was winter, and I don't know where he got them, but they looked good on the mantelpiece.

At about 3 o'clock it suddenly occurred to me that Wendy might be busy, or that she had not got the note, or just did not want to come. I paced up and down the room in an agony – I just could not sit down or relax.

Four o'clock came and went. Nothing. I peered out of the window, but it was getting dark and there was no one in sight. Then a couple of undergraduates walked by, arguing. I was in despair. I sat down on the sofa and munched a biscuit.

There was a knock. I sprang up and opened the door. She was there.

I do not really remember much of our meeting. It was as though I was in a fog. I know I babbled like a fool, made tea, sat down, stood up and asked silly questions.

Wendy sat there, smiling. I told her I was worried that Teddy had upset her but she laughed. "No, I saw through him at once," she said. "I have lived in Italy and in France and I have seen lots of boys like him. They are all the same, a joke."

I warmed to her immediately. It was I who had always been considered the joke. I realised that here was somebody special and that I had better go carefully, and not spoil things by being too intense. For once, I was going to try to build something.

She told me about herself. The daughter of a Director of an engineering firm, she had an older brother who had graduated from Pembroke College some years earlier. She had been invited to Cambridge while he was up and had even been to a May Ball with one of his friends at the tender age of sixteen. This made her determined to follow in her brother's footsteps and in the face of tremendous competition was rewarded by being offered a place.

This was my first indication of her drive to succeed and her determination to accomplish the challenges she set herself. I was entranced. She was like a fresh sea-breeze after the placid and insipid girls I had known.

I also realised just how pretty she was: blue eyes, slim but pleasantly curved, shining brown hair and a natural grace in her movements. There was something continental about her; English girls, in the main, did not seem to know how to walk gracefully and their gestures tended to be rather abrupt and unfeminine. She was different.

She agreed to see me again soon. When she left I was in a daze.

I walked on air, I smiled foolishly and I laughed a lot. My friends noticed and were puzzled. Axel, my huge rowing South African friend stopped me in Chapel Court and said: "What is the matter with you?" He spoke with a strong Boer accent. "I don't know what you've been eating, but can I have some too?"

I told him the story and he wished me joy. Teddy was also, surprisingly, pleased for me. "Good for you," he said. "When you've got her, you can move on. Shouldn't take these things too seriously, you know..."

I told him that, as usual, he was being stupid. "Not everybody treats girls as a notch on your gun or a scalp to hang on your belt! I don't think you know what a friendship with a girl can be."

Suddenly, my luck changed. I was in the habit of keeping my eyes and ears open (as a keen fledgling reporter) and looking for newsworthy events at the University. I discovered that a member of King's had climbed onto the chapel roof at night to join the

Nightclimbers' Club. I immediately phoned the *Evening Standard*, explained my story, dictated two paragraphs to a copytaker and gave my name and address. This was normal practice and everyone did it. After a few days I got a fat cheque.

Also, out of the blue, came a letter from my dear Uncle Max. As usual, there was a £5 note in it. The letter went as follows:

"Beloved Nephew,

I send you a small gift which I hope you will find useful. We are well and your Aunt is as usual. But there is a great storm coming to Baghdad and people are afraid. Many rich ones are thinking of leaving and your Aunt wants to go. It will be sad after so many years here. But do not worry, my clinic is still full of good people and I work hard.

Your loving uncle
Dr Max Makowski Pasha"

I immediately wrote back to thank him for the cash, which I did using our usual code in case Aunt saw the letter. I said I welcomed news of the five foreign friends he spoke about and he understood. I also told him, briefly, about meeting Wendy – I had never before mentioned a girl to him – and told him that this was something very special.

I felt rich. Wendy and I were meeting regularly and now I invited her to an Indian meal. There were few Indian restaurants in England at that time, and Wendy had never been to one.

We went to the restaurant in the evening and I ordered a large meal, expansively and with as much nonchalance as I could muster. When it came, even I was astonished at the amount – a huge dish of rice, prawns, meat balls, vegetable curry and many other things. Wendy was agog, and laughed very much. She ate only a modest amount, tasting everything, and took it in good part when I urged her to try a bright red sauce, saying it was very tasty, but not mentioning it was also flavoured with fiery chillies. I ate up everything that was left.

"Good gracious," she said. "You certainly have an appetite. I have never seen anyone eat so much at a sitting..."

I was barely able to speak and shortly after we finished drove her cautiously back to Girton. I was impressed that she obviously appreciated the charms of Hellcat, and was happy to vault in over the exhaust pipes. I then went home in a happy daze and lay on my bed, unable to move, for some hours. I do not think I ate anything the following day.

A letter came from Mother (a rare occurrence). The parents were currently in Iraq again, Ronnie having been appointed Chief Representative of BP in the country. It told me that I was to come out to Baghdad for Christmas and to bring my friend Mike Pattinson, him of the green MG TF, of whom I was so jealous, to return some of the hospitality his parents had so kindly extended to me. Mother said that Ronnie had arranged for tickets to be sent to me by BP, in London.

I was happy to read that my step-brother and sister, Andrew and Felicity (Ronnie's children) were also coming. I knew them hardly at all and looked forward to establishing a closer relationship. Both were younger than me by some years.

Wendy thought this was all very exciting. She had always longed to travel, having grown up in a wartime England in one small town. She had already managed several trips to the Continent including a six month stay in Italy, and she spoke both French and Italian fluently, with a good accent. I was happy that she felt the same about travelling as I did and wished she could have joined us all in Baghdad for Christmas, but flying was prohibitively expensive, and only the rich and famous and business people flew.

There was a huge scandal. My old friend from school, Mark Boxer, who was a leading light in the Cambridge social and literary scene, and who edited *Granta*, an elegant and sophisticated magazine, got into serious trouble with the authorities for publishing what they considered to be a blasphemous poem. No one else thought it to be in any way offensive, and there was an outcry from the student body, as he was very popular. For his alleged offence the magazine was banned and he was rusticated. This meant he was expelled temporarily from Cambridge (one term) and thus could not fulfil his obligation to spend a minimum number of nights in College. This entailed a whole new term, somehow to be arranged. When I saw him to express sympathy and support, he was very angry.

Cambridge society, principally students and many members of the Faculty, staged a nationally publicised protest, slowly marching down King's Parade in procession, to a dirge, bearing a coffin with GRANTA/BOXER on it. The streets were lined with spectators. Naturally, this had no effect on the authorities, but later, when Mark was Editor of major London magazines and a world-famous cartoonist, he never forgave Cambridge. In any case, the following month *Granta* was reborn under a different name, and continued as before, under a new editor, especially satirising Cambridge authoritarian attitudes.

At *Varsity* we became more circumspect but trumpeted freedom of the press.

The remainder of term passed in a blur. I was happy and busy and life was wonderful.

Wendy was being picked up by her parents at the end of term, to go home to Northwood and suggested I go with them, since I had to get to London. They arrived in her father's beautiful 1937 MG saloon – spotless and shining in the rare sunshine of a December day – and I finally met them. Mr. Joyce was a small man, very intense and a typical engineer. He always referred to a car as a 'chassis', from the days when this and the body were bought separately. He was a filtration expert and inventor and had a number of patents to his name. He had also worked on early helicopters and could be fascinating on the subject. Wendy's mother was just that, a marvellous English mother, warm, generous, kind and comfortable.

What effect I had on them I can only guess. I had had a haircut and polished my shoes and wore a clean shirt. I was badly handicapped, of course, by being a Pole. In the early World War II days, my compatriots had acquired an unenviable reputation, especially in Scotland, of being heartless seducers of pure British girls and thoroughly unreliable – in fact, sort of Teddys, mistrusted by all mothers. I was, if anything, at the other end of this spectrum, but it took several years for Wendy's parents to begin to trust me.

Since I was going to be abroad, I mothballed the Hellcat. The MG appeared at Jesus punctually, having picked up Wendy at Girton, and we drove to Northwood.

I stayed with the Joyce family for a few days. They had a pleasant, modest, tile-hung house with a hillside garden, in what was then a small suburban town surrounded by open countryside, and is now part of Greater London. It was wonderful to be with her all day. We sat and talked a lot and went for walks. Her parents remained wary of me.

Just before I left Wendy said: "Look, I am giving a Christmas party in early January and there is a bunch of Cambridge people and all my local friends coming. It would be lovely if you and Mike come too and you can play your guitar for them. Can you?"

I said it would be terrific and undertook to come, with Mike, straight from the airport. I was, in any case, taking my guitar so I would have it with me.

Mike and I met at the airport and flew to Baghdad without incident. It was his first visit there and, since I considered myself a seasoned traveller, I put on a nonchalant and carefree air. We flew in a DC7C airliner – very much faster and more comfortable than the primitive York (a converted Lancaster bomber) in which I had originally arrived in England from Baghdad, seven years before.

When we landed, both Ronnie and Mother, as well as Aunt and Uncle Max were at the airport. The ladies hugged me to their perfumed bosoms, Ronnie shook hands and bade us welcome, and Uncle Max stood to one side, looking delighted and patting his agreeably rounded stomach with both hands. I called this 'beating his drum', which he did when very pleased. Andrew and Felicity were to arrive the following day.

My parents took me to their large bungalow, and there was Mohammed, Ronnie's long-time major-domo and an old friend, to greet me. He was a small stout middle-aged man, with a rather wrinkled face, grizzled hair and a thick moustache. He was a Persian, self-educated and fascinated by astronomy, who had taught me the Arabic names of the stars and liked to discuss esoteric philosophical points with me. He also always spoilt me utterly.

The Christmas holidays went by quickly. But, somehow, all the celebrations did not seem very real. I thought that it was very ironic that here, in the Middle East where the story of Christmas took place, the festivities should feel artificial while in England, with the wrong climate, culture and surroundings, it seemed real. My mother always insisted that we have a Polish meal on Christmas Eve, *barszcz* (clear beetroot soup), fish elaborately served in a highly-decorated aspic and accompanied by horseradish sauce, and for dessert *makowiecz* (poppy seed cake). She was careful however also to serve a traditional English Christmas lunch on Christmas Day for Ronnie and his children to enjoy. It was very satisfactory to be away from rationing and food was plentiful. Everybody got a token present and the gramophone played Christmas carols. There were some tinsel decorations.

I was pleased at last to be able to spend some time with Andrew and Felicity. Since they were younger, and, at that age, a few years made a big difference, we did not have a great deal to say to each other, but we got on well together. There were parties every night, at which I noticed that they were very well able to fend for themselves. Andrew was a strapping young man with a great sense of humour, and Felicity the best sort of English girl. She had finished school that year and was deciding what to do next.

Baghdad social life reached a seasonal peak. We all went to many parties but there was a dearth of young people of our age. There was one exception. Frances-Mary, the daughter of the local manager of the main cotton factory, a Scotsman, had also come out for the holiday, a very pleasant, quiet girl. She was just starting at St. Andrews University. Since I was wholly besotted with Wendy, who was very seldom out of my thoughts, I decided to play matchmaker for Mike.

I therefore arranged that we go everywhere as a threesome, for appearances' sake, though as soon as we were alone, I would disappear and hover protectively, like a sheepdog, just out of sight, keeping interlopers away and ensuring privacy so that love could flourish.

I was delighted when, two years later, my friends were

married and, with many children, lived happily thereafter.

Naturally, Mother got the wrong idea, and thought I was the one pursuing Frances-Mary. "Darlink," she said. "Are you sure you love this girl?" Her accent, carefully preserved, was still what she herself called 'charmink'. "You are much too young to think about marriage and when the time comes, you must find a girl WORTHY of you!" She often spoke in capitals. "She must be rich and beautiful and a devoted wife – and intelligent. She must not want too many jewels but you must always give her some, to be happy."

I was delighted and sniggered inwardly. But I could see that this was definitely not the time to tell her and Ronnie about Wendy. It would have to keep. So I merely assured her that this was not yet the Real Thing, promised to be circumspect and careful and left her appeased.

There were two exciting episodes, which lit up the holiday for me.

The first was a visit to the King. Faisal had left Harrow and was now a proper ruler, trying very hard to persuade the Prince Regent, his uncle and our "enemy", to stop treating him like a small boy. His Ministers loved and respected him and he seemed to be doing a good job.

Uncle Max had told him I was visiting and thus I was summoned to the Palace and told to come alone. Accordingly, one day, dressed in my best outfit – not very impressively – I set off for the Qasr al Zuhur. I was driven, sitting in the back of Ronnie's gigantic official limousine, a bright yellow Humber Pullman. I was quite lost in the huge car and felt very grand, waving nonchalantly to Arab pedestrians and anyone I saw.

In the Palace, I was shown into an anteroom and then ushered into the large sitting room where Faisal was talking to a group of officials. When he saw me, he grinned and asked them to leave. They did so, but his old Nanny appeared – I had known her from the age of ten. She shook hands with me, remarked how I had grown and actually gave me one of her rare smiles.

Fizz clapped me on the shoulder. "Haven't seen you for a long time. How are you?" he asked.

"All is well. How are you? How was Harrow?" We chatted for a bit, exchanging reminiscences. I asked what had happened to his bodyguards, my old friends, the big Sergeant and the two Unimportant Ones, his companions. Fizz said that they had been taken away from him, and that being King mainly meant – contrary to public belief – that you couldn't do anything at all, let alone what you wanted. He said: "Things are not looking good. I can feel it all round me. Everyone is on the other side." This was an old joke of ours: everyone was either on our side or the other side. His Uncle, for example, had always been on the other side.

I asked after Umm Faisal, his mother, and he told me that unfortunately she was ill but sent her love. She was an enchanting, kind and warm lady and I loved her dearly.

After a short time, with people constantly poking their heads into the room, it became apparent that the old days had gone, that Fizz was very busy with his duties, and that his Harrow education and new friends had caused us to grow apart. This was to be the last time I saw him. We shook hands again and I left, feeling rather sorry for him.

The second excitement happened when an employee of BP who worked for Ronnie, invited Mike and me to go shooting. Mike declined – we had had a date to go on a picnic with Frances-Mary – but I accepted, considering that Mike and Frances-Mary would, by now, be happier without me.

Steve – for that was his name – picked me up at dawn in his Land Rover. The sky was brightening and it was quite cold. Baghdad in winter often went down below freezing while in the summer 125 degrees F were not uncommon.

My new friend had brought a shotgun for me. It was a light 12-bore with a double barrel; as I remembered from my Army days, it was clean, bright and slightly oiled.

He was also accompanied by a young Arab helper named Ahmed, who would assist us in picking up any downed birds and generally be useful.

"We will be going about twenty miles south-west, along the Tigris," Steve told me. "We are after black partridge, which make very good eating and which you can't buy in town."

I had never been shooting or hunting before. I was somewhat

worried at the thought of killing living things but, on reflection, decided that, after all, that was where beefsteaks and mutton came from, to say nothing of chickens and turkeys. So I accepted that it was all right to shoot, if you only shot things you could eat. I felt that shooting or hunting for trophies was very wrong.

We chatted as we drove along the road, and Steve told me about his life in Baghdad, the work he did – he was an accountant – and of his hopes of getting married on his next leave. "Life would be so much better if Shirley was here," he said. "The life of a bachelor can be fun but it does get lonely..."

I also had a few words with Ahmed, and found, much to his and Steve's surprise that my Arabic quickly came back to me. Steve's Arabic was still rudimentary. Ahmed told me that BP was treating him well, and that he aspired, eventually, to a supervisory position in the Company.

We drove through date plantations and vegetable gardens and stretches of scrubby desert. Eventually we stopped by a grove of palms.

"Now we walk," said Steve. "We will go down towards the river, through the palms. Be careful of the irrigation ditches – the farmers won't thank you for damaging the mud walls. Shoot to your front when you see a bird, but let it get up first."

We loaded the guns and started off, about twenty yards apart. Ahmed followed behind. For some distance nothing happened, then, suddenly, there was a loud whirring noise and a bird came up in front of me. I instinctively aimed and fired and the bird fell. It was a black partridge.

"Well done, well done," shouted Steve. "That's the way." Ahmed picked up the dead bird and put it in a bag. I reloaded.

We walked on and on, firing sporadically. I did miss sometimes, but then so did Steve. I also shot a pigeon by mistake, but Steve said that it was all right. We went on for a couple of miles, until we came to the banks of the Tigris, where we sat down to have some sandwiches and warm beer. I remembered my days as a schoolboy in Baghdad, almost ten years earlier, when I used to cycle out of Baghdad along the river bank to sit with friendly farmers eating freshly picked cucumbers and dates.

After lunch, we walked back a slightly different way, to the car. The shooting was not quite as frequent, but we counted more than thirty birds at the end.

We drove back quietly – we were all tired and Steve dropped me off at home with 12 birds, my share. The cook was delighted, but I thought there were too many for us, so I decided to send six to Faisal, to cheer him up and two to Aunt Ina and Uncle Max. We had them some days later and they were delicious. I also got a very kind letter from His Excellency, Tahsin Kadri, the Minister of Diplomatic and Palace Affairs at the Royal Palace, thanking me.

"29.12.53   *Royal Palace, Baghdad, Iraq*

My dear Mike Arnold,

I did not realise that you were so such a good shot until I received the partridges you were so amiable to send to me.

With my hearty thanks,

Yours very affectionately,
Tahsin Kadry"

Mike said that it all sounded like fun, but that he had enjoyed his picnic with Frances-Mary. I tactfully did not enquire further.

I had seen nothing of Uncle Max, who had kept a low profile, it being very much his way not to intrude or interfere. I called him at the clinic and had a short chat with my friend Babu, his invaluable Indian clerk. Babu said: "Oh Master Andrew, what a privilege to hear you. Such a long time – my goodness – it must be years."

We chatted for a couple of minutes, and then Uncle Max came on the line.

I could hear that he was busy, as always, so we kept the conversation brief. He suggested that I come to his house for lunch with him; he habitually ate late – at about four o'clock – and alone. It had always been our habit, when I was living there, to eat together when Aunt was absent on one of her many social engagements. "Come tomorrow," he said. "Your Aunt is at the Swedish Embassy again for the afternoon."

The following day, he sent his car for me and I went to his new house, which I had never seen before. It was a large and imposing mansion on the other, less developed side of the river, Karradat Miriam, with a huge garden and many balconies. It was pale yellow and shone in the winter sun. A few years later, when Uncle and Aunt finally left Baghdad, it became the Iranian Embassy.

All the servants I had known, and who were my friends, had gone. The new lot were very welcoming and pleasant, but it was not the same.

Uncle Max and I embraced and sat down to lunch. I had already eaten mine so I just nibbled, as I had always done, on some Arab bread and drank *shineena*, a watered yoghurt drink.

"Well," said Uncle Max. "So here you are, all grown up. Tell me what you are doing and how your life is at University."

I told him about my life at Jesus, about my Hellcat, about my way of living and the things I did. I also told him – the only one in the family – about Wendy and my feelings for her.

"Well," he said, having listened patiently, "A full life is a good life. You are studying hard, and maybe also learning to manage money, that is very important. It is wonderful that you have found a girl to love. It is pleasant to meet girls, but not many are special, and you say this one is very special." He pondered for a bit, and drank some tea from his glass. He still had the Russian habit of drinking strong black tea from little decorated glasses and sucking it through a lump of sugar in his teeth.

I said that Wendy was very special indeed and that I was going to try to get her to marry me. "I tried before with girls but they were not right. This one is right," I said.

"It is good to be married," said Uncle Max. "There are so many different kinds of marriage. You might want to marry a girl because she had money, or was very beautiful, or very well connected. Some married couples are good friends, some just manage to be content." I thought he looked a little sad. "But perhaps you can be clever and lucky and fall in love and stay very much in love with each other, and make babies and have a family – this is the best." He looked a bit sad again.

"I will certainly want a family. I had only you and Mother and Aunt and I want my own family and my own place," I said.

"That is good," said Uncle Max. "You must love her a lot and give her many beautiful things. Ladies like fine clothes and jewels." I laughed.

"How can I give her clothes and jewels?" I asked. "I have no money, and anyway, she does not want such things."

"In Europe, nobody understands presents," said Uncle Max. "Here we learn from our Arab friends. Gifts are a mark of respect and affection – not because you want anything back." He paused. "Well, maybe sometimes it is good to return a favour."

He leaned back in his chair and chortled quietly. "I will arrange something. Do not worry. Nobody will know anything."

I asked him how things were going in Iraq and how Faisal was doing as a King.

"He is a good boy and is trying to be a good King," said Uncle Max. "But they won't let him, and the Prince Regent thinks he is still a little boy." He sighed. "Nobody likes the Regent and I can see a storm coming to Iraq. Many people are going away and your Aunt is getting nervous. But how can I leave my clinic and my friends? If I go, who will look after all the poor people?" He sighed heavily and drank some more tea.

The day before I left to return to England, I received a small parcel from him with a short note, saying:

"Beloved nephew,

This for your Wendy. Is from Aunt but she does not know yet. Be happy. Get married.

Your loving uncle,
Dr. Max Makowski Pasha"

Uncle Max was a Pasha of the first class, entitled to a standard of three horse-tails.

In the little package was a beautiful bracelet of silver filigree, with large lapis lazuli polished stones inset in panels. It looked to be antique Persian.

We flew back without incident. Mike told me on the way that he had been able to reach an 'understanding' with Frances-Mary and that if he could soften her father up a bit, he thought he might propose, but he had to ask his parents first. I was very pleased for him and congratulated myself on my perspicacity.

Andrew had left some days earlier to go back to school. Felicity, who was in no hurry to get back to England, stayed on for some weeks with her father and my mother, enjoying the sunshine and the parties.

We arrived in England on a dark, drizzly afternoon and drove immediately to Wendy's house in Northwood, for the party to which we had been invited.

The gathering was a pleasant one, typical of the time. A number of young men and girls, both local and from Cambridge who were friends of Wendy, were there. They were mostly formally dressed There was dancing to the gramophone, a tasty buffet prepared by Wendy's mother and some party games.

"And now," Wendy suddenly announced, "here is Mick, whom I have flown in for the party especially from Baghdad to entertain you. He will sing for you."

Since Baghdad was viewed then as the romantic city of the Arabian Nights Tales, this made a great impression on her guests.

I noticed Wendy's parents looking at me rather suspiciously. They still distrusted me profoundly, because of the dubious reputation of my countrymen, and were convinced that I had nefarious designs on their daughter. I noticed, however, that Mike was immediately accepted, since he fairly radiated Englishness and was therefore, by definition, wholly honourable.

I took out my guitar and managed to sing a few songs. It amused me to sing in different languages ending with a Polish folk melody; this made Wendy's parents even more uneasy.

Gradually, Mike and the other guests left and, since I had been invited to spend the few days remaining before term started with Wendy, I stayed behind. It was the first occasion since my arrival that I could be alone with her, so I immediately pulled her into the now deserted dining-room and presented her with the silver bracelet. She was very startled and tried to say that she could not possibly accept such a valuable gift, that English girls were not supposed to do this, that her mother would imagine the worst. After some persuasion, I did manage to get her to accept it, on the grounds that it was a very Arab thing to do and I would be mortally insulted, hurt and lose face if she refused it. It looked marvellous on her wrist.

Term started and we all exchanged news of our holiday activities. Colin had had a quiet Christmas at home, with lots of parties. He was very much a party man, very elegant and courteous, and much in demand as an escort for the young ladies on the fringes of the landed gentry. He always behaved beautifully, and had such exquisite manners that he was often taken for the younger son of some Lord. In fact, his father was Secretary of the Westminster Bank, a charming, polite and considerate elderly gentleman whose passion and hobby was mediaeval church music notation, with its curious square notes and strange symbols. He once confided in me that he could not wait to retire, so that he could devote all his time to his hobby. Colin's mother, sadly, had died when he was a young boy.

Teddy had spent Christmas in a series of romantic assignations, the details of which he uncharacteristically refused to divulge.

This term was mainly notable for the fact that Wendy and I saw a great deal of each other and that the better I knew her, the more besotted I became. The other notable event was Wendy's pantomime.

Wendy has always been a leader, not a joiner. Although there were many theatrical clubs and societies in Cambridge, which constantly put on shows and plays, she decided to form her own society (inspired not least by the fact that girls were then not allowed to join The Footlights) and to put on a pantomime at Girton. All her friends told her it could not be done, it had never been done, it was hopelessly low-brow.

But somehow she persuaded the usually very conventional authorities at the College to allow it, subject only to a preview of the script.

She set to, and wrote a satirical review based on the pantomime format, female Principal Boy with good legs, Good Fairy, Bad Fairy, Dame, slapstick, and a Happy Ending. It was set in New York and Ruritania: there was a scene in a psychiatrist's office. She persuaded leading lights from the Footlights to perform, and our Rooster's President and distinguished scholar Dr Frederick Brittain to be the Dame.

The pantomime, named 'Champagne Cinders' went into rehearsal. I was cast as one of the three traditional broker's men, named in this case, Slim, Slick and Sordid, and appeared in gangster-style clothes, looking both dim-witted and menacing. When Wendy's parents came up to a performance, their doubts about me increased.

After many excitements and rehearsals, the pantomime went on at Girton and was a sell-out for all its performances. It was much lauded in the local papers, including *Varsity*, but its greatest triumph was that Harold Hobson of the *Sunday Times*, London's major theatre critic, came specially up to Cambridge and gave it an unqualified rave review in the national press. I could not have been more proud of Wendy, and even some of the senior academic ladies at Girton had to admit that it was good for the College's reputation, and approved.

I did little studying; somehow my life was so full and so happy that there just was not enough time in the day for everything. I had become Deputy Editor of *Varsity* and this meant added supervisory responsibilities.

But my friends, principally Colin and Teddy (with whom I still sang and gave cabaret shows) were gradually turning against my relationship with Wendy.

They came together to see me in my rooms and sat down, with serious faces.

"Look," said Teddy. "We have been talking this over between us and we think you should listen."

"What?" I enquired. "What is wrong?"

"You see," said Colin, "it is this Wendy thing. You are going overboard about it. She is not right for you and, anyway, you are too young to be taking girls so seriously."

"That's right," chimed in Teddy. "Love 'em and leave 'em,

that's the way. I am not going to get married until I am at least thirty five, if ever. What's the point?"

"Well," added Colin, "perhaps not thirty five, but not yet, anyway."

I sat there staring at them. I am sure they spoke with the best intentions but they were so wrong. How could I get across what I felt, how terrified I was of losing her, how perfect she was.

"Well, thanks," I said after a while. "I understand what you mean but you don't understand what I feel. I am glad you want to protect me, but, believe me, I know what I am doing. I know what I want."

They went on for a while, but I refused to budge and, eventually, they gave up and we talked of other things. Teddy and I intended to make a record and he had found a place to do it and worked out the costs. We would have to sell twenty discs (they were 78rpm graphite) to break even.

This we duly did. On one side, we sang two songs together, on the other I sang two solo. We sold 21 copies.

Later, I found out that Wendy's friends had similar opinions about us and had tried to persuade her to call the whole thing off.

This was also the term when we met George. He was a Lebanese – the first I had met since school in Egypt – and a very charming person. He was older than we were by some years, and had already obtained a degree from the American University of Beirut. He spoke fluent English, French and Arabic and I was delighted to be speaking Arabic again. Wendy also joined in our conversations in French, much to her enjoyment.

George was a sophisticated and urbane man. He was very proud of being Lebanese. "I am not an Arab, you know," he said, "we are Phoenicians; the most cunning and clever traders and negotiators the world has ever known. Never try to compete with a Lebanese; you are sure to lose."

His very wealthy father had sent him to Cambridge for six months to perfect his English, though I thought he did not need it. But he considered it a holiday and amused himself in many ways. His favourite past-time was to infiltrate a group of extremely wealthy Pitt Club young men who fancied themselves expert gamblers. George, quiet and reserved, would allow himself to be drawn into their card games, with apparent reluctance, and proceed to lighten their wallets by considerable sums.

"They really do not know what they are doing," he said. "The more they lose, the bigger their bets and the more reckless they become. Luck is easily offended, and if you do not take her seriously and accord her the respect she deserves, she will not stay by you. But it also takes practice." He chuckled. "My father has often said that mostly the wrong people have money."

He really was an expert gambler, cool, calculating and shrewd. He taught me many of the rules he had developed for himself and they were to stand me in good stead in the future.

But he was also kind, generous and a good friend. On one occasion, when playing for matches with Wendy and me in my rooms, he let her win, much to her delight (though she maintains to this day that she beat him fair and square). He refused to play for money with friends.

We sometimes went out to a meal together, and if it was one of the days when the cold rain lashed the pavements and an icy wind blew in from the Fens, we would gratefully shroud the Hellcat in a tarpaulin and ride with him in his large American car.

The end of term came. Easter holidays were fast approaching and so far I had made no plans. Wendy was off touring Germany with a production of "Twelfth Night" (whose cast also included my friend Dan Massey) and I was at a loss. My parents were still in Baghdad, though Mother said they would be returning in time for the summer.

Just before term ended, Teddy came strolling into my room, looking smug. "I have had a wonderful idea," he said. "I am going to make a new man of you and take away all your troubles. I am going to save you."

I looked at him enquiringly. "What on earth are you burbling about?" I asked.

"I have decided to go on a Retreat," he announced.

"Retreat from what? Retreat where?" I really did not know what he was talking about.

He grinned. "I am a Catholic, as you know, and steeped in sin. In fact, I rather enjoy sin." I nodded; I had noticed.

"So once a year I go on a Retreat to my old school, Ampleforth College, where I confess like anything and am cleansed and can start again with a clean slate." He looked at me seriously. "I think you could do with some cleansing yourself," he said.

"But I haven't been particularly sinful," I said indignantly, "and besides, I am not a Catholic."

Religion had never played a very important part in my life. Although Mother said she was a Catholic, she hardly ever went to church, and was married to Ronnie according to the Anglican rite. At my schools in the Middle East I was in constant company of Greek Orthodox, Roman Catholic, Moslem, Jewish, Protestant, Druse and many other sects and the question of faith never did arise. Of course, I believed in God, but I also believed that it was the same God for everybody, and He could be approached from many different directions. After all, right was right in all monotheistic beliefs, so the ritual, I thought, was not very important. In school in England, I went along with the mainstream, and was duly catechised and confirmed in the Anglican faith. But I maintained my private beliefs.

I decided that it would be interesting to spend a week or so in what was, effectively, a Benedictine Monastery, peopled by monks living a very simple life. So I agreed to go, much to Teddy's delight. This was partly due to the fact that he would get a free lift to the Yorkshire wilds, in the doubtful comfort of the Hellcat and with a companion. I was pleased to find a home for the holidays.

We accordingly set out, on a cold March morning, heading for York. In those days there were no speed limits on roads outside towns and I could let Hellcat have its head – it was exhilarating. We drove and drove, stopping only for petrol and snack meals, until we reached the moors. The weather had not improved, and we were rather wet and cold.

We were travelling on a somewhat deserted road across barren terrain, now not too far from our destination, when there was a tremendous bang, something burst through the side of Hellcat's bonnet and flew across the ground; Hellcat gave a gasping wheeze and expired. There was silence. Teddy and I looked at each other.

"What happened?" he asked after a moment.

"I don't know," I replied. "I'll have a look."

I opened the bonnet: the engine was steaming and covered in oil and water. After examination, during which I got oil on all my clothes, I discovered that the engine-block plug, inserted when the engine was cast, had come loose and exploded through the side of the bonnet; the engine block was cracked and the cylinders wrecked. Hellcat was dead.

"You must go and get us a lift from the village we just passed," I said to Teddy. "After all, this was your idea."

"Yes, " he said morosely. "But it is your rotten car."

After some discussion, he went off up the road while I sat in the drizzle and mourned.

After quite a long time, he returned with a tow-truck. The driver, a mechanic, had a good look at Hellcat, and his face assumed a sorrowful expression.

"Can't do much with her," he said, shaking his head. "I'm afraid she is not really worth repairing – just scrap now."

He scratched his head and thought for a while. Then he said: "Look. If I take you and the car back to the village, I won't charge you anything, but just take the car as scrap in payment."

I had no alternative but to agree to the offer, and we went back to the village, where I bid a sad farewell to a car I had dearly loved.

We continued our journey in a slow country bus, which dropped us outside the gates of the Abbey and College of Ampleforth.

This was a large collection of buildings of various sizes and shapes. It was holiday time so there were no boys about in the school proper. Teddy led me down a drive to a large building adjoining the Abbey Church. He opened the large dark door and we went in.

The rest of the day was spent in meeting large numbers of Brothers and Fathers, as well as the Abbot. All were very welcoming and apologised that, since it was Lent, their Spartan life was even more austere than usual.

Teddy must have told them that he was bringing a potential convert, because that day and the following days, they seemed to pay much attention to me. There was nothing much else to do, other than eat, pray and sleep; thus most of my time was spent in conversation and discussion with my hosts. It was very interesting to delve into philosophy, theology and morality with such learned people.

But soon it became plain that they wished me to accept Roman Catholicism and be brought into the fold. I argued, using the opinions I had always believed in, but these were soon demolished by the Brothers' logic and persuasiveness. Teddy, of course, supported them whole-heartedly.

I do not really remember clearly what happened next or how Teddy managed to insert the subject of Wendy into the general discussion. I do know that I felt that perhaps I should abandon my normal life, join a community and study to become a monk. I had had a varied and unsettled existence and the thought of an uncomplicated peace, rigid routine and the discharging of all my cares on a loving (Roman Catholic) God was attractive.

I must have temporarily lost my reason; the stress of constant exposure to pressure and argument, in an isolated and austere environment must have pushed me over the edge, for then I did something which I have regretted ever since and which nearly ended all happiness in my life.

With Teddy's prompting, I wrote a letter to Wendy, my beloved Wendy, telling her that I thought perhaps we should not continue our friendship, and that I was going to be celibate for the rest of my life.

Within an hour or so of posting this appalling and stupid letter, it began to dawn on me what I had done. I woke from the spell that had seemingly been woven round me, and cursed myself for a naïve and credulous imbecile. I had destroyed the one thing that made my life worth living, that I would never find again, and had put paid to any chance of future happiness, to say nothing of the misery and anguish I had undoubtedly given Wendy. I was in despair; I could not stay in Ampleforth another minute so, briefly thanking the Brothers for their hospitality and ignoring Teddy's questions and remonstrations, caught the first available bus and made my way south.

The rest of the holiday passed in a daze. I went to stay with the Pattinsons, from where I tried to telephone Wendy. I wrote many letters to her, all with no success. She was deeply hurt and miserable and, quite rightly, wished never to see me again. I had an awful feeling of helplessness and guilt, and also a consciousness of having casually broken something that could not be mended.

Another summer term began, with the usual long sunny days to spend on the river, and the usual black cloud of exams, this time the important Part 1 of the Tripos, looming. But I was enveloped in my own black cloud of gloom, and could find no interest in anything. I went through the motions of studying, exchanging monosyllabic greetings with friends and working on *Varsity* so as not to let the others down.

Colin came to see me. He sat down on the sofa and looked at me sadly.

"What is going on?" he said. "Teddy has told me that you went mad in Ampleforth and ran away, just because you broke up with Wendy. Look on the bright side," he added. "I told you, and so did everyone else, that she was wrong for you; you did the right thing."

It was all I could do to be polite. "You don't understand," I said. "None of you understand. You can all go to hell..."

I behaved so badly to everyone that some of my friends, Axel, Sam Brittain and Mike Zander, as well as George, expressed their anxiety and asked if they could help. I avoided Teddy and refused to speak to him.

I even approached some of Wendy's girl friends at Girton, notably Jo – a tall, willowy blonde who was Wendy's closest friend, but she just looked coldly at me and walked away. She had been one of the girls who tried to persuade Wendy to drop me, considering me to be quite unsuitable, and thought Wendy well rid of me.

I contemplated suicide, quite seriously, but came to the rueful conclusion that I was too cowardly to attempt it properly.

In the meanwhile Wendy, who was of a much stronger character than I, both braver and more determined, decided after a period of sadness that she was by no means going to let me spoil her life, and made sure that I saw her going about with a variety of men, laughing and joking, and apparently having a very good time. I began to understand the meaning of true jealousy and found out, for the first time, how sour and corrosive it was.

I particularly remembered a verse which a Persian friend had taught me, from the Rub'ayat (quatrains) of Omar Khayyam which went (in translation):

"*The moving finger writes and, having writ*
Moves on. Not all thy piety or wit
Can lure it back to cancel half a line,
Nor all thy tears wash out a word of it."

I tended to follow Wendy surreptitiously, and noticed she was apparently becoming friendly with an acquaintance of mine at Jesus. Marshall was a weird person, who refused ever to discuss his background or family, who spoke reasonable Russian and was devoted to rather strange books, particularly by Ayn Rand. If I craned out of my bedroom window, I could just look into his main room, round the corner and on the ground floor. I spent many hours, leaning precariously out of my window in the rain, and spying on Marshall and Wendy, as they sat comfortably in his warm room, endlessly chatting.

The term passed slowly. I remember very little of it, except when I had to review a light production, performed by a small group, on a houseboat on the Cam, called the "Riverboat Revue".

I duly went to the first performance and suddenly, to my horror, saw Wendy, in a skimpy top and grass skirt which showed lots of leg, play and sing with a guitar. In fact, she sang very well and looked delightful, but the other acts were appalling, the comics dreadful, the songs boring and the power frequently failing, with unfortunate effect on illumination and microphone. I was forced to pan it in my *Varsity* report, "a brave attempt that did not come off": though I said Wendy sang well. Unhappily, she took the review as a personal attack and I was worse off than ever. She still refused to acknowledge my existence.

I somehow managed to do the end of term exams for Part 1 of my degree (six papers of three hours each), and made my way home. My parents had returned from Baghdad and were living in their house in Chipstead, in Surrey.

I continued to write to Wendy, pleading for us to get together again. There were no replies. I moped about, a nuisance to my parents, who could not guess what was wrong, since I did not wish to tell them about Wendy.

On one occasion, Mother did fix me with a glittering eye and said: "What is wronk with you, my darlink? You can tell your Mother EVERYTHING. It does not matter how serious. I have much experience in the world, and maybe I can help..."

"Thank you," I said. "There is nothing wrong – perhaps it is my age. Many of my friends are also unhappy sometimes."

"Ach," she said dramatically. "Yes, I remember YOUTH. It is very difficult time. You have to learn pain of LIFE!"

I agreed and, thankfully, she let the matter drop.

I had been having trouble with my back; an old injury caused by my playing prop in heavy rugger scrums. It was decided I should have an operation, not long before the end of the summer vacation, to try to remove the nagging pain it caused.

Accordingly, Ronnie arranged to have me admitted to St Mary's Teaching Hospital in London, and for the operation to be performed by the then President of the Royal College of Surgeons, Professor Dixon-Wright. On a preliminary visit to him in Harley Street, he made me strip and lie on my front on a cold leather couch. He peered closely at my back and slapped me hard on the buttocks saying: "Yes, my boy. We can fix this."

I was duly admitted to St. Mary's and put in a large ward. The nurses were charming, although they (and I) were terrified of Matron, who came around regularly, like a thunderstorm. She reminded me of Fizz's Nanny, in Baghdad.

I had written to Wendy telling her about my forthcoming ordeal, somewhat exaggerating its seriousness and hinting at the possibility of not making it through the procedure. I was prepared to do anything to get her back.

The operation duly took place and was uneventful. A day before, the Professor came round the ward, with a large court composed of his many students and junior doctors. I was laid bare and undignified before their assembled gaze, much embarrassed by the presence of the female students, while the Professor explained my case. I suddenly noticed a figure, lurking at the back, doubled over with laughter. On closer perusal it turned out to be Bruce, a good friend of mine from school, who was studying medicine at St. Mary's. My disgrace was complete.

Some days later, somewhat sore but recovering quite quickly, I was reading as visitors' hour started and the assembled families and friends of the patients in my ward came thronging through the door. I had no interest in this, since I never had visitors.

Then, to my utter astonishment, I noticed Wendy coming through the door. I could not believe what I was seeing. I rapidly lay back, hid my book, closed my eyes, assumed an expression of patient pain and suffering and gave small moans. I hoped I was looking suitably pale.

She tiptoed to my bedside and looked at me. I slowly opened my eyes, gazed at her listlessly and said: "Please, please, will you marry me?"

She thought for a moment, standing there and holding a small bunch of flowers.

Then she said: "Yes."

My world, after a moment while I assimilated this huge, stupendous word, exploded into colour. Matron, whose face peered into the ward, was suddenly beautiful; an indescribable feeling of joy burst in me. We kissed. The visitors at neighbouring beds smiled and clapped approvingly.

We sat for the permitted hour, both talking at once, since there was so much to say and so little time. I remember I mentioned that I had been showing the nurses how to Charleston – and almost spoilt everything again, until Wendy's sense of humour asserted itself. It was one of the two or three happiest days of my life.

For the following days, she visited me in hospital. Then I was discharged and we met in London – somehow there was never enough time to talk.

Term started. This was my final year and, sadly, I had to move out of my comparatively palatial rooms in College and into another Jesus College owned house in Jesus Lane, next door to the one where I had lived during my first year. My accommodation was almost identical: the same tiny, freezing bedroom in the attic, the same shabby sitting room on the ground floor, with its sputtering gas fire and decrepit furniture; the same durable landlady with her apron and strict rules of behaviour. But I was so happy that I did not mind in the least.

I saw Wendy every day and our friendship and love grew and grew. It is I think important to realise the difference between the two: it is quite possible to be friends without love, as it is to love without being friends. In our case, we were lucky – we had both.

We spoke endlessly about marriage, its meaning, its responsibilities, children, home, and all the other aspects of our life together. We agreed that the old myth that people who marry must have identical interests, the same hobbies, the same backgrounds, was, in fact, a myth. We thought that different activities and interests brought a richness to life together and each profited from the knowledge and enjoyment of the other.

And thus it proved. Wendy's abiding passion for the theatre, her love of art, her coruscating energy were matched by my deep interest in words, in politics and in journalism. We did share a common desire for a home, children and travel, and a passion for playing the guitar, among other things.

We then had to solve a number of difficult problems. We had to try to obtain approval from both Wendy's parents and mine, and we foresaw many pitfalls. There was the question of the College attitude (both Girton and Jesus) to married undergraduates. My degree would be taken at the end of the year, while Wendy was a whole year behind.

But we decided we could not wait until all these problems were solved by time. We felt that every moment not together was wasted and this was unnecessary. Also, we feared that all the parents would try to delay things indefinitely, in the hope that we would change our minds.

One day, Wendy came to see me in my dingy room, as usual. I seldom went to see her in Girton, where the undergraduates lived in long corridors, and were beset with rules like not closing the door if a visitor was present, not cooking, not singing and so on.

She sat down on the sofa, looking rather ill.

"What's wrong? " I asked in a worried way. "You don't look at all well."

"It isn't anything," she said and stretched out on the sofa, holding her stomach. "I just have an awful pain there."

I remembered something my Uncle Max had mentioned once. "Is it low down on the right side," I asked. "Here, let me show you." I moved over to her and touched the lower part of her right side. She gave a small scream.

"Ah," I said knowingly. "You've got appendicitis. The sooner we get you to hospital, the better. It may rupture and then you would be in real trouble."

After some argument, she agreed to go to her doctor and I took her there. He told me to go to the waiting room, so I sat down and leafed through out-of-date magazines, worrying.

I sat there for what seemed a long time. I looked at my watch and realised that nearly two hours had passed. I peered out of the room at the elderly lady, the receptionist next door. She looked at me in surprise and said: "Good Heavens, are you still here?"

"Well, yes. Is everything all right? The Doctor seems to be taking a very long time."

She laughed. "My poor young man," she said. "The Doctor took your friend to hospital ages ago. They went out by the back door to his car. She is at Addenbrooke's", she added. "They've probably operated by now."

I made my way as quickly as I could to the hospital, and sure enough, Wendy was in theatre. I waited. After some time, the surgeon came out and told me that they had been just in time, that the appendix was about to rupture and that I had saved her life. I felt hugely relieved, and rather proud of myself. He also said I should go away and return the following morning.

The next day, I returned to see her. I had been very extravagant and brought with me a large bunch of flowers and a sizeable box of chocolates. She was lying in bed and looking a bit wan and tired. I tried very hard to cheer her up and succeeded in making her laugh, which made her say "ouch". She said that she would have to stay in hospital for ten days, and thanked me nicely for the flowers and chocolates. I had been helping myself to the latter as we sat and talked and saw, when it was time to leave, that I had absent-mindedly devoured more than half.

She was soon back to her old self, and we began to plan the future in detail.

I suddenly got a surprise. On returning to my digs one evening, the landlady grumpily handed me a brown paper parcel. "This came for you," she grumbled. "Why don't they address these things to College..."

I went to my room and opened the parcel. It was from Uncle Max, from Baghdad. By some sort of magic, and Embassy connections, he had managed to send me a two pound tin of caviar (it seemed all right, since it was winter) and a beautiful silver South Iraqi dagger. There was a note:

"Most beloved nephew,

I am sending to you a small gift and also some good caviar, which I remember you like. Here things are bad. Your Aunt wants to go to Europe and I feel bad also. Maybe we shall go.

You must always be a good man and be happy with your Wendy. I wish very much to see her. Perhaps I will. Faisal is unhappy. The country is unhappy. Why do people not live peacefully together?

Your loving uncle,
Dr. Max Makowski Pasha"

Uncle Max sounded very unhappy and I was worried because I had never seen him anything but quietly content. I determined to ask Mother what was going on.

I was sitting and thinking, and moodily eating caviar from the tin with an old teaspoon, when Wendy came in. She looked at me in surprise.

"What on earth are you eating? Why are you sitting in the dark?" she asked.

"This is caviar," I replied. "Try some. It is the very best Beluga and my uncle sent it, but he sounds very unhappy, and I am anxious about him."

Wendy tried it – it was the first time she had tasted caviar – and pronounced it nice. I told her that one should really eat it on thin toast, with butter and a squeeze of lemon, accompanied by ice cold vodka. Unfortunately I did not have any of these things. We companionably shared the caviar and the spoon and ate it up, while I explained about my Uncle Max.

I talked to my Tutor. I told him I was thinking of getting married.

He looked at me in horrified amazement.

"Are you out of your mind?" he asked when he could talk. "What are you thinking of?" He paced round his study. "You are an undergraduate, for God's sake. You have not finished your degree. You are much too young and have no money."

This was, almost word for word, the litany I was going to hear from everyone to whom I told my plans.

"With respect," I said when he stopped, exhausted. "I know all that. What I would like you, please, to tell me is what the College would do about it. I will wish to live with my wife when we are married, and I will find my own accommodation. Is this acceptable from the point of view of residence qualification and can I still take my degree? After all, I am not living in College now."

Mr. Fisher thought for a bit. "Well," he said. "You seem to be serious. I will do all I can to help. Yes, you can still take your degree, as long as you live within the precincts of Cambridge. At your own expense," he added. "Who is the girl, by the way?"

I told him about Wendy and mentioned she was at Girton. He smiled mirthlessly. "She is going to have a very tough time," he said. "Those old biddies are going to be hard on her."

"Well," he said after a pause. "When you are ready, come and see me again. I wish you luck, though I still think you are being foolish and precipitate."

So it seemed possible, if not exactly welcome.

Wendy had a very much more difficult time with Girton. She related it to me when it was over. She had gone to see her Tutor, a very nice and sympathetic lady, who felt obliged to take her before the Mistress of the College. The latter, while sympathetic, was surrounded by a covey of maiden harpies who were outraged that love should take precedence over academic interests and who were all for throwing Wendy out there and then. After all, women had had to fight hard to be allowed to study at Cambridge at all, and it was only very recently that they had actually been awarded full degrees like the men. Wendy was letting the side down.

The conditions they finally offered were that Wendy could stay on after marriage, provided she lived a celibate life in College and behaved, in all respects (curfew, discipline and so on) as though she were a single undergraduate.

We were twenty two and twenty years old, and very much in love: these terms were obviously unacceptable to us both, so we decided that after marrying me, Wendy would leave the University and, in our view, share my degree, if I got one.

Our friends, even those who had opposed the idea, now gradually came round and agreed that perhaps, after all, we might be happy together. I was particularly pleased with Colin and asked him, when the time came, if he would be my Best Man. He consented with enthusiasm and was, thereafter, a stalwart supporter. Wendy asked Jo, her closest friend, to be bridesmaid and she, also, was willing to help us in every way she could.

Term ended and we went home for Christmas. We had agreed that we would tackle our parents over the Christmas period and try to get their co-operation, if possible. Equally, we were determined to go ahead anyway, even without their agreement.

Ronnie and Mother had rented a flat in Half Moon Street, just off Piccadilly, while Ronnie was sorting things out with BP. He wanted to retire and BP were keen to have him retain links with them, since they were planning to support a new Middle East Association, to form a liaison and meeting place for British business and Middle East enterprises, sadly lacking at the time, and had their eye on him as the man to organise it.

A few days after I joined them in the flat, I tackled the problem. We were in the sitting room, and I was recounting what

I had done the previous term.

"I have not told you before," I said, "but I have met a very nice girl." I paused. "In fact, I have known her for some time but have not mentioned it because I was not sure."

"Not sure of what?" asked Ronnie, puzzled. Mother looked at me and suddenly a light shone in her face.

"Ach, darlink," she exclaimed. "Your Mother knows. You are in Love," she stood up and kissed me on the forehead. "I know about Love! It is Life. How wonderful."

Ronnie raised his eyebrows. Mother went on: "She is a Lady, yes? She is maybe rich... I am sure she is very beautiful. My Son would choose well."

"Wait a minute," said Ronnie. "You have had girlfriends before. What's the fuss all about?"

I had not had a chance to get a word in. Now I stood up. "I want to marry her," I said firmly.

Everyone started speaking at once. Ronnie was telling me not to be silly and reciting the litany to which I had grown accustomed from my Tutor and friends. Mother was torn between the romantic aspects of the occasion, her fear that the girl in question may not be worthy of me, and the practical problems she could foresee.

For the next few days there was a great deal of Talk and Discussion. The situation was analysed, dissected, approved, disapproved, explained, taken apart and put together. The waves of disapproval broke on the rock of my determination. I was adamant. I had lost Wendy once and was not going to do so again. I counterattacked with my last weapon: "If you won't agree and help me, then I shall have to do it alone. You can't stop me. With you or without you I am going to marry Wendy."

This was somewhat melodramatic and colourful, but I knew I had to win Mother over. It worked.

"Ach my Darlink," she cried. "How romantic you are. It is in the blood," she said to Ronnie, who snorted loudly. "Such passion we Poles have; it drives us to a madness."

Ronnie shrugged and looked heavenwards. He knew he was on the losing side.

Mother administered the *coup-de-grâce*: "Bring her before

me," she commanded. "I will examine her and see if she is deserving of my Son."

So it happened that I asked Wendy to come and meet Mother for tea. She had been having very similar problems with her parents. While Mother was not at all convinced that Wendy would be worthy of me, so Wendy's parents were equally convinced that their daughter should not throw herself away on some fly-by-night Pole, since Poles were well known to be untrustworthy and immoral. Good Heavens, this one had actually lived in Egypt and played the guitar! Also, it would mean that she would throw away her academic qualification for which they had saved and planned for so long.

Nevertheless, Wendy stood firm, and they finally agreed, though reluctantly and with many *caveats* about my future behaviour. They would much have preferred somebody English.

Wendy and I met and discussed the various aspects of our parents' attitudes. She consented to come to tea with Mother, and duly appeared, at the appointed time, at the flat in Half Moon Street. Ronnie was on his way out as we arrived, but stayed just long enough to be charmed by Wendy and for Wendy later to pronounce him delightful. He left. As soon as I had introduced Wendy to Mother, she said: "Go now. Do not come back for one hour. Now this young woman and I will have a Talk. It is talk of women, and you must not be here."

I winked at Wendy and left, to walk aimlessly round for an hour.

Wendy told me that my mother began by fixing her with a beady eye and saying, "My son Loves you and Wants you, and what he Wants he must Have." She went on to cross-examine her in the greatest detail. Happily Wendy was amused.

The upshot was that Mother thoroughly approved – as I knew she would – recognising in Wendy the same determination and strength of character which she, herself, possessed. She could also, with her romantic heart, see that we were both deeply in love. Once persuaded, Ronnie was not a problem – Mother took care of that.

The families got together and agreed the logistics. There was some pressure on us to wait until the summer vacation, after my exams, for the marriage to take place. But we stubbornly refused and eventually compromised by agreeing to have the ceremony, at Cambridge, during the Easter vacation. This would give us all some nine weeks to prepare everything.

We went back after Christmas and I started on the administrative details, buying the licence, booking the church opposite my College.

Wendy was busy with organising her wedding dress and that of her bridesmaid Jo: Colin as Best Man had to arrange the hire of morning coats, top hats and so on. The date was fixed for the second week of March, a Saturday. Wendy's father booked a post-ceremony reception at the best hotel in Cambridge, the University Arms, and the invitations went out.

After some thought, we decided to send an invitation to Fizz, in Baghdad. Of course, it was quite impossible that he should find time from his Royal responsibilities to come, but I wanted him to know I was getting married. He was kind enough however to send us his best wishes, together with two silver vases, decorated with Amarah work, and engraved with the Arabic initial "F" and the Royal Cipher.

All our friends were by now happy for us, not least because of the victory of our generation over our parents' one and over the stuffy College rules. There seemed to be no remaining obstacles to our happiness.

But no path is ever completely smooth. In the middle of our preparations for the wedding, Mother told me that Uncle Max had become seriously ill. He had contracted one of those awful muscle-wasting diseases which would cause paralysis slowly to creep up his body until he could no longer breathe, when he would die. There was no cure and, as a doctor, he naturally knew what would happen.

Aunt Ina abandoned her social life, her status as the best hostess in Baghdad, and devoted herself fully to looking after my uncle. She sold everything: the house, the beautiful jewels and carpets, the silver plates and cutlery as well as her furs, cars, and most of her designer clothes. She then said goodbye to her Baghdad friends and took my uncle to Vienna, to a clinic, where he had studied for his degree so many years before and where he still had some very good friends. He was not ever to leave that clinic.

I was devastated. Uncle Max had seemed immortal, eternal. He had in many ways replaced the father I could scarcely remember. He was the rock on which I had depended for so much of my life, my closest and best friend, the only member of my limited family with whom I could speak openly and always be sure of a sympathetic hearing, of understanding and of wise advice. I loved him very much and I knew he loved me. I had desperately wanted him to meet Wendy.

Perhaps it was as well that he had to leave Iraq when he did, although I wish it could have been in happier circumstances. Less than three years later, there was to be a bloody revolution, in which foreigners were massacred, Faisal and his family foully murdered in cold blood, and the military reign of terror begun, which only ended many decades later with the fall of Saddam Hussein.

I do not remember much about the rest of that term. Certainly, I found it difficult to concentrate on any academic work. I resigned from *Varsity*, since I could no longer give it the attention it deserved. My friends did their best to support me, but my mind was so full of dreams and plans – quite apart from a deep, abiding happiness – that there was not much they could do.

Term ended and the day finally arrived. In the morning, Colin and I met for breakfast though he was so nervous and jumpy that I was obliged to eat his breakfast as well as my own. We dressed in our hired plumage and went to church.

I confess I did not notice much of what was going on. I know there were people there, and I recognised some faces, friends of my parents as well as College friends and Wendy's parents. She came in, dazzling in a beautiful white dress and looking radiant. I was lost. She was on the arm of her father and accompanied by Jo, who was but a pale shadow.

Wendy joined me at the altar and smiled. Tears of happiness welled up in my eyes and everything was blurred.

I listened to the wonderful, sonorous old words. When I said 'I do' I really meant it with every fibre of my being. It was as though a curtain had come down behind me and the path stretched ahead, in glorious sunshine, with a huge feeling that everything now was right, and that I had finally come home.

There was the reception, the cutting of the cake, the presents, congratulations, smiles, drinks... I stood beside Wendy and it seemed that we were in our own world, and that everything around us was faintly unreal.

Ronnie had very kindly given me the munificent sum of £40, for a new suit and our honeymoon. The suit was splendid and the remaining sum enabled us to pay for hotels and food and the hire of a car for two weeks to drive down to Devon and Cornwall. The honeymoon was crowned by my cunningly including Helston in our itinerary, where I gorged myself on oysters. Wendy, sadly did not share my passion for them. But she loved the shaggy Dartmoor ponies, the fishing villages, the walks along cliffs overlooking the sea, the cream teas, the wild flowers and our signing "Mr. and Mrs. Arnold" in the hotel registers.

We simply forgot the world; it did not exist. It was a wholly idyllic time.

We went up to Cambridge before term started, to look for a lodging, since I could no longer live in my Jesus digs, nor Wendy in Girton. We could only afford a tiny rent, so after much searching, we found a flat above a hairdresser's shop, for fifteen shillings (75p) a week.

The flat consisted of a small sitting room with a battered sofa, a small bedroom with a sagging double bed and a sort of kitchen with a rusty gas range and a huge stone sink with one, decrepit, cold water tap. The toilet was in a rickety wooden shed at the bottom of a longish garden, full of spiders and other creatures, unpleasant during the day and positively terrifying and freezing at night. We thought the flat was wonderful.

We learnt to sleep clinging like bats to either side of the bed, as if we relaxed we finished in a heap in the hollow in the middle. Wendy learnt to sleep through my snores. The greengrocer next door generously gave us some orange boxes, which we covered with wallpaper and turned into shelves and side tables. We unwrapped, appreciated, then rewrapped and stored away in Wendy's parents' attic some of our grander wedding presents: delicate sets of fine porcelain coffee cups, silver coffee spoons, elaborate table cigarette lighters, crystal ashtrays, and so on, convinced that one day they would come into their own.

But we did entertain. Kind friends would arrive bearing coffee, tins of biscuits or baskets of fruit, which we all enjoyed together. Colin and Jo were frequent visitors, sometimes bringing Pimms and strawberries to take down for a picnic on the Backs, where the College lawns went down to the Cam. Teddy arrived with wine and cheese and the latest girlfriend.

Uncle Max sent his best wishes. He was too ill to write himself. We sent him a photograph of Wendy which, Aunt later told me, was on his bedside table constantly until he died. I wished so much that he could have met my new wife – I am sure they would have become great friends.

A few days after we got back, I was called to see my Academic Tutor, Mr. Rossiter.

He was sitting at his desk in his book-lined study, and looked up as I came in.

"There you are, Arnold," he said with a smile. "So you are now an old married man. Congratulations." He motioned me to a chair.

"You know," he continued, "Much as we approve of the holy state, this University, and this College is principally a seat of learning, though you may not have noticed. It is not a newspaper office, nor a theatre, nor a stage for performances by guitarists..." I just sat there; there was nothing to say.

"You have a good brain," he said. "But the best brain is not much good if it is not used. If you fail your degree, or get a Third Class – what we call a Gentleman's Degree – you will be letting yourself and the College down. There is not much time left before Finals, you know, so you must get down to it really seriously." He grinned. "Of course, I understand that you have removed from Girton, for your own private company, a promising young English scholar. I am sure that together you will be able to produce a decent degree."

I was grateful. So many Dons were humourless, acid and stuffy. But the way Mr. Rossiter, a brilliant scholar, put his message was very acceptable. I promised him that I would follow his suggestion and do my best. I felt that not to do so would be letting him down, and that mattered.

It was a bitterly cold April. We were very poor. There was no heating. So, equipping ourselves with the relevant books and past examination papers, we spent most of our time companionably and warmly in bed, under a great pile of blankets and coats, studying, discussing and arguing about bits of English literature, Greek philosophy and Anglo Saxon poetry. Wendy would examine me by putting difficult questions which I had to answer with suitable quotations, arguments and astute comments.

Weekly, I still had to go to supervisions, but the graduate student who looked after me, actually professed himself satisfied. I know this, since I got a scribbled note from Mr. Rossiter which simply said: "Keep it up!"

The exams finally came: six three-hour sessions, on various subjects from Middle English through to modern poets. I could answer and write short essays on most of the questions, and, at the end, somewhat exhausted, felt I had perhaps not failed.

In the event, I got a Second, much to my surprised astonishment, which, I suspect, was shared by Mr. Rossiter. But I have always considered my degree as joint between Wendy and myself; it seemed only fair that, having studied together, we should share the result.

The usual free time followed, since undergraduates had to complete their residence qualifications, and stayed up for a week or more after the exams. This was the time of May Balls, punting on the river, theatre performances and other amusements. As an old married couple we observed the amusements of the young, and felt smug.

But now it was time to think of the future, and a job. I knew only that I wanted to be a journalist. I had greatly enjoyed myself in the civilised and sophisticated *ambience* of the *Manchester Guardian* during my vacation job there. I thought that, with an English degree from Cambridge, it would be easy to get a good job on a prestigious paper. I could not have been more wrong.

I wrote to all the papers I could think of, and got polite replies saying that, without experience, there was no opening for young reporters. Apparently a holiday job on the Guardian and deputy editorship of *Varsity* did not impress.

I had begun to despair, when it occurred to me, after swallowing my pride (after all, I had to support Wendy), to ask Ronnie for help. He made some enquiries and finally announced that he had found an opening for me on the *Newcastle Journal*. I had never heard of it and I had never been to Newcastle, but there was no other option, so I gratefully accepted. Wendy looked up Newcastle in the atlas, and was astonished by how far north it was. It was practically on the Scottish border. But after all, we were used to cold winters in Cambridge. It was worth a try.

I arrive at Jesus College,
Cambridge

Mike Zander, Axel Ohlsson and
Wendy Joyce in Jesus College

I interview Billy Graham the evangelist
on his first trip to England, for *Varsity*,
the undergraduate newspaper

I enjoy driving my
beloved Hellcat

Teddy Harper and I performing
our cabaret act

Wendy and I become engaged...

...and are married

I enjoy being a newspaper reporter
for the *Newcastle Journal*

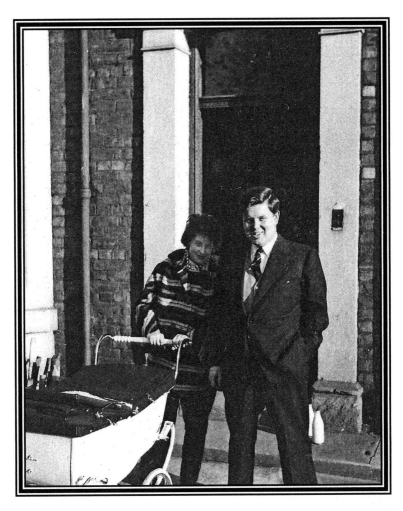

Proud new parents in front
of our Newcastle flat

Wendy sings to our
small daughter Nikki

My induction course into
Shell International Petroleom Company
(I am centre, top row)

The *Reina del Pacifico* on
which we travelled to Chile

CHAPTER TWO

Newcastle
and Shell

We went up to Newcastle by train, sitting companionably side by side like an old married couple, happy and excited at the prospect of setting up house.

We had spent some time after coming down from Cambridge staying with Colin. His father had died and, with his inheritance, he was able to buy a delightful little oast house in Sussex. We were extremely jealous but went to stay and enjoyed ourselves.

Wendy was pregnant. I was ecstatic. All my hopes and dreams were coming true in such a short space of time. I felt it was all more than I deserved, and swore to myself that Wendy would never regret her decision to marry me. I would devote my life to her and to the baby – at last, I had something of my very own.

The journey passed quickly and we arrived in Newcastle on a rather drizzly late August day. We had very few belongings and could easily carry them, so we made our way to a modest lodging house, where we would stay while finding a flat.

Wendy would do the looking, while I went along to my new employers, the *Newcastle Journal*, to sort out the details and find out how much I was going to earn. This was not information I had; I was so relieved to be offered the job that I just assumed conditions would be acceptable. After all, as head of the family I was responsible for their well-being.

The office in which I eventually ended up was exactly as I imagined a proper newsroom to be. There was none of the gentility and polish of the *Manchester Guardian*. It was a huge room, with battered wooden desks and chairs, an atmosphere blue with cigarette and cigar smoke and a perpetual din of shouting, clatter of typewriters, boys rushing about with papers and files and an air of enormous activity. There were many hat stands with damp coats and hats exuding a musty smell and almost everyone was in shirtsleeves and braces.

I was directed to a corner of the room where there was a slightly larger desk. An elderly man, with a seamed and lined face and sparse grey hair was speaking on the telephone. "All right, Joe," he was saying. "Get it all down, and we might get a couple of pars out of it. But get the names right this time, for God's sake." He slammed the phone down and looked up at me.

"Yes," he said. "What do you want?"

"I was directed to come to see you," I said. "You are the News Editor, aren't you?" He nodded. "I am Mick Arnold and I have come to work as a reporter for you. My wife and I," I savoured the words, "have just come to Newcastle and I am anxious to start as soon as I can, please."

He grinned and rummaged on his desk, which was thickly covered with bits of paper, a half-eaten apple, a brimming ashtray and other miscellaneous objects. Also on it was a tall metal spike on a wooden base, with many bits of paper impaled on it. Over the time I worked there, I grew to hate that spike, as did all the reporters, since if a story or report you brought to the Editor was not one he liked, it would be 'spiked'. There was no appeal, no argument; you just went on to another story.

He unearthed a file and looked in it.

"Ah yes," he said. "Straight up from Cambridge, are you?" He did not wait for an answer. "You may think that after the *Guardian* this is a shambles... But I can tell you that this is real journalism – no glory, no 'hold the presses', no posh facilities. This is the real thing: we dig out the news and we tell it. That is what proper journalism is. It is hard, it is often boring, it is not often glamorous, but you will learn about people and that is the most important thing there is; about their joys and their tragedies, their disasters and triumphs, their honesty and their lies. I have been at this desk for more than twenty-five years and

I wouldn't have missed a minute of it."

He took a bite out of his apple. "Lecture over," he said. "George," he yelled, and a young man came over. "This is Mick. He's just come; he is the new cub. Show him the ropes."

I thanked him and turned away. "Hey, wait a minute," he said. "Haven't you forgotten something?"

I stopped. "No, I don't think so," I said.

"Well," he snorted. "You have a lot to learn. What about pay and other minor details? Don't you even want to know how much will be in your weekly envelope?" He turned to George. "It's pathetic," he said. "Whatever will they send us next!"

I felt my face flushing – what a way to start...

"You will be earning seven pounds a week, that is a pound a day. It's a lot more than I started on. How you manage is your own business. If you are looking for a flat, you might care to look in on Jill." He paused. "That's Jill Brookes, a terrific girl. You are replacing her because she is moving to Durham. I am sorry to lose her and you will have to be something special to replace her."

He looked down at his desk again. "Call me Ted," he muttered. "Everyone does."

"Thanks... Ted," I said. I turned and walked away with George. "He is a great guy," he said. "He tries to be frightening but he is really a pussy cat. We all love him and most of us call him father." He grinned. "So long as you do what is wanted and don't try to cheat, you'll get on fine."

George, who had worked for the *Journal* for some years and was a specialist in Council reporting, with truly astonishing shorthand speed, introduced me all round, to the reporters, sub-editors and even office boys. The columnists and editorial staff were elsewhere in the building and I did not get to know them very well.

"Be careful with the subs," advised George. "They lick your story into shape, headline it and so on. If they don't like you, they can make you look pretty damn stupid. They know this, so try not to let them get a rise out of you, which they will try to do."

Just then there was a deep rumble, rising in pitch and making the whole building vibrate. I grabbed the edge of a desk.

George laughed. "It's all right," he said. "Don't worry. It's just the presses starting up for the afternoon edition of the *Chronicle.*" The *Journal*, a morning paper, shared premises with a sister publication, the *Newcastle Chronicle*, an evening tabloid. The staffs of the two papers were quite separate and there was a deadly rivalry, with misleading tricks being played, stories withheld, and life made generally difficult for the opposition. But it was basically good-natured and the staff often met for a friendly drink at the local pub.

George also gave me the *Journal* style-book. This explained in detail the way things were spelled and written in the paper: for example, up to ten, amounts were written out while after ten numbers were used. It also reiterated the news reporter's creed: 'Get maximum information into the first paragraph – where, when, who, what and how. Details can follow.'

George pondered. "By the way, you can claim expenses every week, but they must be clearly described and should have a receipt. Try never to claim anything more than a pound – Ted has forgotten more tricks than you will ever know, and it is one of the few things he gets really ratty about."

The rest of the day passed quickly. I shared a pint and a sandwich with George and hung about the office until Ted said: "Go on, get out of here – get back to your wife. Be here tomorrow at eight."

On the way back to the lodgings, I wondered, as I walked in the drizzle (buses were expensive) if I had done the right thing. Here I was, with a wife, and, before too long, a baby. Quite heavy responsibilities; I wondered if we would manage, and if Wendy would not think me a poor provider.

But when I got back to her, she hugged me and said that she had had an awful day but that it was wonderful to see me and how much she loved me.

She looked very tired but so beautiful that I loved her more than ever.

I told her about my day and all the exciting things in prospect. My wage was somewhat less than I had hoped for, being considerably smaller than my earnings as a National Service officer. But I said I thought that with the almost two pounds a week Wendy was getting from her father, we would somehow manage.

When Wendy went up to Cambridge, her father had arranged a seven-year covenant payment to her of £100 a year. It was extremely advantageous to him from a tax point of view, so I felt no compunction about adding it to our income.

When I had finished telling Wendy about the *Journal* and Ted and George, she related her own adventures. She had been trudging the streets of Newcastle looking for a flat for us, which was why she looked so tired, but, she said, in most cases the landlord or landlady had just took one look at her, said 'no babies or children' and closed the door in her face. Being very slim, her pregnancy was now evident.

This was all sad and discouraging. But it was quite remarkable how resilient I felt. I had always managed somehow alone, and worked things out without much reference to anyone else. But now, with Wendy's warmth and support, the added responsibility was much more than compensated for by having her with me. We could face all these problems together and this gave us both great strength.

We tried to work out a budget, and after discussion, decided that we could afford up to five pounds a week for rent, with the remaining four pounds for everything else. This would mean no entertainment, no luxuries of any kind, no interesting food. But we could exist and, when the baby came, Wendy was determined to breast feed it and we would also have a pint of milk free, according to Government regulations of the day. I was quite determined not to ask for charity from my parents, nor from Wendy's, above the existing covenant.

I told Wendy about Ted's advice to look up Jill Brookes, as there might be the possibility of a flat. She decided to go to see her the next day.

My first working day was not very exciting. Ted had a large book – the news book – in which he listed, throughout the day, ideas and information for likely news stories. These were then allocated by him to the various reporters and, sometimes, photographers to investigate and write up. He was in touch with news services, stringers in nearby towns and villages, hospitals, police and so on, so there was never a shortage of possibilities. His skill was in sniffing out the good stories and sending the right person to write them.

He called me over when I had been at my new desk for a few minutes. "I am throwing you in at the deep end," he said. "You are a la-di-da Cambridge person who doesn't even understand the local Geordie accent and the others are going to look very sideways at you until you prove yourself. So you can do a story which no one ever likes to do."

He gave me a slip of paper with an address on it. "This is where a family lives, in Jesmond (a part of Newcastle). The 19-year-old son was hit by a car yesterday and died in hospital. Go there and get a human interest story, with a photograph."

I gulped. I had not the faintest idea how to go about such a task. But I was determined to 'prove myself', so I took the slip of paper, put on my mackintosh and a trilby hat I affected (as an ace reporter) and went out into the drizzle.

I found my way to the address by using a series of buses (keeping a careful account of the ticket costs) and arrived at a nondescript terrace house in a back street. I knocked at the door and, after a while, this was opened by a lady with her hair tied up in a kerchief, a print dress and an apron. Her eyes were red – she had obviously been crying – and she was sniffing loudly.

"Yes?" she enquired.

"Er, I am from the *Newcastle Journal* and my editor has sent me to tell you how sorry we were to hear of your sad loss," I mumbled rapidly. I really did not know how to approach the problem.

"Yes?" she said again.

I took the plunge. "Well, you see, we would like to write something nice about your son. He will be a sad loss and we want people to know what a splendid chap he was."

She looked at me and sneezed.

"Perhaps I could come in and talk to you about him, and also to his father if he's in. Of course a photograph would be just wonderful and people could see what a good-looking fellow he was." I was desperate. I was not getting anywhere. I must be doing everything wrong.

She wiped her nose on a handkerchief. "I'm sorry, hinny," she said hoarsely. "I don't know what you are talking about. I have terrible hay fever but I don't have a son. You must have come to the wrong address. Goodbye." She closed the door.

I just stood there feeling foolish. I looked again at the slip of paper – I had misread the number of the house. The one I wanted was about ten houses away down the road.

I went there. It was a surprisingly easy visit. The mother was in a state of shock, and wanted to talk about her son. I got my story and the photograph I wanted. I found as the months went by that most people are glad to tell the press about their tragedies and triumphs.

I went back and wrote up my notes. Ted was moderately pleased with my first effort, but the subs mangled the story horribly and cut it down to a single paragraph. The photograph was not printed.

The day passed without further incident and, in the evening, Wendy sympathised with my sad first assignment. She had gone to see Jill Brookes, at the top of a tall building with many flights of stairs. Jill had opened the door and Wendy had been asked in. Unfortunately, the flat had already been let to somebody else, but Jill, who was also pregnant, had asked Wendy to stay and regaled her with coffee and biscuits. She stayed there all day, and it was apparent that the girls would become friends. Wendy came back carrying a big bag of delicious apples. Jill and her engineer husband Mike became two of our closest friends and godparents to our children.

I remained on the early shift at the *Journal* (9 to 6) for the whole month, doing rather boring jobs, some involving verbatim reporting of Council meetings. Without shorthand, I could not keep up, so I asked Ted if there was any way he could help. He said he would think about it.

Some days later, Wendy told me, with a huge grin, that she had found a flat. The next day was my day off, and we went to see it together. It was in a pleasant street in Jesmond, at the top of a large Victorian terrace house.

The landlord, a foxy man with white hair, who gave the

impression of being rather crafty, met us at the house. On the ground and first floors lived a curious man, a salesman, married to a quietly desperate French wife; they had two small children, and another was born while we lived there. We later found that the French wife had an obsession with cleaning everything in sight, with polish, powders, scourers and the like, and tended to give us dirty looks if we left a speck of mud on the stairs or did not polish our door-handle. Her husband had only a finger and thumb on his right hand and, I am afraid, I tried to avoid shaking hands with him.

Up yet another flight and through a door across the stairs, and we were in our new domain. There was a huge cold living room, with an elegant bay window and a large blue velvet sofa sitting in solitary splendour in the middle of the floor, and next door to it a large bedroom with an elderly double bed. Then up half a flight was our bedroom, which overlooked a dreary-looking back yard with clotheslines and dustbins and an outside toilet. A few steps up from this was a very damp-smelling and ancient bathroom, with a prehistoric gas geyser above the somewhat battered tub. There was a permanent, strong smell of gas, and we always felt, when having a bath, that we were risking our lives. Next door to this was a toilet, with a frighteningly decayed wooden floor.

Another half flight, and there was a kitchen – very primitive – and a tiny attic room with a skylight which we immediately decided would be the nursery for the new Arnold, when he/she arrived, and a snug little sitting room with a gas fire and view out over Jesmond Terrace and trees.

I tried to negociate with the slightly dubious landlord and eventual agreement was reached on five pounds a week, payable in advance. We would have to pay for the gas through a coin gas meter. Wonderfully, we were able to move in immediately.

Coming home was a little like mountaineering, but we were both young and reasonably fit, so we managed. We moved our few possessions in that same afternoon, bought some bread and milk, as well as a packet of tea and a pot of jam, and established our first proper household, if you discount the primitive flat we had occupied for three months in Cambridge.

I felt proud and very grown-up: a wife, a house, a job, a baby on the way. What else could there possibly be? My friends at the office, the following morning, remarked on my obvious joy and congratulated me on the flat. We all toasted my success in pints at the pub at lunchtime. Life was rosy.

In the meanwhile Wendy was beavering away, spending our meagre capital on household essentials and some kitchen things. She acquired some orange boxes, which we covered in wallpaper to hide the raw wood. We had the basic necessities and could live, modestly, within our means. After payment of the rent and the gas, we had about three pounds for everything else per week. And on this we somehow managed.

Wendy's mother very kindly sent us a little refrigerator, which was a huge luxury. We could now keep food safely for more than a day, and the milk would not go off. Wendy, having explored the neighbourhood, found that vegetables bought at the very end of the day were cheaper, while day-old bread was much more inexpensive than fresh. Turned into soup and toast, they were fine. All sorts of economies were possible, and we did not mind.

One day, Ted called me over. "Listen," he said. "There is a shorthand class in town which you can attend. It is an hour, three times a week. I think you need the skill if you are going to be a serious reporter."

"That is terrific," I said. "I would very much like to attend these classes." I paused. "But we can't afford them, whatever they cost. We are just scraping by, as it is."

"No, that's all right," Ted grinned. "The *Journal* will pay and you can claim the bus fare if you like." He scratched his chin. "You may not think so, but I was a cub once. I know what it is like."

I thanked him. What an exciting prospect. All great reporters should have shorthand, I thought. And I was going to be a great reporter.

Accordingly, the following day, a Tuesday, I found my way to a rather sordid room on the second floor of an establishment which called itself "The City Administration and Secretarial College". The room was a large schoolroom, with rows of broken-down desks and chairs, facing a raised podium with a desk and a blackboard on the wall. I was early, since this was my first day and I had allowed time to register with the bespectacled middle-aged lady at the entrance. I had equipped myself with a bundle of pencils and a notebook, and sat down expectantly at a desk.

After some minutes, there was a shrill chattering, some giggling and a noise of high heels on the wooden floor. The door opened and a flood of my fellow pupils poured into the room.

They were all girls, some two dozen of them, aged between about 16 and 20, with one exception, an elderly lady of about sixty. They all appeared to know each other and went to their desks. It seemed I had somehow chosen an unoccupied one, so they contented themselves with staring openly at me, and making comments, *sotto voce*, behind their hands as they giggled. The elderly lady glared at them, but with no effect. I was the only man in the class.

That is, until the door opened again, our teacher came in and the noise subsided.

He was a wizened little man, not much over five feet tall, with sparse dyed hair and slightly trembling hands. He sat at the podium desk and peered around myopically.

"Welcome to the new class," he said in a high voice. "You look a likely lot." The girls giggled and a voice at the back said: "Likely for what, then?" There was more giggling.

Our teacher said: "My name is Mr. Gort, like the Field-Marshal." He croaked, and we were to learn that this was his manner of laughing. "I once held the record speed in Pitman's shorthand in the country, but I don't expect you to do that. Seventy words a minute will do."

He looked at me. "Ha, a weed in a garden of roses," he said to a chorus of laughter. "Well, I suppose it doesn't make any difference; not in shorthand, anyway."

And so we started. In spite of his other shortcomings, Mr. Gort was a good teacher. I gradually got used to being the only male, and the girls came to accept me as one of them. They no longer felt constrained by my presence, and freely discussed their most intimate activities and thoughts. I was glad that I was not expected to do the same, after I made it clear that I was unwilling to answer questions about my private life. I dare say they thought me a stuck-up prig, which I suppose I was.

But my colleagues were somewhat mischievous and one day I arrived in class to find, written on the blackboard:

Mr Gort
Likes his port
It's not only his hand which is short.

Mr. Gort didn't seem to mind, and rubbed it out saying it didn't scan. He then made us write it in shorthand.

We were deep into hooks and whorls, positioning and abbreviations. Shorthand was not unlike Arabic, except written the other way, so I did not find it particularly difficult. In fact, I rather enjoyed it and, by the time the course was finished after about six months, was able to do about 110 words a minute, ample for my needs.

On the last day, I was astonished when Mr. Gort said I was best in class and the girls presented me with a box of chocolates, saying I had been a good sport.

Ted was pleased and my reward was to be sent to many boring Council meetings.

But he was kind to me. When I had been at the Journal for about two months, he suddenly presented me with two thick, hardcover books. I do not remember their titles, but he said: "Here. Take these. Give me 250 words on each – a review, you know."

I looked at them – there was a biography and a novel.

Ted went on. "It is an extra perk. When you have finished them, go and sell them; they are yours. I am sure an extra pound or so will be useful."

I thanked him profusely, and from then on was given a couple of books to review, every month or so. I made an arrangement with a local bookshop and sold them for a third of their cover price, which was the accepted amount. This gave me about an extra pound a time. Everything helped.

Wendy was looking forward to the baby and we decided it was time to book a hospital bed for her. She had been to a doctor for periodic check-ups and all seemed well.

She tried every hospital in Newcastle, but all were booked solid and there was no spare bed available at the likely time. We began to get very worried. And tried them again and again, but to no avail. Finally we were accepted by the Salvation Army nursing home who, out of the goodness of their hearts and sensing our desperation, agreed to take Wendy in.

Wendy's parents came up to inspect us (and, I suspect, to make quite sure I was not misbehaving in any, allegedly Polish, ways). They bravely stayed with us for two nights, bought us a large basket of standard provisions, and left. They also, much to our surprise, told Wendy she had been bequeathed £100 (a vast sum) by her recently deceased grandmother. We experienced a mixture of joy and sorrow.

This munificent sum enabled us to buy some second-hand chairs, a table, and some rolls of wallpaper, with which Wendy, now in an advanced state of pregnancy, covered the walls of the nursery-to-be, as well as buying a cot and a small chest-of-drawers for Arnold junior.

We also at my selfish instigation, bought a car. I had visions of driving the family out on my days off, exploring the countryside and being able to visit Jill and Mike Brookes, in Durham, without resorting to the tyranny of the buses.

The car was a tiny, 1932 (thus some twenty three years old), Austin 7. It was in a decrepit state, the brakes were very dubious and required a great deal of foresight, the tyres bald, and exhaust fumes seeped through the rusty floor, which had holes in it. It cost seven pounds, on the road.

I did what I could to it, but to no avail. It was always a lottery if it would start or not, and it was anything but reliable. Sadly, it expired completely after three months and I was forced, to my disgust and disgrace, to pay a man £5 to take it away as scrap metal.

Life at the *Journal* continued at an even pace. As I grew more familiar with my job, and Ted began to trust me more, I was sometimes allocated a job outside the city, travelling, usually with a photographer, in the *Journal* car with a driver. These were mostly to do reports on fêtes, openings of things, centenaries and such. Not very exciting, but a chance to get out of town and see the gorgeous countryside of Northumberland and Durham.

He also entrusted me, at the request of the Features Editor, with the job of writing provocative letters to the *Journal*, under assumed names, to try to induce outraged readers to start a correspondence chain, which was good for the readership. I enjoyed this very much, finally becoming so scandalous that Ted told me to calm it down or we would have demonstrations outside our building. It was interesting to see that our sister paper, the *Chronicle*, copied the idea and was also successful. The exercise gave me a life-long suspicion of the correspondence pages in newspapers.

Finally Wendy's moment came. As always, the contractions started at night. I managed to prevail on our downstairs neighbour, who had a company car, to drive us to the nursing home, where Wendy disappeared into the natal ward. It was most unusual, and somewhat improper, in those days for the husband to attend, so I sat around in waiting rooms and, when the nurse told me it was likely to be a protracted labour, went home.

In the event it did take what seemed a very long time, and poor Wendy, who told me of this later, had an old-fashioned doctor attending her. The whole pattern a birth usually followed was not then explained to mothers-to-be, there were no ante-natal classes or rehearsals for appropriate breathing exercises. Giving birth was seen as a job for the doctor, the woman was supposed to endure without too much fuss, and if she was lucky perhaps be given some gas and air at the worst moment. First-time mothers were therefore very tense and frightened. Wendy's rather elderly doctor arrived late in the proceedings, panicked, and instructed that she be anaesthetised, so she did not see our daughter born. But she was in a charity hospital, and we were grateful they had taken her in at all.

The result was wonderful. There was now a small person, a girl, in the family and I was a father. I was delighted and boasted about it in the office. I even invested in some very modest, thin cigars which I offered to my colleagues, receiving congratulations and pats on the back. This, of course, was grossly unfair, since I deserved no praise for the trauma of birth, but when Wendy came home with the baby, I did all I could to show her how proud, pleased and overjoyed I was at her magic achievement. The assorted parents expressed delight, and Wendy's mother said she would come up soon to help, celebrate, and generally be useful. Mother sent messages of sympathy and admiration, proclaiming herself to be much too young to be a grandmother, a fact which she decided to keep from her friends as long as she could.

We had, naturally, discussed the name we would give our baby, but were caught unprepared. For some reason, we had automatically assumed that the baby would be a boy, and were all ready to name him, grandly, Peter Noel St John Arnold. Now we had a little girl! Wendy wanted to give her an exciting Polish name. I did not want her to be singled out as different. We both wanted a name which other nationalities would find easy to use if we ever lived abroad. So we settled on Nicola, who could be Nicole or Nikki. I went to the registry office to obtain a birth certificate and I told the functionary that we had decided on Nicola Gail as the baby's name; we thought this was a good name, and we were sure it would suit what would undoubtedly be a beautiful, intelligent and loving person. So it turned out.

Nikki gave our life a whole new meaning; this gorgeous, small, pink being perfect in every way, created out of a deep love, was a marvellous gift. Seeing Wendy breast-feeding the baby gave life a perfection, a sort of completion of all wishes and dreams. Of course we were brought down to earth when she woke and cried in the night, by nappies which had to be hand-washed and and somehow dried in the damp air of our flat (it was October) and by being constantly aware of a small person, helpless and dependent, wholly reliant on us.

Wendy's mother arrived, and swiftly taught Wendy all the important skills, how to hold a small soapy baby firmly in the bath, how to fasten a nappy pin without stabbing herself or the baby, which nursery rhymes were the most soothing. Then she left, leaving Wendy and Nikki looking rather apprehensively at each other. "One of the most terrifying moments of my life" Wendy said. But she coped beautifully.

Then I was put on late duty.

This consisted of going to the office at 6pm and staying on for nine hours until 3am. During this time, alone in the office but for the duty sub-editor who slept on a camp bed in the corner, to be awakened by me only if I had a story to be looked at, I was responsible for all night news. This involved an hourly telephone call to a long list of hospitals, police stations (including the Tyne river police), fire stations and ambulance centres, to see if there had been any newsworthy happening, as well as monitoring the news services.

About half of the time was taken up on the telephone but, unless there were news items to write, the rest was idle. I took up this time in writing, for myself, feature articles about all sorts of subjects, ranging from romantic short stories to philosophical discussions on the meaning of truth, and so on. I destroyed them before I left the office as they really were not very good.

It was also at about this time that, during a routine check-up at the doctor's, he informed me that I was becoming grossly obese and that, since my father had died of a heart attack at the age of forty-five, I would soon be dead if I did nothing about it.

I admitted to being just slightly portly – gross obesity was an offensive slander. I told him that my busy and irregular job precluded any exercise other than miles of walking the streets, and asked if he could help me by giving me some medication to curb my normally raging appetite. After some pleading, he prescribed a substance called Dexedrine, to be taken before the main meal, and supposed to depress the appetite – I got a month's supply.

The pills were little heart-shaped affairs, of a pale blue. When I had taken my first one, I felt a striking euphoria and saw life from an exhilarating and exciting perspective. I felt a boundless energy and elation. After a few days, I found that if I took my pill after, rather than before my meal, I could get the best of both worlds. I would bound up the stairs to the flat at 3.30 in the morning, singing loudly and wondering what to do. Wendy did not much appreciate this behaviour, especially if she had only just got a now re-awakened Nikki to sleep, but I found that a few hours' sleep every other night was ample.

It was fortunate that it was just at this time that I met David and his wife, Miriam. He was an Israeli, living in Newcastle in a flat not far from us. I don't know what he did – he was always rather evasive about it – but we became, quickly, fast friends, with our relationship based on a common knowledge of the Middle East and endless friendly arguments on the relative rights and behaviour of Israel and the Arabs. Miriam had a well-paid steady job and supported them both.

We were sitting in his flat one day, after a meal prepared by Miriam (Wendy was at home with Nikki) when David said: "Why don't we write a book?"

"What book?" I asked. "A book about what?"

"A novel," he said and got up, walking noisily round the room (he always wore boots), as was his habit. "A book based in the Middle East. A story of an orphaned kid, and his adventures. We can have a lot of violence and sex – we must have lots of sex, because that is what sells books. I am sure we can do it, with my ideas and your writing skills..."

"Hey, wait a minute," I interrupted. "What do you mean? I also have ideas and you can write as well. But what for, anyway?"

"To sell, you ass," he said. "We can both make a fortune." He looked at me. "You wouldn't mind a fortune, would you?"

So, since I only slept every other night, thanks to my little blue pills, we started to write the novel of the century, to be called "Rahood", the name of the hero. David was content for us to write at night: he then would sleep all day while I worked, though Miriam got a bit difficult after a couple of weeks, and Wendy started to mutter about invisible husbands. We wrote and argued, argued and wrote. What emerged was a travesty, a violent, unbelievable text which would probably be unpublishable thanks to the lurid details; murders, rapes and seductions all provided, much to my dismay, by David's fertile imagination.

After a month, my pill supply ran out and I decided that I would not ask for more. It was obviously some sort of mind-altering drug and living such a hyper-active life was clearly not good in the long run. When I stopped taking my pills, I slept solidly for forty-eight hours, abandoned the "Rahood" project, got to know my wife and baby again, and resumed a normal existence, albeit still being rather portly. Luckily Wendy still seemed to love me.

We had been given a pram for Nikki, like some sort of elegant white coach, and she spent every morning in it, netted against over-friendly cats, snugly tucked in, breathing the fresh air even if it was snowing, in the little rather barren front garden. Wendy, having now resumed her normal slim shape, began to think about theatre again; theatre was never far away from her thoughts. After all, her intention had always been to become a professional theatre director and, had she not married me, would undoubtedly have become a famous and successful one. In the meanwhile she wrote some childrens' stories which were sold to the BBC and read on "Listen with Mother." But now, with her new responsibilities, she cast about to try to blend her two interests. Naturally, she succeeded.

She had been going to our local church, with Nikki, and got to know the church fellowship group, who met each Sunday after the morning service. She managed to interest some members, carefully chosen, in a possible production of a mediaeval morality play, 'Everyman', which she planned to present in local mediaeval churches and in Durham Cathedral. Accordingly, our flat became a haven for strange people, unknown to me, who filled it and wandered about declaiming, in mediaeval English, pious dialogue from the play. Apart from Everyman, the hero, there were notably two enormously tall men, one The Angel, six feet six in his bare feet, with a great shock of blond hair (he was to be clad all in white robes) and Death, nearly as tall, (all in black with a hood concealing his face). Various other Sins and Virtues abounded, crowding the flat. Coming home from the *Journal* was like entering another world.

Colin drove up all the way from the South to see us, in his MG TC. We had not told him about "Everyman". The cast had been trying on their costumes.

As he climbed our stairs at dusk, a tall and ethereal figure arose before him, clad all in black and with no face. It raised its arms. "I am Death!" it pronounced in a sepulchral voice. "Who are you?" Colin nearly fainted, he thought his last hour had come. We revived him with the sherry he had kindly brought us.

The performances were well received and well reviewed, particularly the one in Durham Cathedral. Wendy had somehow managed to persuade the authorities there to allow her to stage the play in its cavernous and beautiful interior. It was a theatrical masterpiece, and caused goose-bumps in the audience when at the end, at dusk, the dead Everyman was borne away , shoulder high, by six robed figures, pacing slowly down the main aisle of the cathedral, preceded by the shining white Angel and followed by the black silent Death.

During this time, one day at the office, Ted called me to his desk.

"Look what I found," he said, showing me a crumpled piece of paper on which I had scribbled one of my late-night features – it was on astrology. He had somehow come across it; it must have fallen out of the waste-paper basket.

"It's not too bad," he said. "You seem to be able to write a bit." I smirked. "I don't want to lose you to the Features Department – you are a newsman. But I have been thinking. If we have a one-off Women's Supplement – just a couple of extra pages – would you like to have a go?"

"But what would it entail?" I asked. "Do you mean I should write the whole thing?"

"Why not?" grinned Ted. "I'll give you a couple of days free and you can try. I leave the contents to you, but they should interest housewives. If you need photos or illustrations talk to Johnny." Johnny was in the photo section.

I thought it was a challenge and, anyway, a change from the rather boring routine. "Fine," I told Ted. "I'll certainly have a go but don't be too tough. I am not a housewife."

So that is what I did. I wrote articles on domesticity, on bringing up children, the care of babies, a recipe for jam (cribbed from a cookery book) and even an astrological forecast. Johnny provided some illustrations of dresses, for which I wrote a very tongue-in-cheek fashion commentary. I also did a piece on household budgeting. Naturally, I wrote under a number of assumed names; I particularly remember that the jam recipe was by Mavis Bloach.

Ted was delighted and, with a few amendments and changes, and help with the layout by the subs, we printed the supplement. Management expressed its satisfaction and gave me a small Christmas bonus.

Our first Christmas as a threesome was a happy time. The parents all sent practical gifts, thick woollies for us, small knitted garments for Nikki, a hamper of Christmas food. We had a modest Christmas meal and Wendy who had never done any cooking, (considering herself to be more intellectual than domestic) still managed to produce a slightly haphazard selection of more or less edible dishes.

She had discovered, through experience and also through the presence of her ever-hungry 'Everyman' cast, that the cheapest and most nourishing food was a sort of everlasting *minestrone*. She had learnt how to cook this in Italy. It consisted of a very large pot of assorted vegetables, tinned tomatoes, pasta, white beans and with luck a little bacon, slowly and permanently simmering on the stove. One took out as many platefuls as necessary, while daily replenishing it with whatever ingredients came to hand. It was nourishing, satisfying, always slightly different and, above all, cheap and plentiful.

After Christmas, life was a little flat, enlivened only one day when Johnny asked permission to bring a rather lightly clad young lady to be photographed in provocative poses on the tiger skin we had been given by Ronnie. I believe this was a free-lance commission, I did not ask for details. My work at the *Journal* was now wholly routine: I knew most of the staff, many of whom were friends. My assignments were all within the narrow range of minor news stories, Council reports and social events. The nightmare late shift came round regularly and there seemed no opening for any sort of promotion. My wages remained the same, though it was said that I would get a rise of ten shillings (50p) a week after a year. I was now generally accepted as an honorary Geordie and my Cambridge manner was no longer ridiculed.

I was wondering what future there might be for me in journalism. I had secretly written to a number of national dailies in London, with my *curriculum vitæ*, asking if there were any openings. There were none.

Our friends Mike and Jill Brookes had bought themselves a little house in Durham, which Mike as a civil engineer had transformed. It was perfect. He had a good job with Durham Council, a good wage, and his life was going somewhere. Where was mine going?

While I toiled away on the *Journal*, and Nikki continued to grow and learnt to crinkle her blue eyes at me, Wendy got a big idea. She decided to gather together our erstwhile colleagues and friends from Cambridge and produce a show at the Edinburgh Festival. Oxford University went up every year to the Festival, Cambridge had never been. As a result, her mother was summoned to come to help, Wendy rushed down to Cambridge to recruit a cast, and then up to Edinburgh to find a venue. This was very difficult: all the normal halls and theatres and school gyms were already booked, mostly by much more prestigious companies and groups, from all over the world.

But, of course, she did find a place: Portobello Town Hall. This was an enormous edifice, some ten miles from the city, accommodating 770 people. No one had ever hired it for the Festival and everyone who was consulted or knew about the Festival, laughed and said not only no one would bother to go there in view of the huge selection within the city, but that it was far, far too big for an amateur and untried group from Cambridge.

But she was able to rent it for a peppercorn rent, and Wendy had faith in her ability to fill it. She borrowed £100 from her father and hired the Hall for the two weeks of the Festival. She then came home to us and began the hard work of selecting her cast (who had to pay their way), writing the scripts of the show, sorting out the musical numbers, and also all the technical side: lighting, props, costumes and the many items connected with any major public performance.

When the time came, again the flat began to get rather crowded. More and more people arrived and an even larger pot was bought for the *minestrone*. This was 'Everyman' multiplied by ten, and most of the actors were staying with us in the two big rooms downstairs. Wendy's mother had given us Wendy's old piano, and it was never silent; there was singing, declaiming, dancing and arguing. In a corner people were amending scripts, peeling potatoes, making costumes and trying out make-up. At night, there were bodies everywhere and there was little floor space unoccupied.

My mother-in-law was a treasure. She came to stay and took complete charge of Nikki (who was now weaned) and took her for long walks in her pram. She did the necessary shopping and was always cheerful and ready to help. I thought she enjoyed it – it was a change from her even, untroubled life on the South coast.

I also noticed that she did not look quite so suspiciously at me; after all, it was her daughter who was the moving spirit of the hullabaloo, while I went quietly about the business of supporting the family.

Finally the move to Portobello came. My mother-in-law stayed to look after Nikki and me. I could not go with the crowd, since I had to go on working, but I did manage to get there one week-end, Ted having pity and letting me take my two days off together.

I found my way to the Portobello Town Hall and stood aghast, looking at the giant building. Inside, it was vast, with a great balcony above sloping upwards towards the roof. The stage was enormous and there was about an acre of curtain.

I found the company having lunch in a large kitchen. It was *minestrone*. The rehearsals were well advanced and everyone seemed both harried and happy. A strong bond had grown in the company and there was very little friction. Wendy ruled with the assurance of somebody who knows what they are doing. She had organised some *ad hoc* publicity in Edinburgh, though there seemed little response. But she was determined to make the show worth while and to make enough to repay the loan to her father.

The plan was, in order to utilise the Hall to the maximum, to turn the meeting hall at the back of the theatre into a morning coffee bar with one of the pianists entertaining the customers, and actors singing songs from the show, and have the major revue in the evening, of some two hours' duration, mainly of sketches and songs. The cast had a hectic schedule.

At night, the girls slept on the stage, while the boys were banished to sleep in the balcony seats. It was uncomfortable but moral.

The time came and the performances started. The front-of-house staff, ticket seller, programme sellers and chuckers-out put on their best bibs and tuckers as they waited for the crowds to come. There was a trickle of some local people, and the Hall looked completely empty. Nothing daunted, Wendy decided to go on. As it happened, one of the leading theatre critics in Edinburgh, on *The Scotsman*, a most prestigious paper, was sufficiently intrigued to trek out to Portobello to see the show.

To everyone's astonished pleasure, the next day the paper printed a 'rave' review, the whole 'Scotsman's Log' unreservedly praising and extolling the performance. It urged the population of Edinburgh on no account to miss this marvel. I remember a telling phrase with which the article ended: "In this case, I say take away the Festival and keep the Fringe." This was the more unofficial selection of entertainments, outside the major Festival programme. The BBC, who was doing a programme on the Fringe, came that afternoon and filmed a fifteen minute piece, and showed it that night.

Attendances leaped remarkably, with crowds for all performances growing and growing until, beyond belief, the final night saw a sell-out; 770 people packed into the enormous hall. Wendy's judgement was vindicated, her father repaid and the cast triumphant, having all greatly enjoyed themselves.

Wendy came home and life resumed its even course. She concentrated on Nikki, who was growing almost visibly, and family life.

I was busy at the *Journal*, with added responsibilities of doing occasional reviews of the more classical visiting entertainments. "Since you are a posh Cambridge person," said Ted, "you probably understand the more weird theatre productions and opera and suchlike."

I therefore happened to go to review a visiting Italian opera group, who performed in Newcastle for four nights. Naturally, I went on the first night and enjoyed the programme. It was not a complete opera but rather excerpts of the better known arias and tunes.

With Ted's agreement, I decided to go back the following day, in late morning, to interview some of the cast and perhaps get a good human interest story out of it.

The cast, some fifteen people in all, were chattering together, in Italian, on the empty stage, drinking coffee out of paper mugs. I addressed myself to the bass, a huge man with a black beard.

"Excuse me. May I have a chat with some of you? I am from the *Newcastle Journal* and I want to tell our readers how lucky we are that you have decided to come to our town and entertain us."

The giant turned to me, and showed large white teeth, like piano keys, in a grin through his beard. "*Bene, bene,*" he said. "Welcome. You have come for to see us so have coffee." He gestured at one of the chorus. "Bring coffee for the gentleman."

The rest of the cast crowded round me and, in a mixture of English and Italian, of which I could make out some of the sense, began to question me about Newcastle, England, what people enjoyed, if they liked Italian songs and operas and so on. I tried to stem the tide – after all, it was I who was supposed to put the questions.

After a while, they quietened down and we all sat on the stage, holding our paper cups, which were constantly refilled.

It soon became clear that they were at the end of a long tour of Britain and France, and that they had not seen their families in Italy for a long time. As a result, they were all very homesick and lonely, in the dramatic way that Italians have. I was sorry for them and I found their showing me pictures of their families, particularly children, very touching and endearing.

The result was that I completely lost my head, and asked them if they might like to come home with me and relax in a family atmosphere, as a change from hotels and lodging houses.

They were delighted. They accepted with alacrity and, like a flock of chattering birds, swept everyone into several taxis and demanded to know where to go. I hardly had time to catch my breath.

We arrived at the flat, and they followed me, thundering and chattering, up the stairs. Wendy was delighted to have an invasion of Italians, she had been so happy living in Italy.

They settled all over the flat, roosting, like birds, on all available surfaces. We still had our giant pot of *minestrone* on the stove, and they discovered this with delight. But they were careful to eat only enough to allow everyone to have some. The tenor, a thin, gangling man, produced from somewhere some bottles of wine, which he and others had surreptitiously brought with them, and the party became merrier and merrier.

Naturally, they began to sing. Then one of them, the soprano, spotted my guitar in the corner and brought it to the bass.

He looked at me. "You play, yes? Maybe you sing?"

"Well," I said, rather bashfully, "I play and sing a bit." It was embarrassing; after all, here I was in the midst of a group of professionals.

"Fine," said the tenor. "You sing, me sing, he sing, she sing," he pointed to various members of the party. "You sing first."

Wendy meanwhile was in her element, chattering away in Italian.

Then Nikki made a noise in the next room. "What is that?" exclaimed the contralto, in her rich, velvety voice. "A baby!"

Wendy fetched Nikki and the whole group crowded round. They cooed over her and sang to her, they passed her from hand to hand, they exclaimed over her beauty; they cuddled her and cried over her. They told us in detail about their babies at home, how much they missed them and longed to hold them. It was very emotional, it was very Italian.

Nikki behaved well, just smiling and blinking and enjoying the cuddles. After a while, Wendy managed to detach her from her admirers and put her back in her cot.

We then began to sing. I was obliged to start, so I thought it courteous to begin with *"Torna a Sorriento"*, which went down very well, with the cast, in harmony, joining in the chorus. It was the first time I had sung with professionals. The tenor then gave us *"La donna é mobile"*, and a duet, with the soprano *"Che gelida manina"*. Wendy sang her favourite Neapolitan love songs. Everyone sang, individually and together.

They stayed until it was time for them to return to the theatre, to prepare for the evening performance. The goodbyes and warm expressions of mutual esteem, thanks, compliments and arcane Italian courtesies (including embraces and kisses by everybody for everybody) finally ended, and they departed in their taxis, singing robustly. I went and apologised to our neighbours downstairs, but the French lady gallantly said she had enjoyed it. The following day, a large bouquet of flowers was delivered for Wendy, with a charming note in Italian.

It was now spring, and Newcastle streets had a smile on their face. Getting up was not so depressing, as it got lighter in the mornings. Nothing very notable happened as spring turned to summer. Nikki grew, and was now able to speak a few words, understand bedtime stories and even take a few very tentative steps.

We became more and more preoccupied with our future. It was not that I was unhappy at the *Journal;* everyone was pleasant, friendly and Ted was a good boss. But the routine was unchanging and my life seemed not to be going anywhere. The matter was clinched for me by Harry.

He was the oldest reporter we had; a man of vast experience and capability as a news reporter on a provincial paper. He had been on the *Journal* for more than 25 years, was Father of our Union Chapel (a curious appellation for the Union to which we all belonged), and respected as a fount of all wisdom. He had never been anything other than a reporter, and seemed to live a grey life, with his grey wife – his grown-up son had absconded to London.

We were having a quiet pint at the pub one lunchtime, when he suddenly said: "What are you doing here?"

"You know what I am doing here. I am a reporter, like you."

"You must not be like me," he said, taking a gulp of beer and wiping his grey moustache. "You are wasting your time. Don't be like me."

I looked at him "I don't understand," I said.

Harry glanced at me. "I am a failure," he said. "I know I make enough to live on, and I can do the job with my hands tied behind my back. I suppose you can even say, after all these years, that I am reasonably content." He took another gulp. "But when I was your age, I also had dreams. A big National, an Editorship, running my own show." He paused. "It never happened."

He sat for a while in silence, while we sipped our beers. "You should get out of here," he said finally. "You are wasting your time. I know you fairly well now, and I am sure you can do a lot better than moulder away as a reporter on a provincial paper for the rest of you life. You have had a good education, you know a lot of things. Now get out and use them, while you can." He drank more beer. "Don't leave it until it is too late; do it now."

I thought about what Harry had said for the next few days. I told Wendy that it seemed to make sense, and she agreed.

"But what will you do?" she asked. "More importantly, what do you want to do?"

It seemed clear that what we both wanted was an interesting life, enough income for comfort, the possibility of promotion and improvement and some security. Wendy, of course, was very keen on travel and said that going off to foreign countries, with everything that this offered and entailed, would be her ideal life.

So the choices narrowed down until it seemed obvious that I should go into oil – I had no engineering or financial skills, so the answer was marketing. I had always been at ease with people, I could speak a few languages, I had experience of travelling and, more than anything, I was familiar with the industry, through Ronnie.

I decided to consult Ronnie. As it happened, he and Mother had come up to see us for a short visit, putting up at a local hotel. They were clearly worried by our Spartan existence.

We were sitting in our sitting room in the evening, when I broached the subject.

"I have been wondering," I said. "I may have got journalism out of my system."

My parents looked at me and Ronnie raised his eyebrows.

"Yes, I know I could do better," I said pre-emptively, before he could say it; it was his favourite phrase to me. "But it is not just a question of that."

Mother looked worriedly at me and nervously grasped Ronnie's hand. "Ach, my darlink," she said loudly. "What has happened to you? Is it bad? Are you dismissed from job? Tell us EVERYTHING!"

"No, no," I reassured her. "I still have job. It is just that we see no future here, in Newcastle; we want to travel and have a more interesting life."

I looked at Ronnie. "I have been thinking of going into oil," I said.

He grinned. "So you have finally come to your senses," he said. Then he looked at Mother. "There you are, you see. The lad has got some intelligence after all." He turned back to me. "Oil is a very good career and I can help. Besides, BP is a splendid company and will give you an excellent career."

But I had already thought it through and also explained my feelings to Wendy. I had a horror of using people and any family influence I might have exerted on BP through Ronnie. It was abhorrent. It was naïve, I suppose as I had accepted Ronnie's help to get the job at the *Journal*. But the case was different: then I had been desperate while now I felt I could manage on my own.

Besides, BP was then mainly renowned for its exploration and production functions, while its geographical spread was limited and it marketed mostly in developed and sophisticated countries. Shell, on the other hand, was everywhere and had a superlative marketing reputation. I had also discovered that Shell thought of BP as an effete bunch of amateurs while BP thought of Shell as a collection of hard-nosed professionals. In my mind there was only one possible choice.

I felt guilty – I was betraying my own father, a journalist, by leaving the *Journal* and now my step-father, by not going into BP.

"Actually," I said, "I think I would like to join Shell."

There was a stunned silence. Ronnie looked aghast and Mother stared at me as though I had suddenly grown horns and a tail.

Ronnie remained speechless. Mother recovered and said: "But you cannot do such a thing! You betray Ronnie who gave us so much. You are wicked boy and must go to BP. What is this Shell.? Only BP is good..." Her voice trailed off and they both stared at me. Wendy maintained a tactful silence.

When Ronnie had recovered from the shock, like the

gentleman he was, he agreed that I had a right to make my own mind up about my future, and suggested somebody in Shell to whom I could write about a job.

So I wrote to Shell, including my details, and asking for an interview for a job in international marketing. After obtaining permission, I gave as referees my Cambridge Tutor and the Editor of the *Journal*. I could hardly give the names of Ronnie's friends in BP!

We waited anxiously, and after some days a reply came, inviting me to the Shell Head Office in London for an interview, and enclosing the cost of the railway fare.

On the eve of the appointed day, wearing my one good suit and with a fresh haircut, I went to London. I stayed the night at my Club, in Piccadilly (I was still a cheap schoolboy member, at £7 a year, paid by Ronnie) and in the morning made my way to the Shell Head Office.

This was situated in St. Helen's Court, close to the Bank of England, in the City. It was a collection of old office buildings, a warren of corridors and dark rooms and it was difficult to find any specific office. But there was a receptionist at the front door, and I was directed to a room at the back of the first floor. After some false turns, I knocked at a shiny brown door.

"Enter!" boomed a voice from inside.

I went in and found myself in a room with a large desk, some wooden chairs, some filing cabinets and a slightly grimy window looking out on a collection of dismal rooftops. Behind the desk was sitting a middle-aged man, in tweeds, smoking a pipe. The atmosphere was blue and hazy.

"My name is Arnold, and I was told to come here and be interviewed for an international marketing job," I said.

"Whoa, whoa," said the gentleman. "Don't rush me; wait a minute. Sit down."

He rummaged in a pile of files on his desk, and pulled one out. He opened it and looked at me.

"Ah, yes," he said. "Arnold, is it? Mmmm..." he pursed his lips and drew on his pipe, almost disappearing behind a cloud of smoke.

"I have your letter here. You seem to have had a busy life so far." I relaxed. The interview, I felt, was not very frightening.

"Why do you want to join Shell?" he suddenly barked at me. "I see your connections are all with BP. It makes more sense that you should go to them." He grinned. "Though they are a bit amateurish."

"Well," I told him. "They seem to market in places which sound a bit dull. After all, European big cities are all much alike and I want to go to out-of-the-way places. I have been in Iraq and Egypt and I have enjoyed myself. Those are the sort of places I would like to work in."

"Perhaps we can accommodate you," he said. *"Ismi Robinson. Tigter takallam 'arabi?"*

"Na'am, sidi," I replied. *"Afham kull shay wa atkallam al logha."*

He had told me his name was Robinson, and asked if I spoke Arabic; I had replied that I understood and yes, I could.

"Et le Français aussi?" he asked.

"Oui, assez bien," I replied.

"Good, good," he said. "we have to check, you know. Some people say they can speak a language, but know just a few words. But I can tell by your accent that you can manage. Languages are very important in our business."

I was to find out, later, that very few Shell expatriates bothered to learn to speak the language of the country in which they worked, and the same was true of the other companies. They tended to believe that if they spoke English loudly and slowly the 'natives' would understand. If you actually could speak the language fluently you were regarded by other expatriates with deep suspicion – only diplomats were supposed to be bilingual.

We chatted for about half an hour and a lady brought in some coffee. He was interested in my escape from Poland and also in my schooling in the Middle East. "Would you like to go back there?" he asked.

"Yes," I replied. "There, or anywhere else. But I don't want to stay in England."

"You have a wife and baby, I see," he said. "What does your wife think about it all?"

"She loves to travel, the further the better and also she is very good at languages," I told him.

He stood up and said: "Come with me."

We went through a connecting door and through a secretary's office into a much bigger room. This was furnished fairly opulently and there was a gentleman at a polished desk, in a smart dark suit and an MCC tie.

"John, this is Arnold. You have seen his file," said Mr. Robinson.

The smart gentleman rose and shook my hand. "I am a Personnel Recruitment Co-ordinator," he said. "Sit down and let us have a quick chat." We all sat down.

After a few general questions and some small talk, he told me that my interview was over. "We will let you know in a few days," he said as we shook hands. As I left, Mr. Robinson winked at me through a cloud of smoke; I was much encouraged.

When I got back to Newcastle, I told Wendy all about my interview. "I feel good about it," I said. "I think there is a good chance they will take me."

She was pleased. "Mmmmm. Travelling, how wonderful," Her eyes got quite dreamy. "Tropical beaches, jungles, deserts, new languages and new people. But I felt I must let you have a go at journalism; you had to get it out of your system."

"I am very grateful. I think it is gone. Very interesting, but not a lifetime occupation." I thought of Harry and his gray life.

After a few days, an official looking envelope arrived from Shell. We opened it together.

It said that Shell was prepared to offer me employment in International Marketing. I would be expected to start in early October, some six weeks hence, and join the autumn intake of new recruits.

It also told me to report to a Mrs Patcham, in St. Helen's Court on October 8, when all the details of my employment would be sorted out. The salary proposed at the start was £735 per annum while in England.

It finished by wishing me a long and prosperous career in Shell.

Wendy and I looked at each other with delight. My income would be doubled; they wanted me; it was International Marketing, with everything that this entailed.

We danced round the room, laughing. This woke Nikki in her nursery and we rushed upstairs to tell her the news, although, of course, she could not understand.

When I went to the office, I wrote a carefully worded letter of resignation, making it clear that it was not anything in the *Journal* which caused me to leave, but rather that I wanted to explore new fields, preferably abroad. I walked over to Ted and handed him the letter.

He looked at it. "Yes," he sighed. "I thought this was coming. You have worked hard, but you are not really suited to provincial journalism." He winked and gave me a broad grin. "Too la-di-da by half!"

He raised his voice: "Everybody, everybody!" The room grew silent. "Mick is sick of us and is leaving. Well, we are sick of him too…" There was a burst of laughter, and everyone crowded round to pat me on the back and enquire what I was going to do. Harry and George, in particular, congratulated me and said that, as an honorary Geordie, I would be a success in whatever I did. "Just don't forget what you learned here," they said.

Ted said there was no need for me to serve out my notice, and that I could leave whenever I wished. We then went, in a body, to our pub where we caroused for a couple of hours – I don't remember much about it, except that I was not permitted to pay for anything.

We gave notice to our landlord that we would quit our flat. We felt quite sorry to leave, it had been our first family home and there were happy memories associated with it, not least Nikki's arrival and Wendy's theatrical triumphs.

We sold our furniture (Shell said we were only allowed to take personal belongings, and a few ornaments and books with us) took the train South, and stayed briefly with each set of parents and Colin. Then it was time for me to go to London to see Mrs. Patcham.

At St. Helen's Court, the doorman gave me complicated instructions how to find her and, again after getting lost twice in the warren, I found the large room where she, and six or seven other ladies were seated at desks in the midst of filing cabinets and office paraphernalia.

Mrs. Patcham, whose name was on her desk, was a gray-haired lady in late middle age. She looked at me through rimless spectacles. "Yes?" she enquired.

"I am Michael Arnold, and I was told to see you today." I handed her the letter from Shell.

"Ah, yes," she said. "Do sit down." She rummaged in her filing cabinet, marked A to D, and produced a folder. "I shall be looking after you while you are in Shell." She smiled. "Most of my brood call me Patch, so you should too. I am your mother-in-Shell, and everything outside pure business and your career progress is my responsibility."

I nodded, not knowing what to say.

"First of all, you should know that you are one of fourteen marketing recruits who will be going on our Induction Course; you know, finding out about the Company, what it does, what it is and so on. It starts on Monday and lasts for nine weeks. Then, when it is over, you will go abroad to your assigned place of work on a one-year contract, as a trainee."

I nodded again; this was beginning to sound like the Army.

"I assume you are happy with the salary offer, since you are here, so we need not talk about it. It will be paid into your Bank account monthly (by the way, I need all your particulars and those of your family: birth certificates, marriage certificates, and any paperwork like College degrees and so on)."

"Well," I said. "I can see no difficulty there, except I do not have a birth certificate."

"How is that possible?" asked Patch. "Everyone has one."

I then explained my circumstances at length: all about Poland, my Naturalisation and subsequent change of name by Deed Poll, my being commissioned during National Service and so on. Patch listened entranced and, when I had come to a halt, said: "Well, I must say! What an exciting past. You are the first I have heard of with such a story and I have dealt with hundreds. If you show me the relevant bits of paper, we will manage somehow. Anyway, you have a passport, so that helps."

After some more interrogation, Patch said: "Now then; have you any preference where you would like to spend your trainee year?"

I gulped. I had not been expecting the question – I thought I would simply be assigned somewhere. I had no idea where I wanted to go.

Patch smiled. "Take a moment to think," she said. "I'll get you a cup of coffee. There is no hurry."

No hurry?! I had to think, both for myself and Wendy, where we would like to spend our first year in Shell. This was important – I might choose wrong and we would have a miserable time. They might not want to send me there. Perhaps it was not on the list... I had found that there seemed always to be a list.

Then I remembered Tony Westcott. He had been my friend at Cambridge and I had met him at the University Cruising Club and seen him perform with the Footlights. He was an Anglo-Chilean and was forever extolling the excitement, magnificence and beauty of his country. "You would love it," he said. "The music is fantastic, you can ski and sea-bathe the same day, the climate is wonderful, the people are terrific." He grinned. "Like me," he added. "And of course I will be there and can show you round and introduce you to everybody. You should try to visit."

This was some three years ago, but I decided to try.

I looked at Patch, who was sipping her coffee. "I would very much like to go to Chile," I announced.

Patch spluttered. "To where?" she gulped.

"To Chile," I repeated. "Lovely country, you know," I added knowledgeably. "Shell does operate there, doesn't it?"

"I don't think any trainee has ever gone to Chile before." She pondered. "But why not, indeed?" She looked the country up in one of her books. "Yes," she said. "They do have a marketing department and I know Jim Maitland, the Sales Manager. I will see what I can do."

After another half an hour of pleasant conversation, we parted. "Remember now," she said as I left. "You can ask me anything you like and tell me anything you want. I am happy to help and sort out any troubles you may encounter. Don't forget."

I went back to Hove with a lot of thinking to do. I hoped very much that Wendy would approve of my spontaneous choice of destination. So far, Shell had come up trumps.

In the event, Wendy was delighted with my choice. She remembered Tony Westcott and we immediately pored over an old atlas in the flat. Neither of us knew very much about South America, or exactly where Chile was, but the same thought struck us at the same time.

We looked at each other and almost simultaneously said: "They speak Spanish in Chile!"

Between us, we had a number of languages but Spanish was not one of them. "Well," I said. "I suppose Spanish is a sort of cousin of French and Italian, and we can speak those. So it shouldn't be too difficult if we try."

"I've always wanted to learn it, anyway," I added. "I would love to understand what I am singing about."

"If they agree that we should go there..." I said.

On the Monday I went to a conference room at St. Helen's Court, as instructed. It was a large room with desks in rows, just like school. There was a small crowd of young men milling about and chatting. I joined one group.

A red-haired man turned to me. "Hullo," he said. "Come for the course?"

"Yes," I replied. "My name is Mick Arnold and I hope to do International Marketing."

"So do we all," said the red-haired man. "My name is Gerry Thompson (with a p), and this is Johnny and this is Tom and this is..." At this moment the door opened and a dapper, elderly man walked in. He strode to the top of the room and turned to us.

"Please be seated, gentlemen," he said. "And smoke if you like," he added.

There was a general shuffling and the scrape of chairs. I sat next to Gerry.

The dapper man introduced himself: "I am Francis Jones, the Training Co-ordinator. I have come to greet you and to give you a brief outline of what this course will cover." We sat forward attentively; he seemed a very senior person. The door opened and another, younger man came in. He stood quietly in the corner.

Mr. Jones sat on a table, dangling his immaculately clad legs. "I don't suppose any of you know much about us." He looked around. "Well, this course is designed to give you knowledge of Shell and what it does. More importantly, what it is. You have not just joined a company, a large industrial concern. We pride ourselves on being more like a family; we believe our relationship should be more than employer and employee. We are interested in your families, your well-being, your problems."

This all sounded very good, but I was cautious now and reserved my judgement. I suspect most of my companions were also slightly cynical.

"Our business is oil," continued Mr. Jones. "Oil in all its aspects: what it is, where it is found, how we get it out of the ground and how we transport and refine it. We will also tell you about the many products we can get out of it, including industrial and agricultural chemicals, dyes, candles and many other things." He paused for breath; it was obviously a well-rehearsed speech, given to course after course.

"We will arrange a trip to Holland for you to look at some oilfields and also to a refinery. After all, we don't want you to get bored." Someone laughed politely. "Now here," he pointed to a table in the corner, where there was a stack of books, "you will find a history of the company. It is quite exciting and we would like you to read it. You are now Shell ambassadors and must be prepared to answer questions from the public about us." He smiled, but rather mechanically. "You can each take one with you when you go."

He stood up. "That's all I have to say, beyond wishing you the best of luck in your new career." He turned to the quiet man in the corner. "This is Mr. Richards, who will be looking after you as a course. He will tell you where to go for your lectures and will go with you on your trips. Any problems – go to him. He is used to it; you are not his first brood..."

Mr. Jones left and Mr. Richards smiled faintly as he came to the table.

"Sorry about that, chaps," he said. "It has to be done." He sat on the table. "Now, I'll tell you what is going to happen. The first five weeks you will be having lectures, here and at the Lensbury

Club, our staff Club on the banks of the Thames at Teddington Lock."

He paused again. "Then we will have a couple of weeks of travelling round Holland. We finally come back for a week or so to wind things up. By then you will know where you have been posted and you get three weeks embarkation leave before you sail."

He made it sound as though we were going to war.

The course was interesting. As well as the British recruits we had a number of so-called 'local staff' on the course, training prior to promotion within their own countries. There were some Europeans, a Japanese, and two Venezuelans. I had long talks with them, finding out about their countries and jobs; they were mostly retail specialists, supervising service stations. The Venezuelans, Pepe and Esteban, were amused by my request to go to Chile and said that, if it worked out, I would have a good time.

"But they speak horrible Spanish there," said Pepe. "They eat the ends of their sentences so you have to guess half the words. But the wine is excellent," he added.

The lectures continued: it was like being back at school with a blackboard, notebooks and diagrams. Fortunately there were no exams. We learned all about anticlines, mercaptans, catalytic cracking and octane indices – many esoteric words and a wide knowledge of the arcana of oil. It involved a great deal of geology, chemistry, finance, and engineering as well as the less scientific aspects of selling, advertising and general management techniques. Then there were the visits to places all over England.

All was going too well to last. One weekend, when we were visiting Mother and Ronnie, they told us that my dear Uncle Max had died in Vienna after fighting his wasting disease for more than a year, lovingly nursed by Aunt Ina, whom I had previously thought so self-centred.

Uncle Max was probably my closest and most loved relation, and his passing left a painful void. I was so sorry he had never met Wendy. I would never forget him.

One day, an envelope was delivered to me by Mr. Richards, who was always present during lectures, which were given by a variety of specialists in the various subjects. "Here you are, Arnold," he said, grinning. "I hope you are pleased with the news." He obviously knew what was in the envelope. I opened it. There was a letter to me from the Personnel Department, saying that I had been accepted by Shell Chile as a marketing trainee and that, after my course was finished, I should go to see Patch about the details.

Pepe and Esteban congratulated me and we all went to carouse at the Club bar after lectures. Other trainees also received their envelopes from time to time, and they seemed happy, except for Johnny, who had asked for a South Pacific Island Company but was offered Nigeria.

That night, Wendy and the family rejoiced. I telephoned Mother who, on learning of my destination, uttered a shriek. "Oh my darlink!" she cried as I held the receiver some distance from my ear. "So far away; the other side of world; we will not see you again."

"It is a beautiful country and we shall be back after a year, anyway. What is a year apart in our family?" I said, thinking of my years at boarding school.

"Ach, but I get older. Time is so precious. And what about Wendy and the beautiful baby? My grandchild will not KNOW me!"

Then it was time for our trip to Holland. We were shown oilfields with nodding hammer-shaped pumps and a refinery, visited the Head Office in the Hague, and were explained the origins of the Shell Company in the 1870s, a partnership between a Dutch company importing seashells and tropical products from the Dutch East Indies to Europe and a British shipowner and exporter of kerosene to the same destination. Hence the Shell emblem of the pecten shell and the original interest in oil.

To round off our visit we went to a local hostelry famous for its pancakes, for a late lunch. The pancakes came. We were surprised to see that they were very different from our expectations. A Dutch pancake, or *pannekuche*, was a plate-sized, one inch thick sort of omelette, with chunks of potato embedded in it, over which you poured a thick, sweet syrup. We washed them down with ice-cold *jenever.*

When I reached my twelfth pancake, I began to feel uncomfortable. Then the owner of the restaurant appeared. He indicated a painted placard on the wall, which contained a list of names, and pointed out that these were the names of the record pancake-eaters in this restaurant for the past fifty years He said "The record stands at thirteen. Eat two more and your name goes on the wall." He paused. "If you break the record your pancakes and the *jenever* are on the house."

At this, most of my colleagues gathered round my chair, slapping me on the back and encouraging me. "Go on, have another..." "Just two more..." "For the honour of England and Shell..." and so on.

The waiter brought two more pancakes and lovingly poured the syrup, while someone replenished my glass.

I made a huge effort and ate one more pancake. I had now equalled the record. The group began to clap their hands rhythmically and shout: "One more, one more, one more..."

I made a supreme effort and ate half of the last pancake. There was a loud cheer as the owner accepted the new record and asked my name, which he carefully wrote down; he said it would be duly inscribed on the list.

I do not remember much about the rest of the day, and I do not know how long my record stood, but I was glad that I had left my mark in Holland, for the honour of England and Shell.

Christmas intervened and we had some time off. We spent it with Wendy's parents and had a quiet, traditional time. Nikki was now stumping about and behaving very well. Naturally, she was the focus of attention and thoroughly spoilt by her doting grandmother.

The course ended shortly after we went back, and we dispersed, exchanging addresses and promising to visit each other in the various countries to which we would be assigned.

After the weekend I went up to London to see Patch, as instructed. She had heard about the Dutch episode and congratulated me on my record. This was the first time I became aware of how quickly and efficiently the grapevine operated throughout this huge Company; there were no secrets and news flashed round the world at astonishing speed, especially so since these were days long before the Internet and e-mails.

Wendy had been very amused by my adventures on the course and was looking forward eagerly to hearing what was going to happen next. Patch was going to tell me.

"Now then," she said. "You will be glad to hear that I have managed to get you on a very special ship to Chile." In those days, air travel being so expensive, expatriates went one way by air and one way by sea – they could choose which. Travel was first-class.

"It is very difficult to find a decent ship for Valparaiso leaving at the right time." She grinned. "So I have been forced to put you and your family into the *Reina del Pacifico*, which happens to be a cruise ship and I am afraid you will have to put up with a five week cruise around the Caribbean on your way there."

I gaped at her. This seemed too good to be true and my opinion of Shell soared. Five weeks on a cruise liner, first-class, stopping at all the romantic places on the way. Wendy would be delighted.

But Patch was not finished.

"As a member of Shell, you have to keep up appearances," she said, eyeing me up and down. "I am going to give you £100 to spend on outfitting yourself and your wife with whatever you need. You do not have to account for it; just go and spend it. It will be in your Bank account tomorrow."

"Finally," said Patch, while I was still reeling, "if you and your wife would like to have some Spanish lessons during the next four weeks, go ahead, and send me the bill. We have always found it useful for our people to speak the local language and you don't seem to have Spanish."

I was still trying to absorb what she was saying. "You have four weeks embarkation leave – you will be sailing on February 15th. I will send you your tickets and various instructions and papers in due course. We will also get you the necessary visas and send the passports to you when they have been done. In the meantime, remember if you need anything, give me a call or come and have some coffee."

I thanked her profusely and went home in a daze.

We enjoyed some happy, leisurely shopping with our bonanza.

We read up on Chile in the local library and found that the climate was not extreme – at least not in Santiago, where we would be living – so the things we bought would be useful wherever we went. We packed all our worldly possessions into twenty seven assorted boxes and suitcases.

We found through an advertisement in the local paper a much-painted and highly corseted Spanish lady teacher, who reminded me vividly of my piano teacher in Alexandria, and we learnt a few rudimentary Spanish phrases, in a stylised Castilian which would be incomprehensible to Latin Americans.

The *Reina del Pacifico* was sailing from Liverpool. Both sets of parents decided to accompany us and see us off so we duly went there by train. It was a typical February day, rather gray and drizzly. Mother, in particular, was working herself up into a great state, muttering "How will I live without you... They will eat you in the jungle... We will never see any of you again..." and making pitiful noises, while clinging on to Ronnie. Wendy's parents, who did not know her very well yet, were rather puzzled, since they took the separation in normal British style, phlegmatically, not wishing to upset their daughter by showing how much they would miss her. We were excited and happy, looking forward to a new adventure in lands we had never seen. Nikki just smiled and took life as it came.

At the docks, the *Reina* shone like a jewel in the murk. She was a large ship of some 17,000 tons, painted a shiny white with two large, mustard coloured funnels, with strings of bright lights everywhere. After much hugging, tears from Mother and promises of frequent letters from everybody to everybody, we parted and the three of us mounted the gangway up to the ship. The luggage had been handed over to a sailor, who undertook to take most of it to the hold, and the one allowed suitcase to our cabin.

We stood at the rail and waved to our family group. After some shouting and hoots from the siren, the ship was unmoored and slowly moved out. The gap between us and the dock grew, the band played and some people threw streamers. The dock slowly faded from view and we were on our way, sailing west to our first exciting posting, to Chile, to another new beginning.

CHAPTER THREE

Chile

We were shown to our cabin, which we found to be tiny; odd, we thought, for first-class accommodation, but we were very tired, it was late and Nikki was getting fractious at the change in her routine and surroundings.

The cabin was about eight feet by eight, with a bunk down each side and Nikki's cot fitting exactly between them. In order to open the small wardrobe one had to slide the cot up to the head of the bunks, to get out of bed we had to crawl to the foot of the bunk and wriggle out. We now understood why we had been told only to bring one small suitcase, and leave the rest in the hold.

The steward who had shown us to the cabin said: "There you are. All snug and comfy. If you want anything, let me know; I am called Sid." He left and we were alone. We looked at each other. The ship was swaying slightly and there was a loud and rhythmic creak in the cabin.

We looked all round but could not tell from where it was coming. Then Wendy noticed a large, six inch wide, strip of copper running across the cabin floor.

"What on earth is that?" she asked. I did not know, so I stuck my head out of the door and called Sid, who was loitering in the passage.

"What is this thing and why is it creaking so loudly?" I asked.

"Oh, that is the ship hinge," he replied.

"What hinge?"

"You see," he explained, "when the ship was built, there were no stabilisers or such modern things, so the designers thought that if you hinge the ship in the middle (the hinge is leather and copper), this will absorb some of the pitching and give us a smoother sail." I looked at him in amazement.

"You can't be serious," I said.

"Yes I am," he said. "It doesn't work, of course, but it was a great idea."

I found out later that he was telling the truth on all counts and we were forced to live with the perpetual creaking for the next five weeks.

We went to sleep that night tucked away in our little cabin. There was a porthole through which one could vaguely see the ocean, but since it was dark, we did not look out. It was a disturbed night, with Nikki crying unhappily at the new noises, smells and surroundings.

In the morning – a rather dark and dismal one – we went to breakfast in the first-class dining room. This was a huge and opulent salon, with elegant tables and white-coated stewards in large numbers, hovering about. We were early and there were not too many people about. A steward approached.

"What would you like for breakfast, Sir and Madam?" he asked. "Oh, I will bring a high-chair for young Madam," he added, doing so.

"What can we have?" I asked.

"We have everything," he said proudly. "I will bring anything you ask." He produced a large highly-ornate menu.

So we had a huge breakfast, and Nikki happily ate the appropriate baby food they provided. We felt that, with maximum availability of wonderful food and only minimal exercise possible, we would have to rein ourselves in, so as not to double or triple our weight during the voyage.

We then explored the ship. The *Reina del Pacifico* was a year older than I was, having been built in Belfast in 1931. She had five decks and carried about 900 passengers, a third of them in First Class. The classes were rigorously separated and I do not remember meeting anyone outside First Class during the entire voyage. The crew was enormous and the service impeccable.

Luxury was everywhere: magnificent dining room, a bar with much chrome decoration, a games room with table tennis tables, some comfortable lounges, a card room, a library and a radio room where the passengers could listen to crackly BBC broadcasts on the ship's radio.

On deck there were chairs, shuffleboard, throwing rings at a peg and a white line for walkers, with distances marked out. There was a modest-sized swimming pool.

There was also a nursery where small children were looked after by competent ladies in uniform. We explored this facility with Nikki and hoped that we could leave her here sometimes. But when we tried to do so, she set up such a desperate crying that it soon became apparent that this was not an option.

I thought about my only other sea voyage, from Brindisi to Beirut, when Mother and I were escaping from occupied Poland. That had been on a smelly, dirty, mostly cargo Italian ship. Now I had my own family with me, and we were travelling in luxury.

I decided to be brave and tackle the Purser about our cabin, to be sure that no mistake had been made in the allocation. I therefore tracked down this individual to his little office and, since the door was open, went in.

The Purser, seated at his desk, was a forbidding-looking individual. He was inordinately hairy, sporting large moustaches and a full beard, slightly grizzled. He wore a dark blue uniform and had a large pair of horn-rimmed spectacles, which, together with his abundant hair, served to cover his face almost entirely. Out of this camouflage there gleamed a pair of black, ferocious eyes.

"And what can I do for you?" he asked severely.

"My name is Arnold, passenger in cabin 172," I said. I had been told always to give my name, rank and number and this was the closest I could get.

"Ah," said the Purser. He looked into a file on his desk. "I have you. Is there a problem?"

"I was just wondering if there has been a mistake in allocation. I think our cabin is very small for three people and the hinge is a great nuisance. Also, this is quite a long voyage."

"Well, no," the Purser rubbed his nose. "It all looks all correct to me, according to this list. There are many different sorts of cabin and you should see some of the Third Class ones!" He grinned without humour. "She was a troopship, you know, and now they want to cram as many passengers on as they can." He leaned forward confidentially. "We are the only ship – apart from our sister ship, the *Reina del Mar* – on this run, so it is a monopoly."

"But can't you move us to something a bit bigger?" I asked.

"Sorry," he said. "We are full up. In fact, I see you got on because of a cancellation." That explained it – we had the worst cabin going. I thanked him and left.

Soon, we were crossing the Bay of Biscay, on the way to our first stop, at La Coruña, in Spain. The Bay is notorious for storms and bad weather, and it did not let us down. The 'Reina' began a complicated corkscrew motion, twisting and spiralling her way forward. It was gloomy, wet, windy and depressing. The hinge creaked and groaned. Wendy felt wretched, and was very seasick, Nikki was bewildered and miserable.

I was lucky enough to be a good sailor and actually rather enjoyed the motion of the ship. I hung around the cabin for a while, making ineffectual attempts to cheer my family up, but it soon became clear that they wanted to be left alone.

I left the cabin and spoke to the steward, asking him to keep an eye on things and to make sure that water and thin, dry toast were always available. I then went on deck.

The weather was wild and exciting. There was white water coming over the bows and a howling wind, driving the rain horizontally across the ship. I stood at the rail and watched for a bit, then, since it was time for lunch, went down to the dining salon.

I was astonished to find it completely empty, with the waiters standing around in clumps, chatting.

I sat down at our table, and our waiter came over. "Welcome, sir," he said. "You are very brave to be eating in this jumpy weather."

"Is no one else coming?" I asked.

"Oh, dear me, yes," he replied grinning. "The officers never miss a meal."

So I sat in solitary splendour and had a large and delicious meal. The officers trickled in, one by one, and after nodding to me sat together at a large table some distance away.

We eventually arrived at La Coruña, our first port of call. The weather had improved slightly, though it was still cold, overcast and drizzly. The town looked rather dull, but Wendy who was feeling better, and had never been in Spain before wanted very much to join an excursion to visit some spectacular cave paintings. So Nikki and I amused ourselves on board. Wendy came back, enthralled by the primitive beauty of the prehistoric galloping horses and bison, though she said she had found the caves rather claustrophobic.

Then off we went into the Atlantic, heading for Bermuda. As we progressed, the weather improved greatly and the sun came out, as did the passengers. They were a mixed lot.

We were by far the youngest people in First Class, which was populated by elderly couples, white haired gentlemen and their wives, on a cruise rather than going anywhere, as we were. They socialised well together, liking the same drinks and food, playing endless games of bridge and mildly exerting themselves at quoits and shuffleboard on the decks. They also sat on deck chairs, wrapped in shawls and blankets, reading the ship's daily newspaper and having tea and biscuits regularly brought to them by their attendant stewards.

There was a muscular young woman, the Director of Activities, who tended to harry everyone to play games, walk rapidly around the deck for exercise and do daily physical jerks. She also ran the daily sweepstake, in which you had to guess the distance travelled by the ship between noon and noon on consecutive days.

A table-tennis tournament was also organised, which I won, being rewarded with a nickel-plated teaspoon with the shipping line crest on the handle.

We did make friends with one elderly couple, who were kind to us and interested in Nikki. We often sat with them on deck and chatted. Their sons were yet to marry, and they desperately wanted grandchildren. Their name was Duck and Mr. Duck was something big in one of the rubber and tyre companies in

Britain. They enjoyed playing with Nikki, and said they hoped they would one day have such a pretty little grandaughter. The weather got warmer, and the sunsets became more and more spectacular, with glorious scarlet and gold skies. As I stood at the rail in my newly acquired white dinner jacket, admiring Wendy in her green shimmery evening dress, Newcastle seemed very far behind.

The weather improved further and the sky was blue for days on end, while the sea was smooth. Nikki, who had been toddling along quite sturdily on dry land, had decided that walking on a moving and swaying surface was not acceptable, promptly decided not to walk any more, and demanded to be carried everywhere.

We finally arrived off Bermuda and had a small adventure.

The approaches to Bermuda are not straightforward and the *Reina* ran aground on a sandbank known as the Devil's Flat. It was the only time she had done so on her many voyages and there was no danger – all that we felt was a sudden slowing down and a loud grating noise as the bows rode slightly up on the sand bank.

The upshot was that, although tugs managed to pull the ship off the shoal without too much trouble, a careful inspection of possible damage had to be made and we were delayed for three splendid bonus days.

This enabled the passengers to roam the island during the day, returning to the ship for dinner and to sleep. We three went ashore and wandered round the town and Wendy enjoyed her first sight of exotic flowers, palm trees and gorgeous gardens. It all seemed otherwise very English, though the houses mostly had white, stepped roofs. The Purser, who had become something of a friend of mine, explained that there was always a water shortage, so the roofs were adapted to catch and save the maximum amount of rain that fell.

We spent most of the time on Horseshoe Beach, a wonderfully protected curve of Bermudan pink coral sand which, when contrasted with the turquoise of the ocean and the blue of the sky, made an almost Technicolor impression. Nikki, finding solid ground under her feet again, gambolled happily in the small surf, while we relaxed with picnic lunches, sunning ourselves in the warm clear atmosphere.

There was no damage to the ship, and we went off on our way to Nassau in the Bahamas. We were now in the Caribbean area and the climate, even though this was February, became mild and pleasant. We saw silvery flying fishes skimming from wave top to wave top, and dolphins weaving and playing in our bow-wave. The evening skies became more and more improbably gaudy.

Nassau was a bustling, West Indian town, with colourful people – especially the ladies in their bright dresses and bandannas – thronging the streets, and many American tourists.

Cuba however was a very different proposition.

We arrived at the quay in Havana and tied up. There was a throng of peddlers and sellers of everything imaginable, mostly of poor quality, to tempt the tourist: mock Panama hats, coloured kerchiefs, maracas, drums, garish paintings (some very improper), straw fans and so on. When we were permitted to go ashore, we fought our way through the vociferous crowd and escaped to the relative quiet of the Old Town.

As we strolled along the main streets, we noticed that the passers-by were somewhat subdued, and that the cafés, which did not seem very crowded, were playing rather gentle music, not at all what we had imagined robust Latin Americans to enjoy. There was an air of uneasiness overall.

We observed that outside banks, Government buildings and major office blocks there were little groups of soldiers, with machine guns, looking restlessly about. We thought that Latin Americans must be very volatile people, if public buildings needed such protection.

All this seemed strange. The buildings themselves, in Spanish Colonial style, were handsome and impressive, as were the parks and plazas we saw. As dusk approached, we hear what sounded like gunfire in the distance, and presumed somebody was letting off fireworks. We sat peacefully sipping delicious *daiquiris* (the amazing iced rum drink, invented in Cuba, and a favourite of Ernest Hemingway's), and eventually strolled back along the deserted quay to the ship.

My friend, the Purser, happened to be on deck and I asked him what the strange atmosphere in town was all about.

"Well," he said pensively. "There is this mad lawyer in the hills, the Sierra Maestra, with a gang of friends, who are fighting a guerrilla war against the President." He scowled. "The man's name is Fidel Castro and he wants to free his country from evil, so he says."

We were quite surprised that the shipping company had not thought to mention to us that a revolution was going on, and on reflection decided that what we had thought was a fireworks display was probably gunfire after all.

Our next stop was Jamaica. We went ashore and found we were again in a very British atmosphere. It was quite remarkable what clear distinction of manners, atmosphere, and even smells and colours there was between the Spanish and British influenced islands, some very near to each other.

Kingston was a colourful, loud city, with British-style policemen directing traffic, busy shopping streets with familiar English names and gorgeous tropical vegetation. In the distance loomed the Blue Mountains, famous for their excellent coffee.

My friend the Purser had mentioned Henry 'Black' Morgan, and his association with Jamaica. I looked him up in the ship's library and found, to my surprise, that he had not been a pirate at all. He had been a privateer, with a license from the King of England to prey upon, loot and destroy Spanish ships and possessions in the Caribbean. A brilliant sailor, he had gathered a fleet of other privateers and also some cut-throat pirates, greedy for booty, and had sunk large numbers of Spanish ships, as well as sacking the main Spanish coastal towns. His greatest exploit was the sacking of Port Royal, on the Panama coast. There he laid siege to the fortified town, sacked and burned it, and returned with huge quantities of gold, gems, silver plate and precious objects.

His share of the privateering profits was enormous, and he became extremely wealthy. He was invited to England, where he was knighted by King Charles II and appointed Deputy Governor of Jamaica, ending his days in fame and comfort.

We looked at the fort and the castle, and were impressed: we could almost see Sir Henry with his beard, boots and cutlass, stalking the ramparts.

Our first sight of South America was of the steep tree-covered mountains rising up sharply behind the port of La Guaira, where we stopped very briefly. We went ashore, and Wendy said she was disappointed to see that grass in South America looked very much like grass in England – she had wanted everything to be totally different and exotic.

We then followed the coast to Cartagena, in Columbia, one of the major coastal cities sacked by Sir Henry. Here he stole a fortune in emeralds, which were locally mined and considered some of the best in the world. But the modern town looked dull, and we were glad to leave for the excitement of passing through the Panama Canal.

The town at the Atlantic end of the canal is Colon, an old colonial city not far from Port Royal, now almost uninhabited. We approached cautiously and entered the narrow confines of the Canal itself, which were just wide enough for two ships to pass. The *Reina* fitted into the locks almost exactly, tugged into place by a 'mule', one of the busy little electric locomotives which tow the huge ships along, and we rose up majestically some eighty feet to the level of the river which flows partly across the isthmus. It was edged with red earth banks and lush green jungle.

We sailed quietly on through the Miraflores Lake, and through more locks to Gatun Lake, enormous man-made reservoirs, which provide water for the locks. Standing at the rail we felt the stifling intensely humid heat. We hoped to see some exotic tropical animals or birds, at least an alligator or two, but only saw a few white egrets flapping lazily along the water's edge.

The whole of the area, for some miles on each side of the Canal, had been leased to the United States in perpetuity (it was actually returned to the Republic of Panama in 2000), and we could see occasional white bungalows with the Stars and Stripes flying above them. The Americans were totally in charge of all operations and administration and were even exempt from custom duties in the Republic.

Down to sea level again, into the many flights of the Gatun

Locks, which were a mirror image of the ones on the Atlantic side, down, down, down and into the harbour of Panama City. This was now the Pacific, which we had never seen. We could understand the excitement of 'stout Cortes'.

The most notable characteristic of the city was the sharks in the harbour and the waters all around. Looking over the side, we saw hordes of them, of all sizes and many kinds, swimming close to the ship and lashing up the water with their tails. The vessels constantly passing through the Canal had the habit of throwing their garbage overboard here (it was forbidden within the Canal Zone), and the sharks had been conditioned to expect a feast with every ship. There were hundreds.

Panama City itself was just as we would imagine a Central American city to be, although there was a strong US influence. The centre was modern, with high-rise buildings, restaurants and hotels, among carefully-manicured tropical gardens.

But the outlying *barrios* were crowded, loud and colourful slums, with music blaring out of cafes and cars honking loudly as they forced their way through the crowds of colourful pedestrians.

Lima, Peru was more elegant. We docked at Callao, its nearest port, and the ship arranged for passengers to visit Lima by coach. This had been the principal city for the Spaniards, where the Viceroy lived. He had controlled not only Peru but also Chile, and there were bad relations between the two countries, with constant border disputes, after independence.

Peru, of course, was also the home of the Incas and all their gold. The story of the brutal repression and near extinction of this civilized people by the *conqistadores* in their lust for the precious metal makes sad reading. Regretfully we did not have enough time to visit the marvellous site of Machu Picchu, but we did stay long enough to sample our first *pisco sour*, a favourite local drink, made with *pisco*, (a very powerful clear grape brandy locally grown and distilled), fresh lime juice, a pinch of sugar and vanilla and the white of an egg, beaten into a froth with crushed ice.

Our next stop would be Chile. The weather was pleasant, on this side of the world it was summertime, and I spent most of my time on deck. My friend, the Purser, was standing at the rail a little way off, when he suddenly called and made violent signs with his arm for me to join him.

"Look, look," he said urgently. "Have you ever seen anything like that before?"

I looked down at the sea and saw, some hundred yards away, a huge grey shape rise slowly to the surface, with a small one coming up beside it. There was a loud 'whoosh', and a smaller one, and a jet of misty air rose straight up for quite a distance, like a fountain, with a small fountain beside it. Then the huge shape gracefully submerged and a vast tail, with enormous flukes, came out of the water and went down with a splash, which concealed the small shape.

"It's a mother and baby," said the Purser. "You are lucky to see them so close; and it was a big one." I rushed down to the cabin to find Wendy, and we hurried back on deck with Nikki, but the whales had vanished.

Our final destination was the busy port of Valparaiso, the gateway to Santiago and central Chile, with long quays lined with cranes, and a lot of other ships already moored. We were too excited to think clearly. We had finally arrived. Chile was to be our home for a whole year and we looked forward to settling down to a normal life for Nikki, whose established routines had all been upset by the trip, though we had loved it.

We said fond goodbyes to the Ducks, and promised to go to see them when we were next in England, tipped our steward, shook hands with the Purser, and went down the gangway, to set foot, for the first time, in Chile.

We were directed to a huge hanger-like customs hall, lined with long tables on which the luggage was being stacked. The customs officials were polite and scribbled in chalk on all our assorted cases and boxes, and we walked out of the cool gloom into the sunshine. We were immediately accosted by a dapper young man, with a pencil-thin moustache and gleaming black hair.

"Are you Mr. Arnold?" he enquired, with a strong Spanish accent. I nodded. He put out his hand, which I shook, and bowed to Wendy. "I am Manuel from Shell. I am here to make sure everything is all right for you and to be certain you go safely to Santiago. I will get your baggage and all will go in that bus. First we go here..." he pointed at a small café nearby "and we have a *copa de vino* to welcome you to Chile *lindo*." Chile was often thus referred to by its inhabitants: beautiful Chile.

He collected our belongings on a trolley and we put our smaller cases on it as well. We had a glass of excellent wine and toasted our safe arrival before boarding a large modern bus for Santiago.

The ride, which took some two hours, was beautiful and spectacular. We went over a small range of foothills and down into a green valley, cultivated and full of wild flowers. Then up and up again over a small range of low dry hills, with the first big cactuses we had seen outside a Western film, as the road twisted and turned, and our cheerful driver went round blind corners without diminishing his speed with his hand firmly on the horn. The other passengers, mostly Chilean businessmen, were relaxed and friendly, chattering away in a Spanish which we hardly recognised. They made much of Nikki, who had settled down and smiled at them, but we could not really communicate adequately, so everyone just smiled a lot.

Over the final hill and we could look down into a huge valley, with Santiago spread out before us, nestling against the feet of a huge, snow-capped volcano: Aconcagua, the tallest mountain in the American continent.

At the bus station in Santiago, there was another young man waiting for us, who might have been the twin of Manuel in Valparaiso. He also greeted us warmly and welcomed us to Chile *lindo*.

"I am Edouardo," he said. "We will get a taxi and I will take you to the house. It is the house of Señor Maitland, the Sales Manager. He and wife are on holiday and he say you can use house. Then you can find your own place." I was astonished; a senior man's house for a trainee? It was a good beginning.

We piled everything into an ancient and enormous American car, with a grinning driver, and, somewhat cramped, drove into the town.

Santiago looked interesting: it had many Spanish colonial

buildings mixed in with more modern blocks of offices and flats. There were trees on the boulevards and a couple of green hills, some two hundred feet high, rose out of the flat plain in the middle of the town. We passed parks and gardens, smartly dressed men and women walking purposefully on the pavements and many shops with exciting shop fronts. But there was little Latin American quality about it and I felt slightly let down. I suppose I was expecting cowboys with clinking spurs, women in voluminous, multi-coloured skirts and horses everywhere. In a leafy suburb we drove through a gate into a large garden. The house was large and looked luxurious. We stopped at an imposing portico and the driver hooted.

Almost immediately a man and two women appeared. The man, smiling, held the door open and helped Wendy and Nikki out. He was tall and formally dressed in a white shirt and black trousers, with very shiny shoes.

"Welcome, welcome Señor and Señora. Please to go in and I will arrange everything."

The two girls at the door were smiling and making welcoming gestures. We went in and found that the interior of the house was luxuriously furnished, with a marble floor and vases of flowers everywhere.

The tall man returned and said something in Spanish to the girls, who went off to deal with the luggage. Edouardo also appeared and said: "I hope everything is good. Today you will rest," (it was, by then, late afternoon), "and tomorrow I will come fetch you to go to the office. This man is called Jaime and he will give you whatever you need." I thanked him and he went off in the ancient taxi.

Jaime showed us round the house. It was extremely lavish and all the rooms were large and beautifully furnished. At the back, in the extensive garden, there was a large barbecue area and lawns with fruit trees.

Jaime brought us some light refreshments and explained that he and the two girls, as well as the cook and the gardener were the Maitlands' staff and would be looking after us during our stay. He spoke good English and introduced the two maids, Consuelo and Alicia. They were enchanted with Nikki –

135

especially her blonde hair – and took her off to walk round the garden while Wendy and I had a short rest in the huge sitting room. To our astonishment, Nikki went off without any fuss and seemed to be enjoying herself.

The following morning, leaving Wendy and Nikki in the care of Jaime, who had given us an excellent English breakfast, I went off with Edouardo, who was only half an hour late. I found that this was a national characteristic: if invited to dinner at 7 o'clock, you were actually expected to appear at 9. The exception was if the invitation specified *hora inglesa*, when you were expected to be only half an hour late.

The Shell office was in the centre of town – a block of grey stone. I was taken upstairs and left in the anteroom of the General Manager's office, with his secretary, a delightful young lady, offering me a cup of coffee. After a short wait, I was ushered into the Presence.

My General Manager turned out to be a tall, slim middle-aged man with great charm. His name was Baird-Smith and he had a most distinguished war record, being a senior pilot of the Pathfinder Group of the RAF. This was a dangerous job and he was much decorated; he walked rather stiffly since he had parachuted out of his burning plane over Germany and landed badly, breaking both knees.

He rose from behind his huge desk and walked towards me, holding out his hand. "Ah, Arnold, isn't it?" he asked. "You must be our very first trainee. I do hope people have been looking after you and that all is well..."

I assured him politely that it was, thanked him for the welcome and mentioned that we were very comfortable in the wonderful house in which we had been lodged.

The GM grinned. "That is Jim Maitland's house; it is pretty nice, isn't it? He suggested that you keep it warm for him while he is away. But do sit down," he added, returning to his chair.

We chatted amiably for some time, and he asked me about my past, especially my childhood in Poland and the Middle East. I was flattered that such a busy and important personage should wish to spend so much time with a very junior trainee, but I found later that he had a keen interest in his staff and kept up to date with their lives and activities.

"Well," he said finally, "it has been very interesting. I am sure you will enjoy Chile – it is quite exceptionally beautiful and friendly. Go and see Rodolfo Muñoz; he is Personnel Manager and will fill you in on everything you need to know." I thanked him, and went out, to find Señor Muñoz.

Don Rodolfo, as he wished to be known, was a grey-haired Chilean with a large smile. He spent more than an hour explaining all the conditions of service, personal details of salary, housing, and all the many items of information which I needed to know on my first Shell posting in a new country.

The gist was that we should try to find a house to rent, and learn Spanish. My job was, for a start, to be attached to the Manager of Santiago District at the main Santiago depot, on the outskirts of the town. He also told me that he would ask one of his Personnel people, called Kiko Diaz, to be my particular guide and that Kiko would help us find a house and also introduce me to Derek Davis, my new boss at the depot.

"Come and see me whenever you want. I am always there to help so don't be shy." I found him an affable, kind man and we became good friends. He was one of the very few Chileans in a senior position in the Company, all the other major posts being filled by English expatriates.

That evening, when I had recounted my adventures to Wendy and told her what everyone had said, she dropped the bombshell.

"You know what?" she said with a big smile. "I am pregnant. Nikki is going to have a little Chilean brother or sister."

My mind came to a full stop. It was wonderful news but completely unexpected; I had been so preoccupied with all the new things in my life that I had not really thought of the possibility of having another child. Then it hit me: I danced round the room, hugged Wendy and laughed with delight. What a wonderful beginning to our Chilean year.

Of course, we talked deep into the night, discussing all the many aspects of the new addition to the family. Finally, Wendy told me to go to sleep; there was plenty of time to decide everything. But it was some time before sleep came.

The following morning, still feeling stupidly happy, I went with Kiko to be introduced to my new boss. We drove to the outskirts of town, to a large Shell depot. It had big silver tanks, an office building, lorry loading racks and pipelines everywhere. There were also lots of red and yellow drums.

In the office we went to the end of a corridor, where there was a modest room, with a desk and some chairs. Derek Davis, the Manager, was seated at the desk and stood up to greet us. As he gradually unfolded himself from his chair, he seemed to go on and on and I realised that he was amazingly tall, some 6 feet 6 inches or thereabouts. He looked down at me and grinned. "Yes," he said, "the air is rather thin up here."

He shook hands and sat down again, folding himself neatly into the chair. "Thank you, Kiko, for bringing my brand new man," he said. "He will be safe with me."

Kiko patted me on the shoulder. "I'm going now. You are in good hands. I will call on Wendy and see if I can help her with a house, maybe, or whatever she needs." He left.

"Call me Derek and welcome to Santiago. What do you like to be called? We are very informal here, not like in Head Office!" He gestured to a chair.

"I am generally known as Mick," I said. "I hope you will have something for me to do. More than anything, I want to learn Spanish – I think I will be pretty useless without it."

"Oh, you will learn it soon enough," said Derek. "We all speak Spanish here. They will try to practise their English on you, but insist on Spanish." He paused. "Now, let us see. You are the first trainee here, so I suggest you spend the first weeks finding your way about. Go out with the salesmen, get to know what we are doing and help where you can. When you are well settled in and can make yourself understood, I will find you something of your own, for which you can be responsible. In the meantime, it is up to you. You can always come and talk to me if you need to."

And so I started work in Chile. The salesmen and other staff at the depot were very friendly and tried to teach me the local Spanish slang; this sometimes caused problems if I used it on more formal occasions, without realising quite how crude it could be. I accompanied salesmen on their rounds of service stations, tried to chat with the peddlers of kerosene, who drove their trucks throughout the slums of Santiago, selling their product to individual households, for lamps, cooking and heating. Then there were the people who controlled the big tanks, who did the ordering and other administrative duties. After about a month, I could make myself understood and after three months I was reasonably fluent. My smattering of Spanish from Hove was useless; local Spanish was very different. The Chileans had the habit of swallowing the ends of their words and this was disconcerting to a learner. The accent was different and there were a lot of local dialect words. But it soon became familiar.

At home, all was going well. Wendy had found a house for us to rent: it was a small cottage, on the very edge of Santiago, facing the orange orchards on the slopes of Aconcagua, the giant volcano, with a spectacular snow-covered peak. The sight of golden oranges, blue sky and the snow on the mountain was magnificent.

We found a maid to help us in the house. She was called Linda. She was small and dark, with a strong kind Indian face, spoke excellent Spanish and was very good with Nikki. Wendy found it strange to have a maid, rather Victorian, but appreciated not having to do housework. We were made much of by the wives of the senior Shell staff, who took an interest in us and helped Wendy, taking her shopping in the local markets, introducing her to their friends, and arranging Spanish lessons for her.

But the most helpful event was when we finally made contact with Tony Westcott, my friend from Cambridge whose descriptions of his country were the reason why I had asked to go to Chile in the first place.

Tony was an Anglo-Chilean, a large group of Chileans of British descent (his family had been in Santiago for several generations), who still felt an allegiance to Britain and carefully cultivated a faint English accent in their fluent, native Spanish. They were all members of a Country Club, run entirely on British lines, of which we, too, became members. There was a swimming pool, afternoon tea on the lawn, tennis, croquet and so on.

There were also many other groupings: German-Chileans, Italian-Chileans and Spanish-Chileans. All maintained their original national characteristics, had their own clubs and were proud of their origins. The main body of Chileans were a great mixture of Indians, inter-group families and immigrants from other South American countries. Finally, there were many expatriates, temporarily resident, mostly American and British, as well as a large diplomatic corps.

The Westcotts appeared to be enormously wealthy. Tony, who was delighted to see us and could hardly believe that we had come there on his advice, immediately took us in hand. He introduced us to his friends and frequently invited us to dinner at his parents' house.

This was a huge villa, standing in a large garden in the best part of Santiago. Mr. Westcott Senior was an industrialist, who owned biscuit factories, textile mills and large plantations. Mrs Westcott was a kind lady with a faintly distracted air, who enjoyed nothing more than seeing a lot of young people enjoying themselves around her. The dinners were spectacular, with some thirty people seated at a vast table in the dining room, amazing food and delicious local wines. After dinner, everyone would go to the drawing room, a cavernous place the size of a tennis court, with two grand pianos and an organ inconspicuous at one end, and arrays of sofas, armchairs and tables scattered around. The Westcotts were very musical, Tony's farther enjoyed playing the organ and piano, and most people gave impromptu performances of one sort or another. Tony and I attempted some duets on the piano and guitar, though there were many far better performers and some professionals. One in particular, a classical guitarist, was magnificent, especially when, after a few glasses of wine, he could be persuaded to play some Chilean folk songs, *cuecas, tonadas* and so on. I thus learned many and enjoyed singing them from then on.

But the best thing of all was that Tony had a car. It was a splendid Sunbeam-Talbot and we went all over the town in it with him. He even took us down to Viña del Mar, a luxurious seaside resort near Valparaiso, where there were white sand beaches and all manner of water sports.

Cars were a problem. Chile, at this time, had a chronic economic problem, with raging inflation and prohibitive import duties: a very much second-hand World War ll jeep, owned by some friends, had cost approximately £30,000 in today's money. So I went to work and came home by bus, as did Wendy, when she went shopping or visiting friends.

I was in Head Office one morning when I saw a tall, distinguished looking youngish man walking towards me. He smiled and put out his hand. "You must be Mick Arnold, the new trainee," he said. I shook his hand and admitted that I was. "My name is David Montgomery, and I am visiting from Antofagasta, where I run the Northern District. But we are coming down here soon, so we must see something of you, and your wife."

We later became good friends with David and Mary, his wife, and it was only after a while that we discovered that he was the Honourable David Montgomery, only son of Field Marshal The Viscount Montgomery of Alamein.

It was a pleasant, relaxed life and we enjoyed it thoroughly. The weather – it was winter in May and June – was mild, but we often burned *leña de monte*, a small tree which grew in profusion on the mountain slopes, in the fireplace at home. This perfumed the whole house with a fragrant, woody smell.

Both Nikki and Wendy grew, especially the latter as her pregnancy progressed. We thought we would like a boy, but were happy to have another girl, if that should be the case.

At one of the Westcotts' dinners, we met an American couple, who were to become our close and lifelong friends. They were a few years older than we were, but, somehow, we seemed to suit each other perfectly. Their names were Bud and Barbara, and they also had a small child, roughly Nikki's age.

Bud was very American. He was immensely proud of his country, generous to a fault and a very merry man, full of quips and jokes. He was extremely active, and hated sitting still.

In contrast Barbara, his wife, was tall, blonde, quiet and intellectual. She was also practical and made sure that Bud's feet remained on the ground. We spent many evenings with them, with Wendy and Bud arguing and joking while I tended to discuss more serious things with Barbara, who showed great and refreshing knowledge and love of literature and natural history. But she would quietly vanish for a few moments, towards midnight, and appear with a freshly-baked coffee cake and piping hot coffee. They were wonderful evenings.

These were the friends who owned the Jeep. Bud kindly drove us to and fro and, on one occasion, later in our time in Chile, we all went off together into the mountains, to a place called *Rio Blanco*, passing on the way up the impressive *Salto del Soldado*, or Soldier's Leap. This was a rock, jutting out over a narrow ravine, hundreds of feet deep, across which a soldier, fighting for Chile's independence, had bravely jumped to freedom, thus escaping pursuing cowardly Spaniards.

Wendy was, by then, significantly pregnant. The way up the mountains, on a loose dirt road between sheer rock face and dramatic precipice, with rather slapdash traffic, was crossed by occasional lively streams cascading over, and partly washing away, the road. The sides of the jeep, driven by Bud safely, but with great *panache,* were open. Wendy spent most of the trip with her eyes shut.

The views were spectacular: snowy slopes, huge crags, and many sorts of strange wild flowers. Chile was a safe place in which to roam the countryside, since there were no stinging insects and no poisonous snakes or spiders; these tended to be on the other side of the Andes, in Brazil and Argentina.

So the social side of our life was pleasant and relaxed. Tony and I developed a double act, similar to my performances with Teddy in Cambridge, and we played and sang at parties. The senior Shell staff were very welcoming and found the presence of a young trainee family intriguing; their own children were grown and far away; we felt we had been adopted.

At work, also, I was enjoying myself. After about three months, Derek called me into his office one morning.

This was an unusual happening and I wondered what might have caused it.

"You seem to be settling down quite well," he said. "How do you feel about your Spanish?"

"Pretty comfortable," I replied. In fact, my entire day being spent with my colleagues, who much preferred to speak in their own language, had made it easy for me to progress to the point where I could converse fluently, as long as the subject was not too strange.

"Good," he said in Spanish; he spoke it effortlessly, without a trace of an English accent – I later discovered that he had been brought up in Argentina. From then on, we always spoke in Spanish.

"Is there anything you specially want to do?" he asked. "It is time you did something useful."

"Well, I would very much like something of my own, for which I could be responsible." I paused. "As long as you think I can do it and leave me to get on with it."

"Hmm," he frowned. "Anything in mind?"

"Well, yes. I have been looking into the kerosene peddler situation. I think I can improve sales and I would very much like to have a go."

He thought for a moment. "All, right," he finally announced. "You can try. They have never been really organised, so there is a lot to do. And they do form quite a significant and profitable segment of the market."

I was delighted and immediately called a meeting of all the twenty eight peddlers for the following morning. I then sat down and thought about how to tackle the problem.

Our Shell peddlers covered all of Santiago, particularly the poorer suburbs. We had been locked in battle with our principal competitor, Esso, for many years and were steadily losing ground. The peddlers were demoralised and there was friction between them, as individual areas were not clearly defined. Finally, their trucks were ramshackle, all different with no unifying or identifying pattern.

I prepared a large map of Santiago, and clearly drew on it the permitted hunting ground of each peddler. These were based on sales potential rather than geography. I then went back to Derek and asked if I could invest some money for my plan of attack.

"Well," he said. "You can have some if you can persuade me that there is a pay-out and tell me what you plan to do."

My plan was simple: I wanted cohesion in the group, through co-operation and mutual support; I wanted money to help them refurbish and paint their trucks, and help, if possible, with buying new ones, on soft loans from Shell; finally I wanted a belligerent spirit with which to attack and, I hoped, decimate Esso, increasing market share.

"I really want our peddlers to be identified as Shell. I have thought of a name we could paint on them: Keroshell. The livery should be Shell, also. Our red and yellow will be visible a long way away."

"Sounds good," Derek grinned. "OK to everything, but we have to ask London about the word Keroshell – patents and things, you know."

Early the following morning we had our first meeting. All the peddlers (except one who was nursing a broken leg) were there. They sat uneasily and muttered among themselves.

I stood up in front. "Welcome," I announced. "This is the first meeting of the new brotherhood: the *Cuadrilla de Buhoneros Shell* or the 'Shell Peddler Gang'. I am your captain and together we will conquer the enemy Esso!"

They looked puzzled and shifted in their seats. "Now listen," I said, "and then you can ask questions."

I unveiled my map and explained my plans to them. It seemed they were delighted – no one had ever before bothered with them or tried to help. There were some minor arguments about areas, but the promise of repainted and refurbished trucks and also support in their replacement, excited them a lot.

"Very well," I said. "That is what I will do for you. But what will you do for me?"

They sat there. Finally one said *"Capitán..."* everybody laughed. "We will sell more. So what is good for us is good for you."

Everybody, to my surprise, stood and clapped.

"Thank you," I said. "But I am going to set you sales targets. If you do better, you get a pat on the shoulder and a small present. If you fail, you get a kick in the other place."

They all laughed loudly and we had some coffee to seal the bargain. Then they broke up into small groups and chatted about the new plans; I wandered from group to group, joking and finding out what a peddler's life was like. I also tried to get to know them individually, each with his particular problems and difficulties.

There was a little money left over from the painting budget, so I told the gang that if they wished to get schoolboys on bicycles to follow and record the movements of the Esso peddlers, we could plot their habitual routes and precede them, taking away their customers. Everyone thought this was a good idea, and before long I could put the Esso routes on my map. From there it was easy to pre-empt them at every turn. The freshly painted, red and yellow trucks with Keroshell written in large letters on their sides (permission had been obtained from London), swarmed into the suburbs.

I got some of my colleagues, retail salesmen who had company cars, to drive me around so that I could see what my gang was doing. The salesmen thought my plan was a great joke, but indulged me since they also had Esso competing with their service stations.

The upshot was that, within three months, our market share had increased by 18 percent, to 60 percent of the kerosene market.

There were, of course, some minor problems with the Esso peddlers, but I avoided getting personally involved, simply telling the gang to sort things out themselves. They did so, and I believe only one case had to be hospitalised.

Derek called me into his office. Now that my Spanish was fluent, we had reverted to English. "I don't know what you have been doing, and I don't want to know. I have noted that the sales have leapt, so I suppose you got something right. But the General Manager has told me he wants to see you; you better have your story straight – he does not like problems caused by junior staff."

I went to Head Office the following morning, and waited outside the General Manager's office for about half an hour. His secretary then told me to go in.

Baird-Smith was sitting behind his huge desk. He looked at me, scowling, and did not invite me to sit down.

"I had a visit the other day from the General Manager of Esso," he said in an icy voice. "He told me that you had started a kerosene war in Santiago. He said that you were using sly and underhand methods and stealing market share which has traditionally been his. What do you say to that?"

"Well, sir, all I have done is some marketing. Naturally, methods have to be adapted to circumstances and I have not been underhand. All is fair in war and selling kerosene."

Baird-Smith was not amused. "You have caused me a great deal of irritation. I had to pacify Esso, and I don't like having to do that." He scowled at me some more; I waited in trepidation.

Suddenly he grinned. "Well done indeed, young Arnold. I was just like you many years ago. Always take the fight to the enemy. Derek is very pleased with you and so am I. But please be a little more discreet in future. Now sit down, have some coffee and tell me how you are getting on."

I was much relieved and told Wendy the whole story that evening. She laughed and said that it was a good job I had an understanding General Manager.

During this time, Wendy and Tony had been plotting to present a Revue to the public of Santiago, and at the same time raise money for local charities. They got their heads together and wrote sketches, songs and music, added some of the songs and acts from Wendy's Cambridge pantomime, and some Footlights material.

The casting was fun. Bud, together with Dick, a drunken American CIA agent, would be in it, as would many of Tony's Chilean friends: two sisters did a spectacular Hawaiian hula. One of the cast was David Montgomery, who had returned to Santiago from Antofagasta; there was a very funny sketch of a British general presenting medals to undeserving soldiers and he bravely undertook to be the general, notwithstanding his father. David's wife Mary had a beautiful singing voice, and sang enchanting duets with a local expatriate banker who was married to a Chilean girl. The guitarist and pianist were professionals.

There were only two disasters: on the last night, Dick escaped from Bud's supervision, and made his first entrance so drunk he could hardly stand. Happily he was still funny, and the audience thought it was part of the act when Bud snatched him off the stage with a hook. The other was when a custard-pie-in-the-face sketch missed the target and, instead, landed full on the huge crimson velvet curtains. The cleaning would have cost a fortune, but was kindly donated by a local firm, so the Revue – which was bilingual, Spanish and English – was a great success, and a large sum was raised for local Santiago charities.

Just after this, we had to move house and found another, without the magnificent view, but with a garden with orange and lemon trees. There were also *chirimoyas*, trees of twenty feet or more, bearing a delicious fruit tasting like a mixture of banana, pear and apple. Nikki loved the garden and pedalled her tricycle up and down the paths, accompanied by the maid who could not be torn away from her. This lady used to put lemon juice on Nikki's already very blonde hair, to make it even more golden.

There were also, during this time, two outstanding episodes in my life. The first was when I discovered, through my friend Rodolfo Muñoz, the Personnel Manager, that, as junior expatriate, one of my duties was to be 'The man in the garage'.

"What on earth is that, Don Rodolfo?" I asked, puzzled.

"It is the General Manager's wish," he said, smiling broadly. "As you know, Mr. Baird-Smith is not married, and his elderly mother visits him frequently from England. This lady is very superstitious and, since she becomes his hostess, and the dining table seats fourteen people, she is terrified that a guest will not turn up, and she will be left with thirteen." He paused, and smiled even more broadly.

"So it has become the custom that the junior expatriate, dressed in his dinner jacket, is brought by the GM's car to his house, and sits in the garage until all the guests have arrived. If one does not, he joins the party. If they all come, he is taken home again." He laughed. "You are the junior," he chuckled.

I had to do the garage trick twice, but on both occasions all the guests turned up. However, the second time, the cook was kind enough to send me a large dish of ice-cream, which I devoured before being driven home.

The second episode was the visit to Chile of Field Marshal The Viscount Montgomery of Alamein. David's father had decided to accept his son's invitation to visit and the General Manager extended both welcome and hospitality, on behalf of Shell, to the Field Marshal. There were, of course, many parties and dinners given in his honour by both Shell and local Government dignitaries, as well as tuft-hunting society hostesses.

The General Manager announced that the Field Marshal had consented to give a lecture on Leadership to all the Shell expatriates and some selected senior Chilean employees.

On the day and at the appointed hour, we all assembled in a lecture room in Head Office, and found a place in the rows of chairs facing a podium. We had been told, on pain of dreadful punishments, to be early, so when the door opened to admit the Field Marshal's party, we were all seated expectantly and waiting.

The party consisted of the man himself, with the General Manager and David, looking embarrassed, bringing up the rear. They proceeded to the podium and the Field Marshal stood, with his hands behind his back, ramrod stiff, at the podium. The General Manager said: "Gentlemen. I am proud and pleased to present Field Marshal The Viscount Montgomery of Alamein, who has honoured us with this visit. I am sure he needs no introduction."

He bowed slightly to the Field Marshal and sat down in a chair in the front row, beside David.

The Field Marshal glared at us; we were about thirty in all. He was a lean, small man, rigid and unmoving. He scowled rather than smiled, barked rather than spoke, and marched rather than walked. He exuded an air of unbending discipline and had an outsize charismatic effect on his surroundings, which he wholly dominated.

"Put out those cigarettes," he suddenly barked loudly. We all jumped, and the three or four people who were smoking hurriedly stubbed out their cigarettes. The Field Marshal continued, in an abrupt, sharp voice. "I don't approve of smoking. Hate the smell. Bad for you. Like drink. Must keep the body pure. And sit up. Slouching will wreck your spine." His sentences were short and often verb-less.

Having got us suitably cowed, he launched into a discourse on the virtues of leadership: the duty towards one's men; the leading by example; not allowing set-backs to deter one from the goal; victory at all costs. He cited the battle of Alamein as a perfect example of perfect leadership and unblushingly stood silent when there was a ripple of applause, started by the General Manager.

He spoke for about half an hour, while we sat rigid, not daring to move as his piercing eyes roamed over our faces. When he had finished, no one dared ask him any questions and so he departed with his entourage in tow, after the General Manager thanked him for his enlightening and uplifting lecture, of immense value to all potential leaders. We stood and clapped until the door shut behind them, then lit up, and dispersed. Later, David came up to me and said: "I am sorry. The old man is very set in his ways and used to talking to soldiers. There is nothing I can do about it."

The following week, Derek called me into his office. When I had sat down and coffee was produced, he looked at me and smiled.

"I am quite pleased with you," he said. "You have done your gang of peddlers a lot of good. But I think that it is time to move on."

I was puzzled. I was enjoying my work and had made good friends with most of my peddlers, who had become known as 'Mick's Gang'. We were constantly refining our campaign against Esso and the results were improving.

"Not that there is anything wrong," said Derek hastily. "That is, beyond the fact that the Esso District Manager, who used to play golf with me, now no longer even speaks to me." He grinned. "No big loss," he added.

"But your training must go on," he continued, "so I am going to give you a service station district – about seven of them that you will have to look after. They need a lot of work – that is the bad news. The good news is that you will get Company transport. You can start next week."

The new job sounded exciting, especially the transport. I was to find out that this was a rickety, ancient Standard Vanguard open van and that it was to be used exclusively for business and never taken outside the city limits of Santiago. Nevertheless, it would be extremely convenient; hitherto we had had to depend entirely on the goodwill of friends and on public transport.

The news went around the District and León, one of the natural leaders of my gang, came to see me in my little office.

"Capitán," he said. "We hear that you are leaving us. I come to tell you that you have helped and that we are sad that you are leaving. But now we can manage by ourselves – those *maricones* in Esso are giving no more trouble." He grinned. "We will not tell you why."

"But we wish to mark your departure. We invite you to a *parrillada* on Saturday. We all very much hope you can come and be with us."

A *parrillada* was, effectively, a barbecue and I was much gratified that the gang should wish to do this for me. "One o'clock at La Paloma, then. I am afraid it is for men only," he added.

Saturday came, and I duly presented myself at La Paloma, a large open restaurant with a tree-shaded patio at the back. I arrived at 1.30, since León had specified *hora inglesa*; thus one was expected only half an hour late. I was directed to the patio at the back, where I found most of the gang present, scattered around huge trestle tables with long benches on the outside, since they were formed into a large circle – so everyone was looking inwards. The tables were bare wood and there was a knife and fork at each place, as well as a bottle of wine and a glass.

León came forward to greet me and the others all clustered round, shaking hands and patting me on the back. Others arrived and then, on a loud invitation from León, we all sat down. I was placed between León and Papa Juan, the most venerable of the peddlers.

We chatted and drank wine. One of the great pleasures of Chile was the abundance of excellent wine, principally Cabernet Sauvignon. There were many long-established wineries, some dating back well over a hundred years or more. The vines had originally been brought by immigrants, principally from France, and had grown amazingly well in the Chilean Mediterranean climate. It was ironical that, when *phylloxera*, a deadly nematode, attacked and destroyed the vast majority of European vines in the second half of the nineteenth century, the stricken wine growers brought back cuttings from the New World, slowly to re-establish their vineyards.

This was before any serious exports were attempted and, at home, we bought very acceptable wine in *chuicos*, ten gallon glass acid bottles, with the price being around twenty pence a gallon. The bottle on the table before me was of medium quality, strong, aromatic and slightly astringent.

Then a troop of waiters and waitresses appeared, bearing small braziers, about eighteen inches in diameter, and filled with glowing charcoal. There was a metal grid on top. These were placed in front of each guest, together with several large lumps of bread.

Finally, large trays were brought with many different pieces of meat. There were steaks, chicken, mutton, veal, and also liver, kidneys, parts of cows' udders and bulls' testicles.

One of each sort of item was placed on every personal brazier, where they began to sizzle and give off an irresistible smell of grilled meat.

"*Buen provecho*, start eating, drink some wine," echoed round the tables, and everyone began to arrange their meat until it was cooked to their satisfaction.

I was very hungry, and so began to try everything, between gulps of wine. The meat had been spiced and perhaps marinated, so it made one thirsty – the wine then renewed one's hunger.

I ate steadily, listening to the conversation and jokes flowing all round me. I also answered many toasts, drinking with my friends.

Then I noticed that the waiters, hovering round, would replace whatever piece of meat had been eaten with a new one. Also, when my bottle was empty, it was immediately replaced by another full one.

"You must be very hungry," remarked Papa. "You must have a very big capacity, like my truck..." he chortled.

A guitar was produced, and passed around. It seemed that almost everyone could play, and they were expected to entertain the others with song. Most were folk songs, but there were also some scurrilous ones, adapted to insult and poke fun at the Government, Esso, and other targets. These brought howls of laughter and applause.

I had pretty well eaten and drunk my fill, but then I noticed that the others were eating very slowly, with long pauses, and drinking fairly sparingly. I turned to León and asked: "How long do these *parrilladas* go on for?"

"Hard to say. If everyone is having a good time, we usually stop about midnight."

Midnight!? A barbecue lasting twelve hours? I felt quite faint. It was only three o'clock and I felt I could hardly eat another mouthful or have any more wine. What could I do for the next nine hours?

"I wish you had told me before I started," I complained to León. "Now I am full up and very merry and what shall I do?"

He laughed loudly. "Come on, Capitán," he said loudly. "You can do better than that. Just slow down a bit and have fun."

He waved his arm across the circle. "Hey, Pepito, bring the guitar for the Capitán and he will sing us a song, before he passes out."

There was much laughter and I was handed the instrument. I managed a couple of folk songs, including *Bajando pa' Puerto Aïsén*, a Chilean one which I had learned. This was greeted with enormous applause, slightly alcohol-enhanced and loud cheers.

I cannot remember much about the party after that, beyond a muddled memory of speeches, including a drunken one by me. What I do remember is being delivered to my house in a Keroshell truck, and falling into bed, to wake, uncomfortably, fairly late on the Sunday morning. When I explained the circumstances to Wendy, she forgave me.

We wrote to both sets of parents weekly; or at least Wendy did. Her mother wrote regularly, but mine was somewhat disorganized. From her we learned that my step-siblings, having finished their education and going out into the world, were busy and seemingly happy. Andrew was working for an oil drilling company in Austria – so family tradition was maintained. Felicity had married, and had gone with her husband to live in New Zealand.

With no more school fees to pay, Ronnie had decided to retire early from BP and was going to spend his life painting, as he had always wanted. He had gone to Paris as a young man to be an artist, drink absinthe and lead *la vie bohémienne*. But, much as with me, he had found it difficult to make ends meet, and had joined BP.

Mother had written earlier that they were going to try to live in the Canary Islands, where the light was supposed to be marvellous. But this move was not successful and, after a relatively short time, they had moved to Cascais, a little fishing village just north of Lisbon, and had hired a house, where they were now installed. We were invited to stop there for a week on the way back from Chile.

Before the end of the week of my *parrillada*, Derek called me again. "Your taking over of the service stations has been slightly postponed," he said. "Don Rodolfo – the Personnel Manager – wants to see you first thing tomorrow morning."

"Why?" I asked. "Is something wrong?"

"You will find out," said Derek and with that I had to be content.

At home, that evening, we wondered what it could be. There was no way of knowing. Everything seemed to be all right; as far as I knew everyone was reasonably satisfied with my performance; there were no administrative problems. My salary was being paid regularly every month, with the normal monthly increase of a few percent.

This monthly adjustment was due to the fact that Chile was going through one of its economic convulsions, with astronomical inflation of several hundred percent a year. Thus salaries had to adjusted monthly, to try to keep pace with the galloping inflation. In fact, since we were paid in Chilean pesos, it was everyone's habit to rush to the bank as soon as the monthly cheque was received and change it into any available currency: dollars, pounds, francs, lire or anything else, maintaining only a minimum balance in the peso account. Then, when there was shopping to be done, or any expenditure envisaged, a sum of the foreign currency could be changed back into pesos and immediately spent.

Odd things happened with this type of inflation. A friend of mine, Joaquín, had a mortgage with a permanently fixed monthly sum to pay. This monthly instalment was fairly onerous at the start, but, by the time I met him, had been eroded to less than a penny a month; the mortgage company finally wrote to him to say that they no longer required payment and that the house was his, fully paid.

I went to see Don Rodolfo, still puzzled and slightly worried. He ushered me into his comfortable office and turned with a smile.

"Welcome, Don Miguel," he said in Spanish. "I understand that you are now quite fluent in my language."

"Well, I suppose I understand most of the everyday talk," I said. "But then, everybody helped me and I really enjoy learning it. Especially the slang," I added.

"So soon we will be having you speak like a real Chilean *campesino*, or peasant," said Don Rodolfo. "But you should learn the proper Chilean Spanish too. We have winners of the Nobel Prize for Literature, you know."

We drank some coffee, which had been unobtrusively provided. I waited nervously; this social chatter was all very well, but why was I there?

"I suppose you are wondering why I asked you to come," he said, stating the obvious. "It is, I think, good news. The General Manager is pleased with your work, and the way you and your wife have merged into Santiago's social life. Derek also speaks highly of you and Jim Maitland, the Sales Manager remarked to me the other day how much everybody had enjoyed Wendy's show. In fact, the General Manager has asked me to tell London that we would like new trainees every year, following you."

I was flattered and did not know what to say. Fortunately, he continued: "Once a year, I ask Kiko (you remember Kiko, my assistant who met you when you first arrived?) to do a tour of the country, making sure all is well with our staff everywhere and meeting a few major customers, to try to find out what is generally thought of the Company. He goes all the way, from top to bottom; it takes about three weeks."

He paused for a moment. "The General Manager has asked me

to tell you that, if it interested you, you could accompany him on this trip. Consider it half holiday and half reward. Derek agrees and can wait for the three weeks before you become a retail salesman."

I was speechless. I had wondered what the rest of Chile was like, and was sad that probably I would only get to know Santiago, the immediate coast and the foothills of Aconcagua. Now here was a princely offer for me to have a conducted tour of the whole country.

Don Rodolfo smiled. "You don't have to say anything," he chuckled, "just nod."

I nodded vigorously. "Oh Don Rodolfo," I said. "What a marvellous invitation. Of course I want to go. Please thank everybody on my behalf. How very kind..." I went on babbling for a moment until he put up his hand. "Stop, stop," he said. "I understand. Get together with Kiko and fix it up. I hope you enjoy it – my country is very beautiful."

I rushed out to find Kiko. He was in the main Personnel office and I hurried up to him. He saw me and smiled.

"Don't say anything," he said. "I know all about it. Sit down and have a cup of coffee and we will talk about it."

This was the third year that Kiko was going to do the tour, so he knew quite a lot about the various places we were to visit.

"There are two main things to decide," he said. "The first is whether we do the South first or the North, since Santiago is in the middle and I usually break the tour up – my wife would be very fed up if I didn't have a two or three day break in the middle."

I agreed that Wendy would probably feel the same. I was feeling guilty that I would go off and have a good time, while she had to stay at home, feeling the effects of her pregnancy. But it was August, the middle of the Chilean winter, and the weather was very pleasant.

"Well," said Kiko. "I suggest we go North first and leave the best till last. You just wait till you see the volcanoes and lakes."

So we first flew up to the small port of Arica, on the northern border of Chile and Peru – in fact just twelve miles away from the border itself. Arica was a small town, very dusty and with undistinguished adobe houses. It was a port and was quite old, having been in the past the outlet for the famous Potosi silver mines at the time when the Spanish Viceroyalty of Peru had dominion over what is now Chile

Chile is an odd country, geographically. It is like a long string bean, some 2,200 miles long (excluding the Antarctic) and, on average, only 120 miles wide. Its northern border with Peru has always been a source of friction and has moved up and down with the centuries. In the south, there was Cape Horn and Tierra del Fuego, with its glaciers, volcanoes and dangerous seas.

This thin strip of land is bordered in the east by the Cordillera of the Andes, huge mountains (mostly volcanoes, some active) with many topping 10,000 feet and permanently snow or glacier covered. On the west the land plunges into the Pacific, into a deep trench a few hundred yards off shore, where the cold water from the seasonal Humbolt Current provides a playground for whales, sea-lions, green turtles and seals, as well as a multitude of fish.

But what might be called the trademark of Chile are the volcanoes and earthquakes.

Our first acquaintance with earthquakes was the second day after our arrival in Chile. No one had thought to warn us, and we were enjoying breakfast in the palatial home the Sales Manager had lent us, when I noticed concentric circles in my coffee cup. There was a slight tremble, and the chandelier began slowly to swing to and fro.

"What on earth is going on?" asked Wendy.

"I don't know," I replied. There was no heavy traffic passing by, and there were no underground trains.

Just then, one of our two borrowed maids came in, holding Nikki by the hand. Also at this moment, the earth gave a sort of convulsive hiccup, and the cutlery clinked.

Nikki had just got over the moving floors on the ship and had again begun to trust her feet. She screamed and clung on to the maid.

"*No te preocupes, mi tesoro*," said the latter, hugging her. "*No es más que un pequeño terremoto...*"

So it was 'nothing more than an earthquake'! Of course, after a day or so, we got used to them, though Nikki still regarded them with great suspicion and uneasiness. There tended to be several tiny ones every day, as the precariously balanced shelf of land which was Chile tried to even out the pressures between the high mountains and the deep ocean trench. Happily there were no major earthquakes while we were there, though there was a huge one shortly after we left, which devastated towns on the coast.

Manuel, Shell's resident representative in Arica, drove us in his battered pick-up truck, out into the country towards the mountains, on rutted, twisting dirt roads. In arid, rocky terrain, we came across herds of creatures, which all looked like small slim llamas, but which Manuél explained, laughing, were quite different.

"A llama is a big, nasty-tempered beast of burden – like a camel," said Manuél. "Always approach it from the side; from the front it will spit a smelly spit at you and from the back…well, I wouldn't." He and Kiko laughed loudly.

"These are guanacos," said Manuél. "They are a bit smaller and have an even worse temper. Then, even smaller, are the alpacas. They have nice hair for making cloth, but are no good to eat."

Kiko took over, as we drove bumping along the track, leaving a big dust cloud behind us. "But the aristocrats of the family are the vicuñas," he said. "They live very high, on the *Altiplano*, and are very difficult to find and catch. They have a small tuft of hair on their chest, which makes the finest, softest and warmest cloth in the world. I heard that in New York a *vicuña* jacket can cost ten thousand dollars."

After some more dusty miles, we turned round to head back to the coast. The panorama was breath-taking. You could see for a huge distance, right down to the blue of the Pacific. The rocky countryside was wild and bare, just a few stunted trees and bushes. And behind us, a looming presence, the snowy volcanoes, going high into a pure blue sky.

"My wife has told me to invite you for dinner," said Manuél. "There is really nowhere to go and she said she wanted to show you some good Chilean cooking."

I was grateful. The hotel (if one could call it that) was very rudimentary – just a bare adobe room, with an iron bedstead and a basin on a chair. The bathroom was down the hall.

We thanked Manuél, who undertook to pick us up in the evening and take us home.

In Chile it was the habit for guests, instead of sending flowers and a note to the hostess after the visit to say thank you, to do so before one arrived, on the morning of the party. Unfortunately there was no way of finding a bouquet, but Kiko managed to procure a rather old and dusty box of chocolates, which we sent on ahead, by means of a bedraggled boy who was hanging round the hotel entrance.

Manuél arrived and drove us to his house. This was a spreading bungalow of adobe, on a smallish plot, on which an attempt had been made to grow some shrubs and trees. There was a goat tethered in one corner and some chickens running around.

Manuél's wife came to the door to greet us. She was a merry-looking lady, small in stature but sturdily built, with a smiling, perfectly round brown face and jet-black hair, pulled tightly back. She wore a colourful skirt and blouse.

"*Bienvenidos, bienvenidos,*" she said. "How nice to see you again, Don Kiko." She turned to me. "And you must be Don Miguel," she said, holding out her hand. "Manolito has told me so much about you."

I shook hands, made a suitable response, and we went inside. The main room was gaily decorated with brightly striped pieces of cloth and there were some religious pictures on the walls. The furniture, like its mistress, was sturdy and practical. Through an open door I could see a collection of large dark eyes peering at me.

Manuel gestured towards the open door. "Come in, children and be presented to our guests." He turned to me. "I have six, all boys," he said proudly. "Maybe we have some more..." He grinned at his wife, who laughed. "Enough is enough," she said. "God has been good to us; don't tempt Him." She turned to me. "Thank you very much for the chocolates. The boys have wolfed them all down."

The six boys filed in shyly, and stood in a row. Then they all bowed. They looked so alike that it would have been difficult to tell them apart, other than by the three or four inches difference in height between each and the next one along. Doña Carmen, our hostess, asked us to sit down. "Manolito said that you were interested in our country, and in our cooking," she said to me. "So I have made a very Chilean *campesino* meal. It is very modest, but it will give you an idea. Anyway, I wanted to cook something for you that you will remember when you have left Chile – it is a good way to remember a country."

The meal, when it appeared, served by a succession of sons, who ranged in age from fifteen to four, was anything but modest. Kiko expressed himself as astonished. "What a marvellous meal," he said to Doña Carmen. "Even I, a Chilean, will always remember this. You should be a fat man," he added to Manuél. "No wonder you are so lazy."

Manuél grinned. "You should come more. I never get to eat like this." He served us generously with wine.

We started off with tiny *empanadas*, half-moon shaped tiny pastries, filled with a tasty mixture of meat and olives, sultanas and hard-boiled egg and baked in an earth oven, and *humitas*, corn leaves, stuffed with seasoned grated sweet corn, tied up and steamed. The main dish followed. The famous Chilean *pastel de choclo*, grated sweet corn mixed with chicken, onions, olives and a touch of sugar. Doña Carmen explained: "I love this dish," she said. "I come from the pure Indian tribes of this area, the Inca and the Araucanians, and this is our food. *Choclo* is the Inca word for *maíz*.

She turned to Manuél. "You are nothing special," she looked at him fondly. "You are lucky to be married to a pure Indian."

Finally the dessert came, a rich pudding made by boiling down condensed milk until it becomes a sort of soft toffee, and sometimes called *dulce de leche*. To drink there was *cola de mono* (Monkey's tail), a powerful mixture of fiery brandy, milk, coffee, and sugar with a sprinkling of cinnamon.

I felt very comfortable and the meal had been delicious, my first proper introduction to Chilean food. I thanked Doña Carmen profusely and, when we left, I remember the three of us singing folk songs, rather loudly, all the way back to the hotel.

We flew back to Antofagasta the following day, in the same rickety plane in which we had made the four hour flight from Santiago. The flight that morning was only some ninety minutes, and we flew fairly low, between mountains and sea, over a varied landscape. On the way, Kiko told me the history of his country: about the brutal Spanish Conquistadores, who pillaged and destroyed the tribal civilisations, especially the Incas, whom he considered much superior to the conquerors.

"The worst thing was that it was all done, officially, in the name of religion. The priests, especially the Jesuits, felt it was their duty to convert and manage all foreign people, even if it killed them, which it often did. The people, I mean. Of course, the real reason was loot and slaves."

"But we stood up to them as much as we could," he continued. "The Araucanian tribes in the south were never actually conquered by the Spanish and only accepted, with reservations, to be part of the free Chile long after independence in 1810."

"Anyway," said Kiko. "It was only thanks to an Argentine hero, San Martín and an Irish adventurer, Bernardo O'Higgins, who chased the Spaniards out and made us a Republic. Sort of," he added with a grin.

I could see, on the left, the beginnings of a huge, dirty yellow desert stretching up into the foothills. It lacked the romantic appeal of Arabia and just looked grimy and dull.

"That is the Atacama," said Kiko. "You will see it properly later on."

We landed in Antofagasta at midday. There was a choking cloud of dust over everything and the small airport was very primitive. Antofagasta, which I had seen from the ship on our way to Santiago, was principally an outlet port for the copper mines of the interior, and had little pretence to beauty or interest. There were some colonial buildings and a few gardens and parks, but the whole was dominated by large cranes, nodding and swaying along the sea front and grimy ships crowding the harbour. I wondered how my friend David

Montgomery had stood it for many months, when he was Manager of the Northern Region.

We were met by Gonzalo, the acting manager of the region, in a typical rusty, decrepit American pick-up. He and Kiko were old friends, and they gave each other a healthy *abrazo*, the Latin-American greeting hug.

"Well, *viejo*," said Gonzalo to Kiko. "It's that time again, is it? Come to snoop around?"

"Of course. How can you be trusted on your own, without a master..."

Gonzalo turned to me. "I suppose you must be the Don Miguel that I have heard about. Kiko wrote to me about you. You won the war of the kerosene peddlers in Santiago? Well done, well done." He clapped me on the shoulder. "We have a lot of trouble with the *pendejos* here."

He drove us to the hotel, where we washed off some of the dust and had an undistinguished meal. But we did have some local wine, which was a mistake, since it made me drowsy all afternoon.

Kiko was merciless. "We have to stay awake and Gonzalo will drive us to the mine," he said. "This is the most important customer we have and Esso keeps trying to take it away. The miners are all *gringos*, so they sometimes succeed, but then we get them back."

So we got into the pick-up, with bottles of water and sandwiches, and drove to the mine.

As we climbed steadily on the dusty road into the Altiplano, the High Plateau of the Andes, the scenery grew bleaker and bleaker. We were entering the fringe of the Atacama desert, one of the driest areas on earth, in many parts of which rain had never fallen. Although it seemed boring it held many surprises.

"This is the great treasure house of Chile," said Gonzalo. "There is everything here: gold, silver (although in small quantities), huge amounts of copper, and most other minerals. In fact," he added, "about thirty percent of the world's copper lies around you."

"And that is not all," said Kiko. "There are vast deposits of salt and all sorts of chemicals too. But just wait, we will show you."

We drove on, and suddenly I noticed a train running slowly down the mountain, parallel to the road. It was amazingly long, with what seemed like a hundred wagons, and was pulled by two electric locomotives. It just went on and on.

"That is the copper coming down from Chuquicamata," Gonzalo told me. "It is also carrying other stuff, but most of it is rough copper ingots, thousands of tons of them, down to Antofagasta to be loaded onto ships."

As we went on climbing, we began to see on both sides of the road, and stretching into the distance, vast salt pans, with the salt making curious wind-sharpened sculptures, and ant-like people scattered about, gathering the white crystals. The scale of everything was incredible: vast volcanoes towering ahead, desert all around, the blue of the ocean behind. A few white clouds floated in an achingly azure sky.

We stopped at a ramshackle *cantina* for a cold drink and to stretch ourselves. Our journey from Antofagasta to the mine was about 150 miles, and we were half way. There were some corn cobs grilling on a brazier and I had one; it was sweet and tasty.

The mine, when we finally reached it, was astounding. It was difficult to assimilate the scale of everything, since there was nothing to give that scale.

We first drove through the little town which had grown around the mine; adobe buildings, a few *cantinas*, some stunted trees and the odd shop selling everything. Then onto the mine itself. On the edge of the pit, we stopped at a group of office buildings.

I got down from the pick-up and jumped up and down for a bit; I was feeling rather stiff after our fairly long and bumpy drive. I suddenly felt dizzy and faint and had to sit down hurriedly on the ground.

Kiko and Gonzalo laughed loudly. "Ah ha, ah ha," they chortled. "You have to be careful. Remember, you are now about 10,500 feet above sea level and the air is pretty thin. Take it easy!"

After a minute or two, taking deep breaths, I stood up, rather cautiously. From then on, I moved slowly and managed to avoid what is known as altitude sickness. It was interesting, when I later found out that the Indian tribes, who lived on the Altiplano, had developed extra large lungs to cope with the lower air pressure. I had no such advantage.

We followed Gonzalo into the office, which was cool, well organised and busy. He asked the receptionist, a young Indian girl, if Spade was there and she called some other office. After a few minutes, a grizzled, elderly American came in, dressed in faded jeans and a khaki shirt which had seen better days. He also had a pair of dirty, scuffed boots on as well as a worn and sweat-stained cowboy hat.

As he saw Gonzalo and Kiko, he came forward with a wide grin and gave each a big *abrazo*. "Hey," he said. "Here you are again. By golly, time passes fast when you're having fun! Who is your friend?"

Kiko introduced me and Spade shook hands. "You sure keep bad company, boy," he said. "Don't believe anything these two tell you and only half of what they show you..." Everyone laughed merrily.

"This is our usual visit, to see if everything is OK," said Kiko. "I suppose it is, or we would have heard you in Santiago."

"Yup," said Spade. "The luboil is fine and the supplies are good. Gonzo here looks after us well." Gonzalo grinned.

"We will be spending the night, so we have to fix that up. I thought maybe you could give Don Miguel a quick look over the hole while there is still light. We have to leave early tomorrow."

"Sure thing," said Spade. "Come on with me. Gonzo, come back and get him in an hour."

He led me outside and we got into a filthy jeep, which, to my surprise, started first time. "Can't call you Don Miguel," said Spade. "What is your usual name?"

"Mick," I replied.

Spade looked at me in astonishment. "You Irish?" he asked.

"No," I said. "There are just too many Mikes."

Spade pondered for a while. "Yup," he finally said. "Makes sense. You call me Spade. In the old days I was prospecting in the Rockies – yeah, mule and everything. Then I got old and got this easy job. Pay is good," he added.

By then we had driven to the edge of a colossal crater. "This is it," said Spade proudly. "The biggest hole man ever made on earth, about two and a half miles long and two miles wide and half a mile deep – so far, anyway."

The mine was immense. It was difficult to get a sense of scale in the innumerable terraces as they slowly narrowed down to the distant bottom. There were tiny toy trucks, carrying ore, laboriously climbing the steep dirt road which zig-zagged up the side. I was astonished to find that the tyres dwarfed me when I stood beside them, they stood ten feet high. The soil was reddish yellow and shone in the setting sun.

"This copper has been worked for centuries," said Spade. "Long time before we came. The Indians here – they were Chuqui and Aymara – used it to make weapons and tools." He paused reflectively. "Then we come and rip everything up. "

He then showed me the various processes: smelters, sorters and other mysterious plant, up to where the rough, heavy copper ingots were loaded onto the trains. Work never stopped, and as the sun went down, huge arc lights turned the dark into brightness. The many workmen I saw were principally local Indians: short, stocky men with enormous barrel chests. We drove past the living quarters and I saw some expatriates playing tennis.

"Yep, you're surprised," said Spade. "I know, you can hardly breathe can you? It takes a good while, maybe three or four weeks to get acclimated to this thin air but in tennis, wow, you should see those balls fly!" He chuckled.

Back in the office, Kiko and Gonzalo were waiting for me. As we climbed back into the pick-up, I thanked Spade very much. He clapped me on the back and said: "Come back and see us real soon."

I waved as we drove back into the little town, to our lodging, which was fairly basic. The bar, where we ate, had several people in it, drinking *chicha*, a fiery local brandy, and beer. Most were Indians or *mestizos*, of mixed blood, but all were cheerful and one was strumming a guitar in a corner.

We sat at a small table and the landlord, a swarthy man, who looked like a bandit, with straight black hair down to his shoulders, came over.

"Well, Don Gonzalo," he said. "Back again to see the *gringos* in the big hole. I hope everything is OK."

"Thanks be to God, Chico," said Gonzalo. "I see you in good health."

"All is good."

"I have brought two friends to sleep and eat here. I see you got my message."

Chico nodded, and we all shook hands.

"We are hungry," said Gonzalo. I suddenly realised I was ravenous. "Bring us your best food and also *chicha* and beer."

Chico grinned and went off. A little later, he came back with two outsized platters: one with a large heap of roasted somethings (it looked like rabbits). The other had a selection of *humitas*, roast corn on the cob and *empanadas*.

"*Buen provecho, hermanos*," he said. "Eat well and enjoy."

We fell upon the food like starving wolves – it was truly mouth-watering.

"What are these small animals?" I asked Gonzalo. "Some kind of *conejo* or rabbit? "

Gonzalo and Kiko laughed. "You couldn't be more wrong," said Kiko. Then he laughed so much that Gonzalo had to explain.

"The things which look like rabbits are *cuyos*, what you call Guinea pigs. These are good ones. Everybody has *cuyos* – each family grows thirty or forty in special little houses. They like to make love all the time so they provide constantly very good meat for the families. But the wild ones are lean and tough and hard to catch. These here are the best domestic ones."

I thought about this for a moment, decided that any doubt was only in my mind, and that they tasted really good. I continued to tuck in. The *chicha* and beer helped and, when we could eat no more, we went up to our rooms and went to sleep. It was bitterly cold – well below freezing – but I managed to borrow from Chico a thick blanket of llama wool, rolled myself up in it and slept soundly until dawn.

The following morning, as the sun rose over the Cordillera, we gulped down a light breakfast, with some amazingly strong coffee, and set off for San Pedro de Atacama, some distance away. "There is no business there," said Kiko, "But we thought you should see it – not many foreigners bother and they don't know what they are missing."

We climbed the dirt road steadily, going north. There were salt pans all around and even so early, people were already busy filling sacks and loading carts and pick-ups. The scenery was barren, but the volcanoes looked majestic and beautiful, some with curls of smoke or steam rising from the peaks.

We drove and drove and then, as we crested a rise, saw spread beneath us, amazingly, a large, green valley. There were cultivated fields all round us, corn, vegetables and trees in profusion as well as small wild flowers. It was truly a Shangri-la – unexpected, beautiful and startlingly out of place in the desert. Some distance away there was a small town, with proper buildings and trees, some small streams and a feeling of lushness about it. This was San Pedro.

We drove on and Gonzalo explained: "This is the crossroads of Atacama. There is a road up to the cordillera and one back to Antofagasta. But there is also the main road used in ancient times to go north to Peru and the Incas and to Bolivia. South, you follow the mountains and find mineral deposits."

Suddenly, he pulled over to the side of the road and stopped. I looked round but there was nothing special. Then I looked again and saw two small posts on each side of the road.

"Let's get out for a moment," said Kiko. "I want to show you something."

We got out and Kiko pointed to a painted white line across the road; it was faint and grubby and just discernible.

"Guess what this is," said Gonzalo.

"No idea," I replied. "Perhaps a provincial border or something?"

They laughed. "No," said Kiko. "This is imaginary. You can't see anything. It is the Tropic of Capricorn." They both laughed, and stood with one foot on each side of the line. "Come on," they said. "It will bring you luck."

So I did.

After a brief stop in San Pedro, we went on towards the Andes. Climbing steadily, the landscape again became barren and we came to the geysers of El Tatio, the highest geysers in the world; we were at about 14,200 feet, the air was really thin and still volcanoes towered over us, going up to 20,000 feet. The geysers were in a series of shallow lakes of hot water, of a corrosive blue-green but very beautiful, reflecting the equally blue sky.

"Don't be tempted to swim in these pools," said Gonzalo. "Above all, don't put your fingers in or drink a single drop of water from them; beautiful though they are; they are deadly. They are all saturated with sulphur and arsenic." I kept well away.

All around us, in a lunar landscape, there were little cones of fumaroles, all emitting gentle clouds of sulphurous smoke.

It was downhill all the way back to Antofagasta. As we got lower and left the thin mountain air behind us, the pick-up engine stopped spluttering and coughing and ran sweetly. We reached the town in the early evening and went straight to bed, after a rapid supper.

The following morning, Gonzalo took us to the little airport. We said goodbye and I thanked him very much for the trip.

"It was a pleasure, Don Miguel," he said. "Chile is a beautiful country, I know you will enjoy seeing the south now. Go with God."

He gave me a warm *abrazo* and we could see him waving as the plane trundled down the dirt runway and lumbered into the air, going south.

Back in Santiago, I told Wendy all about my wonderful trip and also how much I was looking forward to going to the south. She, in turn, told me that she had booked herself into the Clinica Alemana, a German-run clinic, which she said was full of very nice and efficient people, many German, and with an excellent reputation, as confirmed by all our Chilean friends. The doctor there ran classes in 'natural' childbirth, which Wendy had been going to, where she was learning special exercises and breathing techniques which should help prevent the pain and difficulties she had experienced having Nikki in the charity hospital in Newcastle.

Our very best friends, Barbara and Bud, were being very

helpful and supportive. Barbara had had her second child, Rolf, a few months earlier, but had not managed to get to hospital; Rolf had decided to arrive precipitately and Bud had to deliver him at home, alone and unaided. But it had all gone well, and Rolfito, as he was known, was a rosy, round bouncy baby with a huge smile. His older brother, Douglas, though something of a handful, nevertheless seemed pleased to have a brother. Nikki was very excited and demanded to have a brother too – we said we would do our best.

I went to Don Rodolfo and told him how much I had enjoyed the trip and what a wonderful place his Chile was. He smiled and said: "You should say 'our Chile' now. You are becoming a Chilean by adoption. And wait till you see the south – your eyes will drop out."

So, a couple of days later, having assured myself that all was well with Wendy, Kiko and I set of southwards, in another pick up, along what was grandly named the Pan-American Highway.

This was a road, paved with cement in long patches, which was planned eventually to run down the west coast of the Americas, all the way from Alaska to the tip of Chile. There were many gaps in it, for example in the impenetrable rainforest of eastern Panama, but the project was gradually being completed.

We drove south, through the town of Rancagua, a pleasant typical Chilean colonial town, regretfully missing out a visit to the vast underground "El Teniente" copper mine nearby with its 500 miles of underground galleries, since it was in the firm grip of our rivals, Esso.

We reached Curicó and found it was delightful. With cornfields, alfalfa grass and vineyards everywhere; it was the central part of the wine growing region of Chile's delicious wines. I was looking up at the snow on the volcanoes on my left, when Kiko suddenly pulled over to the verge and stopped.

"Come on," he said. "Let's have a little break."

I climbed out and noticed that, beside the road, there were long trestle tables with glasses and jugs on them. We were outside the Viña Undurraga, an old-established winery.

Kiko filled two glasses from one of the jugs and gave one to me.

As I drank the refreshing wine, he said: "The wineries all put out jugs and glasses of their wines on the road, to refresh the travellers and also hoping that you will like their wine so much that you will drive to the main house and buy some. Naturally, it is free."

"But don't people steal the wine?" I asked.

Kiko looked horrified. "Of course not," he said. "That would not be nice at all!"

I thought Chile to be a very civilised country.

We drove on, and I saw some *huasos*, or cowboys, riding beside the road on small, rather shaggy horses. They were resplendent in brightly coloured, *mantas* (a sort of short poncho) striped in red, blue, green and yellow, though some had full length ponchos draped down over their ornate, high-pommel saddles. They all wore large black sombreros, and waved as we drove by. As we passed close to one, I noticed his spurs. These were huge, silver sharp-spiked stars, which jingled as he rode.

Kiko said: "They are going off to a fiesta. They work very hard all week, and then they go to the local town or village for the rodeo. That is where they can show off their skills as cowboys and dance the *cueca*, which, as you know is the national dance."

"What about those huge spurs?" I asked.

"Ah, they are the Chilean musical spurs. They are all tuned to a different note when they are made, so they are bought to harmonise with each other as the *huaso* dances. It makes a pleasant sound. After that they go to the *ramada*, a sort of open enclosure, roofed with green branches for a good *parrillada* and lots of wine."

I remembered the *parrillada* my gang of peddlers had given me in Santiago, and thought enviously of the *huasos*.

We then drove on to Linares, the centre of fruit growing and also rich in other crops. The cathedral, brick-built and impressive, was relatively new, but stands on the site of an ancient one, totally destroyed by an earthquake.

We stayed the night at an acceptable hostelry, ate well and slept in comfort. I enjoyed the fresh cherries, apples, *chirimoyas* and other fruit. The hostelry was run by a young couple, friends of Kiko, whose five year old daughter had a pet chinchilla, which she showed me. This was a delightful little animal, indigenous to Chile, with thick, soft fur. It looked somewhat like a *cuyo*, but had a pretty bushy tail and long whiskers. When I held it, it cuddled itself into my chest and surreptitiously bit my finger.

We detoured to Talcahuano and the coast, some miles from the inland road on which we were travelling. This was a small fishing port, colourful, with some Araucanian Indians wandering about. The fishing boats, drawn up on the beach, were selling an impressive variety of fish and other sea creatures, which the buyers were sampling raw. The *corvina*, a sizeable fish resembling a large trout, seemed the favourite buy, but I was content to eat several oysters, some other molluscs and an abalone. Kiko had the same.

We spent the night in Concepción, just down the coast, and visited the Shell representative who covered the whole coast. Guillermo (or Willy, as he insisted on being called) had spent a year in California and was very American, to the extent of being regarded with some suspicion by his countrymen.

His house was brick and looked comfortable. His wife, Doña Elena, was rotund and merry and not at all American. She was of Araucanian stock and had a string of black-haired, stocky, cheerful children of assorted sizes. She welcomed us to her house with a glass of *chicha*, which gratefully burned its way down my throat and made my eyes water.

"You will eat with us," said Doña Elena. This was as much instruction as invitation, and Kiko and I accepted. "Willy will take you to the hotel where you can clean up (we were dusty and travel-stained) and then you will come back and I will feed you *seviche*."

It was evening, and the town was lit up; there were lights strung in the trees of the little central plaza, where boys and girls, separately, were strolling about, pretending not to notice each other. On the benches sat the *dueñas*, keeping a very beady eye on their young female charges.

I had never eated *seviche* before, and when Dona Elena described it to me, I wondered if I should like it. Raw local fish was marinated overnight in a mixture of lime and lemon juice with sliced onions and tomatoes, and served sprinkled with chopped coriander. It proved to be delicious . Lobsters and fresh fruit completed the meal, accompanied by a strong white wine.

Doña Elena was very proud of her Indian heritage. "We are really the *Mapuche*, a huge nation divided into many parts, both here and in Southern Argentina. Araucanians is a name that the Spaniards gave us when they came to destroy and enslave us; we, in turn, call them the *huincas*. They never discovered that in our language this means thieves!" She smiled, rather bitterly, I thought.

"Over the centuries we have fought the Incas, the northern Indians, the Spaniards and, finally, the Chilean independence people, until we finally signed a treaty with them, quite recently. Our wars have lasted 350 years!"

By now, Kiko and Willy had stopped talking and were listening. "Are your people Christians?" asked Kiko; he seemed to know little of what Doña Elena was telling me.

"No. We believe that the supreme beings are a celestial family of gods, each responsible for a different thing: people, animals, mountains, ocean and so on. If they are pleased, there are good harvests, good health and the people are happy. But if we make them angry then we get earthquakes, volcano eruptions, draughts and floods. We have rituals and speak with them on the *kultrun*, which is a holy big drum with different rhythms." She smiled again. "They usually listen."

One of the children brought *chicha*, and we sat and sipped and listened. I was fascinated.

"The Spanish brought us many new things," continued Doña Elena sardonically. "We learned about firearms and horses and so on, which make killing more efficient. They also gave us some unwanted presents: yellow fever, measles, smallpox, which killed hundreds of thousands of my people. But although the soldiers were bad, with their massacres, rapes and enslavement, the worst were the priests. They did very many terrible things 'for our own good'." She spat in disgust. "Although," she added, "they introduced the poncho, which Chileans now wear."

Kiko looked surprised. "The priests introduced this?" he asked. "Yes, to cover our nakedness," said Doña Elena. "Indians are proud to show their bodies. The priests did not like that. We wear clothes for warmth and ornament, not from shame."

"Finally, I should tell you that we do not like the Spanish language. We have our own, called *Mapundungun*." She said a few words, mellifluous and musical; they reminded me of the sound of wind in the trees. "The words came from imitating natural sounds, the sea, the wind, animals, streams, thunder and so on. The *Mapuche* have always lived close to nature. It is the best way."

We talked late into the night. I had a lot to think about: I wondered if our so-called civilisation was really the best way of life, if we should not be closer to natural things and also integrate our faith with our surroundings.

The following morning, we drove on, back on the inland road, through the colonial-style town of Temuco to Valdivia. We passed through forests of strange trees (half of Chile's flora and fauna was indigenous and existed only in that country). Notably there were groves of *araucaria*, the monkey-puzzle tree and several other curious ones, which Kiko said were medicinal, and widely used against various ills by the Indians.

Valdivia on the Calle-Calle river, was a fascinating city. It was one of the oldest in Chile, but, unlike the others, was settled by German colonists in the 1850s. They seemed to get on well with the *Mapuche*, and brought to the area their ethos of hard work, craftsmanship, house styles, food and social ways. Thus there were German shops, selling German food, German clothes and even a German newspaper. The houses were mainly A-frames, with eaves down to the ground, because of the heavy rainfall.

Valdivia became famous two years after my visit when it had what was agreed to be the biggest earthquake ever in the world. With the epicentre 100 miles off the shore, it practically destroyed the city. Fortunately, the death toll was not as high as it might have been, since Chileans are used to earthquakes and the strong tremors before it, as well as thunderous noises beneath the ground, caused the population to flee for the mountains.

Kiko and I had a pleasant dinner of *bratwurst,* cabbage and potatoes, finishing off with a large cream *torte*. We had this in company with Nugi, a young Shell representative, who lived there and assisted Willy in the region. Nugi was also a *Mapuche*, and because I had said I was interested in knowing more about his people, took us, the following morning, to visit his Indian village. This was a small collection of adobe huts, roofed with branches, in which some eight families lived. They were a handsome people: the men, brown and strong, had straight black hair cut short, and wore loose clothes in sombre colours, always with a blanket or poncho over one shoulder. They had wide brimmed black hats.

The women were plump and happy, and the children which surrounded them were small replicas of themselves and their husbands. They wore long dresses in plain colours, decorated with colourful embroidery. They also wore an embroidered band round their foreheads and had long, black plaited hair, down to below their waists. Some carried babies, strapped to their backs on a sort of wooden trellis. Everyone seemed to have perpetual smiles on their faces.

I was introduced to the *lonka*, or clan chief. He was taller than the others and wore an embroidered band round his waist. He had scary eyes: their irises were so black that the pupil was indistinguishable, and they looked empty. But he exuded an aura of power and authority; I was rather nervous.

"You are welcome in my village," he said in passable Spanish. "Nugi says you are interested in my people. If this is so, then I will tell you about the two serpents."

"I should be most honoured to hear a story of your people," I said. Kiko nudged me with his elbow. "You are lucky," he whispered, "he must like the look of you."

We sat on some tree logs. The *lonka* lit a clay pipe and said: "The world here is controlled by two giant serpents: there is Cai-Cai Vilu, who is wet and shiny and controls the ocean. Then there is an equally huge one called Treng-Treng Vilu, who is dry and hot and controls the earth. They are very jealous of each other and when the world was made, by the Great Sorcerers, who are now volcanoes, the serpents were ordered to stay apart."

He puffed on his pipe. We listened silently.

"But you can never trust serpents. Soon they began to fight and caused great convulsions of the earth and ocean, which continue to this day. We call them earthquakes, giant waves and eruptions of lava, but it is the serpents."

We were offered some *chicha* and roasted corn cobs, and left soon afterwards after thanking the chief for the story and the hospitality. "It is best not to outstay one's welcome," said Nugi. "My people do not usually entertain outsiders, however well-disposed. You were fortunate the *lonka* liked you and told the story."

We left early the following day for the last leg of our southern journey. The forest closed in on the road and I was told there were many strange animals to be found in the area, as well as *colo-colos*, big ginger wildcats and of course puma, but we did not see any.

We stopped at Osorno, because Kiko knew a young man there who had a small plane in which he was employed to look out for forest fires. We drove out to the airstrip and met Charlot, who had French antecedents, although he could not speak a word of French. His curious habit was of singing, loudly and non-stop, once he was airborne. Perhaps his many solo flights were boring. But Kiko managed to persuade him to give me a ride, for half an hour, particularly to see the spectacular Osorno volcano.

After a short chat, we climbed gingerly into the little two-seater Cessna, which looked rather decrepit although Charlot claimed it had never let him down. "Besides," he chuckled, "I never go very high so it is not so far to fall!" This did not help, since I had never before gone up in such a tiny flying contraption.

We took off and climbed towards the Andes. As we rose, the view became more and more spectacular – volcanoes, crystal lakes, lush green forest; all this in a clear blue sky with fleecy white clouds. It was all so perfect that it felt artificial.

We circled the crater of Osorno, rimmed with snow but with a curl of smoke rising from it; dived low over the lake that mirrored its perfect cone, and skimmed the forest tree-tops, only to soar again to a neighbouring mountain. It was exhilarating and exciting and I no longer felt nervous. Charlot was singing Chilean songs at the top of his voice and I could not ask him anything, what with the noise he was making, the roar of the engine and the swish of the wind.

We landed and taxied to where Kiko was waiting with the pick-up. I thanked Charlot profusely (he had stopped his singing as soon as our wheels had touched the ground). "It is nothing," he said, grinning. "I love showing my beautiful country to everybody."

On we went through Puerto Varas (a little old fishing port) to Puerto Montt, which was really the bottom end of Chile, before it turned into a vast archipelago of thousands of islands. There was the large island of Chiloë, temptingly isolated from the mainland, said to be full of extraordinary people and animals, which I wondered if I should visit, but decided that there was really no excuse for the extra day and night the trip would have taken.

Kiko said that this was a great centre for whaling, and that I should go to see where they processed the whales they caught. Accordingly, we went down to the whaling station and observed several whaling ships moored some hundreds of yards offshore. I could see grey whale bodies attached to their sides and, as we stood there, we saw a boat towing a huge carcass up to the concrete slipway beside which we were standing.

A chain was attached to the tail and the huge body was slowly winched up to where the flensing and butchering was done, as it was drawn onto land, by men in rubber boots with razor-sharp flensing knives on the end of long poles. Great slabs of blubber were pulled away on chains, and soon, the carcass was just a jumble of meat and the blood was running in streams freely back into the ocean.

I did not stay very long, although Kiko was very interested. The sight horrified me and gave me a disgust, from then on, for the hunting and murdering of whales, giant creatures that did no harm and were peaceful by nature. I remembered the whale and her pup whom I had seen from the ship in Northern Chile, and felt very unhappy.

This was the end of the line for us, though it was the gateway to Chilean Patagonia. A long, long way south was the settlement of Punta Arenas, in lower Patagonia, beside the Magellan Straits and not far from Cape Horn. It meant a lengthy flight and, although I very much wanted to go, there was really no justification.

We spent the night in a small, comfortable hotel, run by an ex-Irish couple whose forebears had sailed over with Admiral Cochrane, the Earl of Dundonald, an English seaman who commanded the first Chilean navy in the War of Independence, in support of the Liberator, Bernardo O'Higgins. As with Charlot, they did not speak their ancestral tongue, but only Spanish. Their name was, I think, O'Connell. The only notable event was that, for dinner, we were served roast *huemun*, a small brown deer. The venison was tender and full of flavour. The only other deer around, the O'Connells said, was the *pudu*, a tiny animal, much loved by everyone in the south.

In the morning, we drove out to the small airport. With us came a young student from Santiago, who had been visiting his parents. Kiko had arranged that, with the payment of expenses, he would drive the pick-up back to Santiago for him.

The plane, a relatively small 16 seater, took off on time, and after a long flight, we landed in Santiago in good order. The flight had been uneventful, but interesting. Through the small window I could see the volcanoes on the right, the ocean on the left and beneath, the emerald green canopy of the rain forest gradually giving way to more organised nature, with fields, vineyards, orchards and villages, as well as lakes and rivers. Even today Chile remains the most beautiful country I have ever seen.

Back home, the arrival of our second baby was theoretically only just over a month away. Wendy wanted to hear every detail of my trip. She seemed well and everything appeared to be going right. Nikki was very excited by the thought of a new brother or sister, as were the maids.

I went into the office the following day, to thank Kiko and Don Rodolfo for the trip. Both said it was a pleasure, and Don Rodolfo remarked that Jim, the Sales Manager, wanted to see me.

Accordingly, I went to his office and reported to his secretary. She made me wait for five minutes and then ushered me in. It was only the second time I had been in his office and had forgotten how opulent and impressive it was. Jim rose, shook hands and motioned me to an armchair. I sat down, but suddenly noticed, sitting unobtrusively in the corner was the General Manager. I sprang to my feet, but the motioned me to sit down again.

"Well, Mick," said Jim. "So you are back from your travels. What did you think of it all?"

"It was terrific... wonderful... unforgettable," I gabbled. "I am most grateful to you for letting me do it. I am afraid there was not much business to be done so I do not think it was really justified, but I thought it was great."

Jim smiled and the General Manager said: "We think the expenditure is well justified. It is an investment in you. We want our young men to know their way about and I am sure that all experience is good experience." This was good sense, but then he spoilt it by adding: "It will help to make you a good Shell man."

The next day Barbara had invited Wendy to tea, for, unbeknown to her, an American-style baby shower, when lots of friends would bring clothes and gifts for the new baby. Wendy had begun to feel some contractions, and was in bed, so instead Barbara brought the whole surprise party to our house, and Wendy had a merry afternoon. Our son arrived the following day: our calculations had been a month out. The baby clothes proved very timely.

In the early hours, I took Wendy to the Clinica Alemana and, she, with every stage talked-through and explained, with back massage and the reassuring company of a trained natural childbirth councillor, at lunchtime next day produced Robin, a fine, rosy boy. Wendy said it had been a wonderfully happy experience, she had not needed pain-killer, and she was proud to have been able to remember her Spanish and have a conversation with the Spanish-speaking doctors while giving birth.

We were over the moon. The clinic was clean, efficient and friendly; the doctors and nurses expert and sympathetic. A far cry, indeed, from the kind but primitive charity hospital and old-fashioned doctor in Newcastle who had ushered Nikki into the world.

Back home, with constant visits of congratulations and delight from all our friends, including all the baby-shower ladies and all the Shell senior staff wives, we settled down to enjoy our expanded family. Bud and Barbara were never far away and Tony, who was always seriously thinking of getting married himself and then getting cold feet at the last moment, spent much time with us.

After a couple of days, when life had settled down a little, I had to go back to the office. I took a customary box of cigars and offered them round, to much clapping on the back and congratulations from everyone. My gang of kerosene peddlers sent a bottle of old rum, with instructions not to drink it all at one go.

My new job was looking after eight service stations. I was allocated an ancient van to drive around, and told to get on with it.

It was easier than I thought, and the dealers were all friendly and interested. I got to know Santiago very well, driving all over it.

Together with my dealers, we plotted and schemed on how to get the better of Esso and thought up many ingenious ways both to boost our sales and, where possible, put a spoke in their wheel. Derek expressed himself satisfied and the Retail Manager seemed content. Life was good.

But I was approaching the end of my Chilean idyll, for so I considered it. I was anxious to know where we would go next – it could be anywhere.

Christmas came and went, in summer sunshine. It was now 1958, almost three years since Cambridge. It seemed far away.

Time passed quickly. We were enchanted by Robin and found his care, with the help of our kind maid, much more easy than in a cold flat in a Newcastle winter. Nikki was rather bewildered by this extra being, and was surprised rather than jealous. The weather was warm and fresh, the mountains were scorched golden brown and, on our occasional excursions down to Viña del Mar, the coastal resort, we could bask in the sun and watch the water-skiers dashing by.

I only made one more trip. This was a one day visit to

Pomaire, a small village not far from Santiago. The village was famous for its pottery and the shops were brimming with colourful confections made out of the local clay and decorated with traditional designs.

What attracted me was a small hut we passed on the way. This was really a broken down hovel and, sitting on the ground outside it was a woman making pots. There was a small dirty child nearby and what I assumed to be a grandmother sitting with them. This lady had a huge goitre on her neck and I could see a smaller one on the pot-maker. Apparently there was no iodine in their diet.

We stopped and walked over. I politely offered cigarettes all round and the ladies each took one and lit up. I suddenly noticed that the clay with which the younger woman was working was coal black; I had never seen the like. I also saw, on a small shelf beside the hut, some animal sculptures, simply decorated, in this selfsame clay, but fired.

I found one I liked, a pig with huge ears, and bought it for a few pence. I have never seen the black clay, or such artefacts, anywhere else. We still have it.

A month before we were due to leave, Jim called me into his office. "I have news for you," he said. "You better sit down."

My heart sank. What awful thing had I done? I racked my brains. Could it be Esso complaining again?

Jim grinned. "No, no," he reassured me. "There is nothing wrong. It is just that we have now been advised of your next posting." He paused deliberately; I was holding my breath. "It is..." another pause. "Africa!"

Africa. I could hardly take it in. My only experience of Africa was my school in Egypt, now twelve years ago. That was Arab Africa, not Africa proper.

"Where in Africa?" I enquired.

"Some place called Dakar, in Senegal," said Jim. "I don't know anything about it except that it is in the French area of Shell, and controlled from Paris. I didn't think we had any Englishmen there. But you will find out, no doubt. Patch will tell you all about it, at home."

I told Wendy when I got home. It was exciting news. We got

out the atlas again. I hoped it would be as beautiful and friendly as Chile had been. We discovered that it was the westernmost point of the African continent, and that the towns round Dakar had very strange names. It was also not too far from the Sahara.

We were booked to fly home (since we had come out by sea) and I asked that we break our journey in Lisbon for a week. My parents were living in Cascais, just north of the capital, and had asked us to stay. They had also mentioned that my aunt Ina had, after my beloved Max's death, come to England to live and had bought the lease of a house in Clarges Street, off Piccadilly in London, where she intended to run a select and genteel bed and breakfast establishment.

Soon it was time to pack up and go. There were many farewell parties. The hardest goodbye was to Bud and Barbara, with whom we had become very close. We were determined that wherever we went we would not lose touch, and we are still now nearly fifty years later close friends. We also bid farewell to Tony, whom I thanked for having spoken so glowingly of Chile when we were at Cambridge, and who thus was the direct cause of my asking to go there. We had made these good friends Robin's godparents, and so part of our family.

On my last day, I met Don Rodolfo. I was very touched when he gave me a book of poems, by Gabriela Mistral, the Nobel Prize winning Chilean writer. It was inscribed: "To our dear friends, the Arnolds, honorary Chileans, with happy memories. Come back."

The airplane turned out to be a huge DC7C, a four engined monster, which was to take us all the way to Lisbon. We flew first class – in those days all expatriates did – and it looked comfortable. Wendy had never flown before, but the constant attention demanded by Nikki and Robin, kept her mind off any frightening thoughts. A final wave, and we were off.

Piston-engined planes did not fly at enormous heights, so we circled gently out over the coast, climbing steadily towards the Andes. It was difficult for the plane to fly over the higher volcanoes, so the pilot wove his way through valleys and ravines. It was strange to see the snowy peaks not beneath us, but beside us; Wendy's eyes were very round, and she was very quiet. It was her first ten minutes ever in the air, and she was was flying over Andean snowfields, where any downed plane would never be found. Nikki was dreamily cuddling her toy rabbit, Robin was sound asleep. After some hours, we landed in Buenos Aires, having crossed South America from west to east, for refuelling. Then there was a short hop to Montevideo, to pick up some more passengers. Night gradually fell, and after we took off for Rio de Janeiro, our next refuelling stop, we discovered a wonderful thing. The stewardess, having given us a pleasant dinner, pulled on the overhead rack and produced two suspended cots, discretely curtained like sleeping berths on a train, into which we could climb to sleep. Shell had kindly booked these for us.

We clambered up, Wendy taking baby Robin in with her, as she was breast-feeding him, while I had to cope with a very wriggly Nikki. It was nice to stretch out, but I did not get much sleep.

On through the night to Rio, a brief refuelling and on to Recife, on the easternmost tip of South America, prior to the long flight across the Atlantic to Lisbon.

All we remember is a succession of meals and drinks, and the children becoming ever more tired, but not sleeping much. The stewardesses somehow remained cheerful and bright, and brought us picture books, crayons and small toys. But we were all completely exhausted when we landed at Lisbon. We had been flying solidly for 18 hours and there had been periods of turbulence and also a storm, with lightening flashes, and sudden gusts of the high winds which tossed the aircraft around. Piston-engined planes could not fly above the weather.

My parents were there to meet us and bundled us into the car for the short drive to Cascais. Mother prattled away, with Grandmotherly exclamations and dramatic pronouncements on the beauty and intelligence of the children. She actually had little empathy with children but felt it her duty to be very enthusiastic. She therefore made Polish noises, saying: "Ach, my darlinks! You have come such a dangerous journey just to see your Grandmother who loves you. See the little man," this admiringly to her new grandson.

Ronnie, my step-father, looked quietly pleased to see us all.

They had rented a nice little villa with a small garden, and a maid was there to welcome us. The children were tired and whiny, so we put them straight to bed, following them soon after.

The following morning, at breakfast, we all sat and talked non stop for a long time. Ronnie and Nikki seemed much taken with each other, and walked round the garden. Mother assumed maternal poses and gingerly held Robin, exclaiming: *"Borze moj,* what a fine boy. How smiling! How like his father! How very HANDSOME!"

Ronnie had retired from BP and taken up his real love, painting. He was amateurish at the beginning, though he improved rapidly to become a wonderful artist. Portugal, with its clear light, white painted houses, colourful fishing boats and blue sky and ocean gave him plenty of material to paint.

I had arranged, before leaving Chile, that we might meet George, the Operations Manager, in Lisbon. George was English, but with a Portuguese wife, and would be on leave while we were in Cascais. Accordingly, I called him and he invited us to dinner in Lisbon. Sadly, Wendy could not go, since she was still breast-feeding Robin. So I borrowed Ronnie's little car and set off. I was to meet George at a fado cellar, whatever that was.

The cellar proved to be just that. Down below the street, there was a large subterranean restaurant; it was smoky, dim and there were tantalising odours of food. George and his wife were already at a table, so I joined them

"Well, nice to see you," said George. "You can't come to Lisbon without listening to some fado."

"What exactly is this fado?" I asked.

"The fado represents the soul of Portugal," said George solemnly. "The Portuguese are a naturally very melancholy people..." He winced as his wife kicked him under the table. "With exceptions of course," he added hurriedly. "But the fado are the national songs, full of sadness, tragedy and misery. In Portuguese, the word is *saudade*, which expresses longing for things that have passed and will never return." He paused, much moved. His wife grinned and said: "George always exaggerates everything, but the idea is about right."

"Let us have some port," said George. "After all, this is where it comes from." He spoke to the waiter, who brought us some dryish white port, which was excellent. He then ordered a meal for us of a dried cod soup, assorted seafood and an elaborate and very sweet pudding, with a rich red port to wash it down. The waiter brought the bottle, and we sat there chatting, replete and happy.

Suddenly there was silence, and a lady appeared through the curtains at the back. She wore a black dress, and over it was draped a long black shawl. Another, made of black lace, covered her hair. She was followed by two men, one with a full size guitar and the other with a small, thin one, rather like a mandolin.They came to the centre of the room. The guitarists struck up a steady, rhythmic tune and the lady began to sing.

The hairs stood up on the back of my neck. The song was beautiful, unutterably sad, with a wonderful tune. The rhythm of the guitars was hypnotic. I was transported and my whole being was concentrated on the music.

"You like it?" asked George. "I suppose you do, because you have not moved an inch since they started. Have a sip of port, for heavens' sake."

I was totally mesmerized. We sat through the night, drinking port and listening to the fados. Since that day, it has remained one of my very favourite song styles.

When everything was over, a little after midnight, I thanked George and his wife very much for a fantastic experience and said I would never forget it. George's wife said she was delighted to have a new convert to Portuguese culture and we parted after an evening I had enjoyed very much; my only regret was that Wendy was not there to share it.

The week passed quickly. We told my parents what a wonderful time we had had in Chile and that we were now destined, after leave in England, for Africa.

Mother gave a little scream. "But Africa is very dangerous, full of lions and elephants. And cannibals who will EAT you! My darlinks, the diseases; you will all get the sleeping sickness and the fevers. How will I live if you never come back! And my God, the little ones..." Fortunately, Ronnie patted her hand and reassured her that things were not as bad as all that.

Wendy and I managed to slip away once together between Robin's feeds, as Wendy very much wanted to see something of Portugal. Ronnie was very kind and lent us his little car, so off we went, early one morning, firstly down to the beach. This was full of brightly coloured fishing boats and fishermen in clothes straight out of 'Pirates of Penzance': pantaloons, shirts and waistcoats and long stocking caps. We noticed that every boat had a large eye painted on the prow. We did not know why, but supposed it was to help the boats to see where they were going.

We then drove inland, along dusty roads lined with tall eucalyptus. We passed several donkeys, grossly overloaded with hay and a couple of ox carts lumbering slowly along. There were very few cars.

Suddenly Wendy said: "Stop!" and I pulled to the side of the road. There beneath us was a truly Biblical scene: a man, walking slowly behind a wooden plough pulled by two sedate oxen, turning the rich brown earth in a deep furrow. Behind him walked another man, with a large cloth bag over one shoulder, regularly plunging his hand into it and scattering seed, with a circular sweep, into the furrows. I imagined that nothing had changed for thousands of years. The Portuguese seemed very different from the other bustling, busy Europeans and I liked their unhurried and placid way of life.

The week was soon over and we were off to the airport again. The parents were sad to see us go and Mother was in tears, convinced that Africa would do its worst and she would never see any of us again.

The short flight to London was uneventful, and easy after our recent marathon. Wendy's parents were at the airport to greet us and take us to the flat in Hove, to which they had moved from North London. It was good to feel English soil beneath my feet again. On the way to the coast I reflected that Chile had been a wonderful posting, that I now had two children and that soon the family would be going off to Africa, on a new adventure.

CHAPTER FOUR

Senegal

Back in England on leave, we soon settled down with Wendy's parents. M, (as I called my mother-in-law), immediately developed a profound bond with the children, and with Wendy took them on happy expeditions to beach, playgrounds and rowing lake. My father-in-law, whom I called D, was still commuting to his office in London, although approaching retirement.

After a few days of lazing round, I decided I would go and see Patch, at the Shell headquarters, and see what I could find out about my new posting to Dakar.

Accordingly, I went up to London and to the office which Patch shared with other mothers-in-Shell.

She seemed to remember me, and as I sat in the familiar chair in front of her desk, she produced a cup of coffee without having to ask me how I liked it.

"Well," said Patch. "So here you are again. How did you like your first contract?"

"Terrific," I replied. "The country is gorgeous, the people fantastic and in Shell everyone was extremely helpful and friendly – the only improvement I can think of is to make it two years instead of just one; it isn't enough."

Patch nodded. "I am glad you had a good time. There have been some things filtering back here: it seems they were very pleased with you and have asked for another trainee. In fact," Patch continued, "you may find that your good impression on

Shell may be a two-edged sword." She frowned slightly. "They were particularly impressed with your language skills and the way your family managed to blend into the country – it seems you were much liked by the Chileans." I was pleased to hear that.

"What this has caused is that you are to be used as a sort of ambassador." She smiled, without humour. "The situation is this: the Shell companies in French West Africa and French Equatorial Africa – in their colonies – are not run from London, but from French Shell in Paris." She paused while I took this in. Why did they want to send an Englishman (for so I now thought of myself) to a French-controlled area?

Patch answered my unspoken question. "It seems there has been great resistance from the French managements to accepting any but Frenchmen in their companies; London has tried to put people in but with no success. The French think London wants to take over and they don't like it."

"So?" I prompted her. "What does this mean for me?"

"It means that London has insisted (it went up to the Board) and you are the first London marketing person to be posted there. Your reception may be a little frosty..."

I thought back to my Shell superiors in Chile, all of whom had become friends. "Oh, I am sure it won't be so bad," I said. "I'll manage." Little did I know.

Patch then told me of the arrangements. At the end of my leave, I was to fly to Paris and change planes for Dakar. I had received a salary rise and this would be reflected in my local pay. The contract was a little strange: twenty months without a break and then four months' leave. Patch strongly recommended that I go out alone for some weeks and prepare everything for the family, who would arrive later.

I told Wendy all this, and we wondered what it would be like. I felt that Patch was trying to warn me, but could not do so openly. We pored over all the information we could get about Senegal, in atlases and the public library, but there was not very much.

We saw some old friends and had a happy, lazy time. M took a lot of the work associated with the children, who adored her, off Wendy's shoulders, although they mostly did everything together. D was also enchanted with young voices again in the house, though we tried to keep these quiet when he was working in his study.

Colin had met and married Carol, a beautiful model, and settled down to the profession of insurance loss adjuster. Teddy had gone to live in Spain and married a very much older, but wealthy Spanish lady. We were surprised he had allowed himself to get hooked. Sadly, being a diabetic, as we later heard, he died at forty.

Before we knew it, it was time for me to go. I had bought some khaki shorts and bush-shirts, and some stout shoes. On the appointed day, we all went off to the airport and after many goodbyes, and instructions from Wendy to take care of myself, I went off to the aircraft. I had told her that I would be writing frequently. I was going to miss my family – this was our first real parting.

The flight to Paris and the change of plane to an Air France Constellation went without a hitch. I started to speak French to the cabin staff, to practice, since I had got a little rusty. But soon I felt comfortable in it again.

We flew through the night and, as dawn came up, we were near Dakar. We skimmed the town, which seemed to be a sprawling, mostly white spread of low houses with small gardens and palm trees. In the centre there were more substantial buildings, including some ten or fifteen stories high. The sea and the port passed beneath, the sea a clear azure, the beach of yellow sand. Then there was a bump and we landed in Africa.

The airport was some way from the town, but as we taxied in I could see a solitary tall building on the nearby beach. This, I later found, was the Hotel N'Gor, Dakar's most luxurious hotel. We could never afford its prices.

After tedious explanations in Immigration and Customs, who regarded me with great suspicion as an Englishman who spoke French, I finally got out into the public concourse. There, among the crowd, I saw a little man with grizzled grey hair, holding a placard which said 'Shell'. He was a very dark indigo black, as was everyone around.

I identified myself, and he told me to follow him, together

with a porter with my two suitcases. There was no word of greeting or any other talk.

We got into a taxi, and he spoke to the driver in a strange language, which I later found was Wolof, the main language of Senegal.

I tried to speak, but received only monosyllabic answers, so I stopped and looked out of the window. We passed through a suburb of pleasant looking houses and flats, set in green gardens with trees and flowering bougainvillea, then on to the main part of town. I thought the houses looked inviting and that the family would be happy here.

We drove through a shopping area, with not very many shops and on into a poorer section of town, which gradually degenerated into a sort of slum. The houses were of rough concrete, with wooden doors painted in bright colours, the street was narrow and rather dirty, with the odd goat and rather impoverished-looking Africans wandering about.

To my surprise, we stopped at one of the doors, crudely painted blue, and the driver turned off the engine. I noticed many ragged figures squatting along the walls of the houses, on the pavement. They looked shabby and ill.

My guide got out and said: "Here we are," and then spoke to the driver.

"What do you mean?" I asked. "And what are all these lines of people squatting about? Is this a clinic or something?" I remembered my Uncle Max's clinic in Baghdad where he treated, free, large number of poor Arabs.

"No," said my guide. "This is your house. And don't take any notice of these people; they are just beggars, mostly lepers and polio victims. They are everywhere."

The driver had taken my cases out of the taxi and stood there, waiting. "There must be some mistake," I said. "I can't live in this place."

"Well, this is where the management told me to put you. You have to spend the night here and you can argue with them tomorrow. It is nothing to do with me, anyway."

He opened the rough wooden door and went in. I did so too, followed by the driver with the cases; he put them on the floor.

There was a passage with a door on each side. These revealed smallish bedrooms, one with twin beds and one with a double; each had a small cupboard. At the end of the passage there was a medium-sized living/dining room. It was furnished with a table with six chairs and a settee with two armchairs, upholstered in a shiny, mustard – coloured plastic. There was also a rather primitive bathroom.

Beyond this was a small kitchen and a narrow paved area, with a high wall all round it.

"There is a refrigerator in the kitchen," said my guide. The driver had gone. "I have not put anything in, but you can get something yourself. Here..." he handed me an envelope. "There is money in it, I will collect you tomorrow morning at eight and take you to the office. You can work everything out then." He turned away. "Oh yes, and here is the key. You should keep the door locked at all times."

With this he left and I sat down on a warm sticky plastic armchair to think about everything. It was hot and humid and there was a persistent beat of drums in the background, from the compound over the fence. We were to find that these never stopped.

After some moments, I decided to make the best of it, and started to explore. The refrigerator, a small, rusty affair, was not working, but made a satisfactory whirring noise when I turned the switch.

The heat was oppressive. There was no air-conditioner in the sitting room, but there were two small ones built into the front walls of the two bedrooms. I turned one on and it worked: a cloud of dust was the first emission; it took some time to begin to cool. The house had heavily barred and shuttered windows in the bedrooms looking out on the street, one in the sitting room, looking out on a blank wall some four feet away, and a window and glass-panelled door leading out to the scruffy back yard. Altogether it was a very unprepossessing dwelling and a very far cry from what I had expected after Chile. In fact, the whole arrival was disappointing and worrying.

I looked in the envelope; there were some notes in it, CFA francs, the local currency. I decided to get some food and drink, and ventured out of the front door, carefully locking it behind me.

The assembled beggars immediately set up a pitiful whine, those who had hands were holding them out and two small urchins, in rags, began pulling at my clothes and looking at me with huge eyes, with flies clustered round them.

I had no coins, so I said "Wait, wait, when I come back," in French and some of them must have understood, because the noise subsided.

After some walking, I found a little, broken-down shop and went in. The items on sale were not very many and looked rather old and dusty. There was an enormously fat lady, in a shapeless flowery dress and turban, behind the counter.

"Good day," I said politely. "I would like to buy something to eat and drink, please. I have just moved in down the street."

The lady gave a huge grin. "Aha," she said in the French pidgin dialect which would become very familiar. "So they put you in the Shell house."

"It seems so," I said. "But I won't be there long." The lady gave a guffaw. "Ha ha, that's what the last one said. He was there for a year..." As she laughed, her body rippled, like waves on a colourful pond.

I looked around. "I will have two tins of those sardines and some bread and half a dozen bananas, please."

I then spotted some bottles of mineral water. "And six of those."

"Well, if you promise to come back and shop," said the lady, "I will lend you a basket to carry the things. I will also lend you a tin opener."

I paid, making sure I had some small coins, and, after thanking her, took my loot home. I gave some of the coins to the beggars and urchins.

After further exploration, I found a pair of dirty glasses and plates in the kitchen cupboard and a corkscrew. The water from the tap was a pleasant light brown, but served to wash my crockery.

I sat at the dining table and had my modest meal, firmly deciding that I would sort things out in the morning. I was still convinced there had been a mistake. I then cleaned the house as best I could, sweat dripping from me, and unpacked the cases.

That evening, feeling depressed, when I went to bed (there were some worn sheets and blankets piled on them), I lay awake and planned what I would tell the management, rather forcefully, in the morning.

The following morning, my silent guide arrived punctually in a taxi, and took me to the head office of the Société Shell de l'Afrique Occidentale, or SSAO as it was generally known. This was a large, modern building of many floors. The Company was much larger than the one in Chile and looked after the whole of French West Africa which included many colonies: Senegal, Mauritania, French Soudan and so on. The equatorial colonies were controlled by the Equatorial version of Shell, based in Guinea, which looked after the remaining colonies. Both reported to Paris.

We went up in the lift and I saw large numbers of Frenchmen bent over their desks in various offices. None looked up as I passed or made any comment.

On the top floor, we went through a series of secretarial desks to a large and opulently furnished office, where my guide motioned for me to sit down.

"This is the office of Monsieur Morineau, the Personnel Manager. He will be here shortly."

With this, he turned on his heel and left the room. I never saw him again.

I looked round. There were colourful pictures of African scenes on the walls and a number of beautiful wooden carvings on shelves and tables. The view from the window showed a panorama of palm trees, other office buildings and, in the distance, blue sea and sandy beaches.

The door opened, and Monsieur Morineau came in. He was a smallish, dapper man, with swept-back, oily black hair and a little moustache. He was impeccably dressed in a well-fitting grey suit and made me feel shabby. He reminded me of the Regent of Iraq, whom I had particularly disliked.

He went behind the large desk and sat down.

"You are Arnold," he stated, looking at me coldly.

"Yes, "I said. "There are many things I want to ask you, please."

"That can wait. First of all listen to what I have to say." He leaned forward, his elbows on the desk, and stared at me. The air-conditioning hummed softly.

"We did not particularly want you here," he started. "You are the first English person on contract to join us here in Dakar, and that is only because London asked us to take you. All conditions of your contract, pay, accommodation and so on will be according to Paris rules, not London. No one else complains, so there is no point in you doing so..."

"But all this is not my fault," I interrupted. "If you didn't want me, why am I here?"

"There are reasons," he said. "Anyway, as it happens, we have found a job for you. You will find it takes you out of town quite a lot, but it may be of some interest. You should limit your contact with this office to a monthly report of your activities; that will be sufficient."

"What will be the job?" I asked.

"I will tell you presently. You must also understand something else." He paused and stroked his little moustache. "As you know, you are paid a basic salary by London, which is converted into local currency and adjusted for cost of living in different countries." I nodded. The Chilean salary had been comfortable.

"Here, your London salary must first be adjusted by Paris before the local amount is calculated." He smiled thinly. "We have not done this before, but I expect it will be enough."

"Oh, and another thing," he added. "Individuals may not, by law, send money out of Senegal and you are not a member of the French pension scheme. You have to arrange to send your own pension contribution to London – we will not do it for you."

"But how can I do so, if it is illegal?" I asked. If my contributions to the Shell pension were not made, I would not get one.

"That is your concern," he said coldly. "And you may bring your family whenever you want. You have seen the accommodation."

"It is not good," I said. "Is there not some mistake? It will be difficult for my family to live in such conditions and in such a neighbourhood."

"It is what is available," he said. "If you start your time here by complaining, you will not do very well. And, by the way, it is not permissible for you to communicate directly with Shell in London, under any circumstances. If you do so, you must expect stern disciplinary action. Any further complaints must be addressed to this office."

This was all very different from my reception in Chile. I could hardly believe my ears: no welcome, no introduction, very onerous terms and frightful housing. Things began to look very bleak indeed.

"Now about your job..." said Monsieur Morineau. He pressed a button on his desk and said into a box: "Tell him to come in."

Almost immediately, the door opened, and a young man came in. He was dressed all in white (as I later found out was his permanent habit). He was slim, of medium height and had a crew-cut. His clothes were impeccable: white bush-shirt, perfectly creased, white shorts, white stockings and white shoes; he positively shone.

He came towards me with his hand out, as Monsieur Morineau said: "Monsieur Puligny, this is Arnold, your replacement."

We shook hands. "Jean-Claude Puligny, at your service," he said.

"Mick Arnold," I answered, shaking hands. "Very glad to meet you." I was. He was the first person to greet me in any way.

"Very well, Arnold," said Monsieur Morineau. "That is all. You may go. Puligny will show you what you need to know." He pulled some papers towards him and began to read. Jean-Claude, to my astonishment, winked at me and motioned with his head. I followed him out.

"They are not all like that," he said, when we were some distance away. "Some are much worse." He laughed. "Thank God I never have to go to the office; you will be glad too."

"But what is this job?" I asked. "What do you do?"

"I am the Retail Inspector for four countries," he said. "It is not nearly as wonderful as it sounds – wait till you see the countries. But I hope you enjoy driving in deserts and jungles, because that is what I do. And you will take my place."

We had come out of the building and were walking towards an extremely muddy Land Rover, which had all sorts of things fixed to it everywhere. Beside it stood a tall, slim African with a huge grin. He was dressed in khaki shirt and shorts.

"This is Sarr M'Baye," said Jean-Claude. "This car will be your home and Sarr will be your ever-present companion. He is the mechanic, cook and many other things. Quite useless!" Sarr grinned even more widely.

I shook hands with him. "I am happy to meet you," I said. "Me too," said Sarr. He spoke the pidgin French mainly spoken by the Africans. "He is not good boss." He giggled.

We got into the Land Rover. Jean-Claude drove, with me beside him while Sarr sat somewhere in the back, among a great pile of boxes, bits of metal and jerricans.

He started off. "Oh, damn it," he suddenly said. "To hell with the instructions; let's have lunch." He caught his breath and looked at me out of the corner of his eye.

"What instructions?" I asked. "What are you talking about?"

"Nothing.. nothing," he babbled. "Some old rumour... we hear a lot of them... nothing important... forget it..."

I looked round at Sarr, but his face was impassive.

"I know," said Jean-Claude. "I will take you to Mère Marie. That's some of the best cooking in Dakar. And it's my treat," he added.

It was just as well. I had been given a cheque, an advance on my salary, and told to open an account, but I had not done so yet. It was given to me by a clerk just outside Monsieur Morineau's office.

The restaurant, very like a typical French bistro, was pleasant and crowded with Frenchmen. Jean-Claude was obviously well known and greeted on all sides. In fact, the proprietress came out to shake his hand and he introduced me. Sarr was told to go and get his own lunch and return in an hour.

"Now Marie," said Jean-Claude. "This is a *rosbif* who has come to us. We must show him what real food is like."

We had a splendid meal. There was proper French bread, a

first course of *charcuterie,* and a main course of a impressive steak, with potatoes and salad. The steak was succulent and delicious, though with a strange, rather sweet, extra taste. Jean-Claude told me, after the meal, that it had been horsemeat. It was the only time I ever ate it. There was also a strong red wine. Jean-Claude explained that everything I had eaten, including the bread, was flown in daily from France. "This makes it rather expensive, but really, the food eaten here is horrible. The *bougnouls* (a derogatory term for black Africans) have no idea."

This was my first encounter with the racial attitudes of colonial France. Overtly, they seemed more enlightened than British colonists – there were many Africans in quite senior administrative posts in Government, business and the army. Inwardly, most colonists considered them to be inferior beings and, between themselves, used many nasty terms to describe them, legally, however, every inhabitant of French Africa was a Frenchman; a citizen of metropolitan France, just as though he was in Europe, and Senegal even had two Deputies in the French Government.

During the meal, Jean-Claude told me a bit about himself. He was a bachelor and had been in Dakar for two years. He lived in a pleasant flat in the Mermoz area, where most of the French staff lived, in modern housing with greenery and trees everywhere. It was also close to the beach at N'Gor, where expatriates tended to gather.

"Now, thank God, I am going back to Paris. I've had enough of this place. Especially the *petits fonctionnaires*, the little petty Napoleons who run the Company. You will have to be very patient and forgiving."

"I think the house they put me in is pretty foul," I said.

"I'm not surprised," he said enigmatically. "Try and stick it out; it may get better. But you will have to organise some friends for your family, when they come. You may find the beach is a good place to meet people outside the Company. And make sure your wife has a car; she will need it. I will help you get one."

"Tell me about the job," I said.

Jean-Claude leaned back in his chair and lit a small cheroot. He had offered me one, and I also lit up.

"I've really never understood it," he said. "You are responsible for the petrol stations in the area, which is huge – about the size of Europe. The stations are very few, separated by many, many miles of dirt tracks and sometimes no road at all. You are expected to visit them all at least once every six months. The ones in Dakar proper are looked after by someone else." He paused and puffed meditatively at his cheroot.

"I don't know why we have them. Perhaps it is some service to the French Government, or something. They sell very little, and are hard to replenish – the trucks always get stuck and take weeks to fill up the far ones, especially in the rainy season. But if you like wildlife and local tribes and customs, you will enjoy it. I have got bored with the whole thing, and anyway, it is hard to keep one's clothes looking good." He smoothed his immaculate shirt front.

I wondered why Shell should wish to employ an expatriate, and a local mechanic and use an expensive vehicle for what seemed a useless task. This was a question which was never answered.

After agreeing to meet the following day, Jean-Claude took me home. I went back to the little shop and got some more basic provisions, and then settled down to write Wendy a long letter. It was hard to decide how honest I should be. My first impression of the Company and my circumstances was most unfavourable and I did not want to depress her. On the other hand, I did not want to raise any false hopes in her mind.

I thought that she should come, with the children, after about a month. This would give me time to work things out, get the house as straight as I could, and find out about general living in Dakar. In the meanwhile, I emphasised how important it was that she should pass her driving test (Wendy did not drive) since otherwise she would be stuck in the house. Public transport was crowded and haphazard.

In the event, she stayed with Colin and his new wife, Carol, who helped look after the children while Wendy took driving lessons every morning and afternoon and passed her test with flying colours in just three weeks.

The month passed, rather slowly but with interesting

interludes. Jean-Claude was as good as his word and shepherded me through the logistics of opening a local Bank account and buying a car. I got Wendy a little, feisty Renault Quatre Chevaux which seemed cheap, fun and suitable.

Jean-Claude also showed me Dakar, the beaches, the shops and so on. We went to the beach at N'Gor, where there were masses of people in tiny bikinis, both girls and men, mostly French. But there were also some African *fatous*, as Senegalese women were called, fully clothed in colourful sarongs and turbans, often with babies strapped to their backs, wandering about selling peanuts and other small eatables. It seemed a strange contrast. The sand was golden and hot, the sea a perfect clear blue.

He also explained about the Land Rover. It reminded me very much of Mr. Ginger's 'Explorer' in Baghdad, in which he had taken me and his sons on a visit to Babylon. I decided to christen my Land Rover by the same name and, much to Sarr's astonishment, also tended to bow slightly to it at the beginning and end of each journey, in thanks.

"This poor old thing is practically dead," said Jean-Claude. "As a last good gesture to you I have persuaded the idiots in Head Office to authorise a new one for you. You should get it just after I leave."

I thanked him. Sarr grinned broadly. Jean-Claude said: "But it will need many modifications. You are going into pretty rough country and all sorts of things are necessary. Sarr will fix it, if you want him to."

But we did use the old vehicle at first. Jean-Claude wanted to 'blood' me and introduce me to what was generally known as The Bush.

For a first trip, he decided that we should do a loop through three towns not far from Dakar, and with decent roads. Accordingly, we set off one early morning in the direction of Kaolack, inland.

The road, more or less paved, led us through a sad collection of slums out into the open country. There were palm trees, bushes and savannah, grassy and dry. The driving was dangerous: there were small, busy buses, crammed with passengers both inside and outside, on the roof and clinging to the sides. They looked very unsafe as they swayed from side to side on overloaded springs, driven with great abandon by cheerful drivers. There were donkey carts, and many *fatous*, trudging along the sides of the road, with large bundles of firewood on their heads. Bicycles, wobbling dangerously, some with three people aboard, were everywhere – there seemed to be no rules of the road.

"We should really have left earlier," said Jean-Claude. "I usually try to get away just before sunup because it is cooler and there is less traffic."

"And there are less birds then," chimed in Sarr from where he was wedged in the back, among all the paraphernalia, which I now noticed included a shotgun.

"True," said Jean-Claude, nonchalantly driving off the road to avoid being hit by an oncoming bus with a blaring horn. "The birds are mostly vultures, though there are crows and other things. They come out and sit on the road at sunup, eating the dead snakes. These come out at night and lie on the road because it holds the heat from the sun; then they get run over and the birds eat them in the morning." He tooted the horn. "Nature is very tidy."

We drove on, and got to Kaolack at lunchtime. There was a petrol station there, with two pumps, and Jean-Claude stopped to introduce me to the owner. This was a large, cheerful African who expressed himself pleased to see us and told us that sales were as usual and there were no problems. Since we were only some forty miles from Dakar, he was visited frequently. We then went to a little restaurant and had lunch. Sarr was, as before, dismissed to find his own sustenance.

We had a simple meal of fish with peanut sauce and millet, washed down by some rather sour red wine. So far, I could see nothing very frightening in travel in The Bush.

The town was not very prepossessing: low, whitewashed buildings, dusty streets, dusty trees and dusty people. It was quite crowded, and there was an open market selling mostly different items of food, as well as sandals made from old tyres, woven hats and brightly-printed cloth. There were beggars everywhere and there was a plague of flies.

I noticed a mosque and asked Jean-Claude if there were many Moslems. "Oh, yes," he said. "The Wolofs, the main tribe in Senegal, are almost all Moslems. But quite a large number are also animists, who worship many things in nature. There are even some Christians," he added.

I was embarrassed; he spoke as though Sarr were not there at all. This was, I noticed, the way French expatriates tended to treat the Africans; they were not rude or unpleasant, they just ignored them as though they were not there.

"But it is very different in the Real Bush," he said. "You will see."

On the way out of town, I noticed a huge enclosure with trucks and people buzzing around enormous mounds – some fifty feet high – of stuffed brown sacks.

"Look at that," I said. "Great mountains of sacks. What on earth is this?"

"Oh, it is nothing," said Jean-Claude. "It's peanuts."

"It's not peanuts," I said indignantly. "There are mountains of sacks."

"I know," he replied, grinning, "it's just as I said: peanuts. This is the main collecting point for peanut production in the hinterland. From here, the peanuts get trucked to Dakar for export all over the world. It is a major crop."

I subsided, chastened. But the quantities were impressive and I later saw the same mountains of peanuts on the docks in Dakar.

We drove on to Djourbel, a small town some miles away, swinging back towards the coast. This was much like the previous stop; same dust, same flies. "We will spend the night here – no reason to hurry," said Jean-Claude.

He seemed to live his life at a very leisurely pace. I calculated that we could easily have got back to Dakar that day.

After a somewhat uncomfortable night in a small boarding house we set off again, heading for the coast.

We got to the sea at lunchtime, near a town called M'Bour. There was another pump to inspect, and then we went off to the beach. Jean-Claude, impeccable as always in his pristine white clothes and shoes (I was wearing my khakis), stopped, and taking off his long white stockings and white shoes, carefully put them in the car, and began to stroll along the beach. I took off my sandals and followed him.

We stopped at a group of fishermen, who were dragging their boat up onto the sand. "Good catch?" enquired Jean-Claude.

"Good fish," said a burly fisherman, naked but for a rag round his waist, his black skin shining in the sun. "Tide good, wind good. See here..."

He pointed to the boat and we craned over the side to see a great mass of wriggling fish, of all sizes and shapes, gleaming on the bottom of the *pirogue*, as these boats were called. I noticed particularly a large ray, with a span of some three feet, flopping about on top.

After a further stroll, and a half-hour rest sitting under a palm tree and staring at the waves gently lapping the brilliant white sand and chatting, we climbed back into the car and drove home. I felt this would not be a very demanding job.

I decided to go to the office to see if I could get any help with the house and to find out when the new Land Rover would be delivered. Jean-Claude was off somewhere, so I went buzzing up in the little Renault.

The man at the reception desk was not at all helpful, but eventually directed me to the Administrative Department, on the third floor.

The Department consisted of a large open space, full of desks, with some little offices on the sides. I had been told to see Monsieur de Frescheville, and found him in one of the small offices.

He looked up and smiled as I knocked on the door. He was the first person to smile at me in the office (other than Jean-Claude).

"Come in," he said. "I think I know who you are. You must be Monsieur Arnold, recently arrived from London." He spoke a beautiful French, extremely literary and correct.

I told him I was.

"Please sit down" he said. "What can I do for you?"

I explained about the house, the car and the general vagueness about the job, though I told him that Jean-Claude had been very friendly and helpful. I did not say that no one else had been.

Then, as he showed sympathy and was friendly, I found myself telling him of my disappointment, my worries about how the family would manage and the apparently very low salary I was to receive.

"Well," he said when I had finished. "You surely have received a bad impression of us." He frowned. "I am not surprised." He was the second person to say that. "You will find that Shell politics are a complicated affair and that they affect us all."

"I don't understand," I said.

"You will in time," he answered. "Now, about your house. I am afraid it is the only one available and, while in an unpleasant district, is adequate, in the opinion of Management. You must get yourself a *fatou* to clean and cook and that will be all right."

He paused. "I am the Deputy Administration Manager," he said. "But even I can't do everything." I found that everyone in the Company had a resounding title and that the hierarchy was formally and rigidly observed. "As far as your salary is concerned," he sighed, "that's decided in Paris and we cannot tinker with it."

"My wife was brought up by an English nanny," he suddenly remarked, out of the blue. "You may like to visit us sometime." I was staggered; an invitation, though not specific. "I would be truly delighted," I said. "It would be a great pleasure."

"Good," he said. "I am sorry I have not been of much help."

Throughout our meeting, I could not help noticing what beautiful French he spoke. There was no slang, the grammar was perfect and the sentences harmoniously constructed. A far cry from Jean-Claude's careless *argot* and lazy elisions. I looked forward to listening to him again.

We went on two or three more unmemorable short trips and the time passed. There was the beach, there was exploration of the limited facilities in the town. I found a good bookshop with some interesting books: life was leisurely to the point of lethargy.

Finally, Jean-Claude departed, leaving me, as his legacy, the battered Land Rover and the agreeable companionship of Sarr. Just before he left, he said: "I have had this shotgun for years and it is very useful in the wilder parts of the Bush. I do not want to take it to France, so perhaps you might like to have it?" "I would be delighted," I said. "But I am afraid I can't pay you very much for it."

"No, no," he laughed. "Have it as a gift. You will also find some boxes of cartridges in the Land Rover. I am certain you will find good use for them. Besides, you will discover that Sarr is an excellent tracker." Sarr grinned.

He also helped me to find a *fatou*, since the family's arrival was now imminent, and I asked her to clean the house properly. I also acquired odd bits of additional furniture and some native knick-knacks. Our luggage from Chile had arrived, but I did not embark on a full unpacking.

The *fatou* was rather fat and very languid. She moved slowly and, whatever I said or threatened, just smiled lazily and continued in her way. I was sure Wendy would want to find someone more energetic, but I had no time to do so myself.

So the great day finally arrived. I had not slept the night before; I was both delighted and anxious, happy to be reunited with my family (it was the longest we had been apart) but desperately worried that I was bringing Wendy and the children into an unpleasant situation, so very different from Chile.

I was at the airport early, driving the little Renault with Sarr following in the Explorer, to carry the luggage.

We waited and waited. It was hot and humid and there were lots of flies everywhere. Sarr tried, in his own way, to cheer me up but I still felt apprehensive.

Then we saw the plane land and the waiting got worse. I was thankful that Wendy's French was so good since I could do nothing to help her through immigration and customs.

Finally, the family emerged and stood blinking in the harsh, bright African sun. I rushed forward, while Sarr quietly organised the luggage into the Explorer.

Everyone spoke at once. I was embracing all of them. Wendy was babbling about the flight and the delay in customs; Nikki clutched my legs and talked non-stop about the airplane; Robin lay in his mother's arms and grinned.

The journey home passed in a flash and suddenly I was ushering the family, past the beggars and lepers, into the house. We went into the sitting room and collapsed into chairs while Sarr brought the luggage in and discreetly disappeared.

I produced cold drinks and showed Wendy the house; it only took a moment. She was very brave and accepted everything as it was. In her own way, she always made the best of everything and, after I had explained everything to her said: "We managed in Cambridge, we managed in Newcastle, we will manage here. Don't worry. What is important is that we are together again."

"I can take a couple of days off and we can drive around and I will show you the main things: the shops, the beach, the bank and so on. But you must not expect any help from Shell – they don't seem to want to have anything to do with us. It is very strange."

"Never mind," said Wendy. "I expect there is a reason. Besides, they are not the only people in town."

I gave her a map of Dakar, and we spent the next three days driving round, going to the beach and shopping. She made the acquaintance of the *fatou*, but I could see she was not impressed.

The children settled down well. Nikki was very excited by all the new sounds (especially the drumming and wailing from the African compound on the other side of our back wall), the new smells and sights. She chattered non-stop and asked innumerable questions. Robin just sat, smiled, and dozed happily.

Wendy was very proud of her newly acquired driving skills and was soon at ease in the little Renault, in spite of having to drive on the 'wrong' side of the road. So I did not feel too guilty when I finally had to go on my first proper trip up-country, which would last about five days. Wendy assured me she would be alright.

Just before dawn, Sarr arrived and we got into the Explorer (the new Land Rover was promised for the following week).

After consultation with him, I had decided to make the first trip to Rosso, north of Dakar, on the Senegal river, which formed the border with Mauritania.

Sarr had told me that the best road to St. Louis and Rosso was parallel with the coast, some fifteen miles inland. He said it was a good road, which ran through the main towns in the area.

"This is road which Monsieur (he called Jean-Claude Monsieur) always took. It is easy and quick. Monsieur never went on difficult road if he could avoid it. Also, he never went where there was no Company business."

He grinned. "French people do not have interest in Senegal, or people or anything. Only work and food and beach." He looked at me. "Maybe you want to see more? Maybe you are different?"

"Well," I said. "Of course I am interested in everything and I would like to see it. I think there is no use to go to a country and not look or find out..." I found myself talking in Sarr's slightly pidgin French.

"There is also a road, not good but nice, which is along beach. Between Dakar and St. Louis there is a beach of sand and it is not very far, maybe 260 kilometres. But villages of fishing people are there and sea. Maybe we stop to fish?" He looked at me sideways. "Very good fishing there."

"All right," I said. "We will go there on the beach and come back on the road. "

We set off, seated companionably side by side in the front. Sarr had told me that Jean-Claude always insisted that he sit in the back. "He just call me *bugnoul*, he think that means a bad thing. But he did not know it only mean 'black' in Wolof language." He laughed. "All French use such words in a bad way."

I decided to find out a little more about Sarr; after all, I was going to spend months alone with him and he seemed an interesting person.

He told me that he was born in a village close to Dakar, the eldest of a family of seven children. His father was a carpenter and his mother had a stall in the market where she sold *faneaux*, the colourful sarongs, blouses and head-dresses worn by Wolof women. "We were very poor," he said, "and everyone had to work. I managed to get to good Jesuit school and have work in the evening. But the Fathers teach me much and so I speak French and I can read and write. Wolof language has no writing, only speaking, so this is a big help for getting me a good job."

"But Jesuits are all Catholics," I said. "Are you a Catholic?"

"No, no," he said, laughing. "Sarr is a famous ancient Wolof name and Wolofs are almost all Moslem – well, sort of Moslem," he added. "We change Moslem religion a small amount to also pray to natural things, and we have *marabouts*, holy men, to speak to Allah for us." He paused and thought for a bit; I listened, fascinated.

"I tell Fathers that I believe in Christian thoughts, but this is only my mouth speaking not my heart feeling. I believe that religion means respect for people and natural things – so if you are a good man, it is no matter what name you give your religion. Good is good and bad is bad always everywhere."

This seemed to make very good sense. We sat in silence for a while, while I negotiated my way out of town, going north towards the ocean. There was the usual hurly-burly of traffic: overloaded taxis and busses, carts, pedestrians courting suicide, and errant goats and dogs everywhere. The harsh, glaring sunshine of Africa bathed everything in bright colours and there was a great din of horns, yells and barking.

"What do you want I call you?" asked Sarr suddenly. "I do not want to call you Monsieur because you not like other Monsieur."

"Whatever you want," I said. "Arnold or Mick are my names. I call you Sarr, which is your name."

Sarr looked embarrassed. "I can not use your name, because you are my chief..." He brightened. "That is what I will call you, if I may; I call you Chief?"

"All right," I said. "Chief it is." Sarr then explained to me that in the Wolof culture, greetings were extremely important, and full names had to be used. Without this, a person would be deeply insulted and even friendships could be broken. So morning and last thing at night, he would call me Monsieur Michel Arnold. I said I would also greet him in his full name of Sarr M'Baye Diouf.

As we drove out of the town through the *bidonvilles* (slums) on the outskirts, the road deteriorated to a track and we soon found ourselves on the sandy beach, which stretched unbroken as far as the eye could see. At Sarr's suggestion, I engaged four wheel drive and the tyres gripped the sand.

We soon passed through the first fishing village, Pikine and on to a second, larger one called Fas Boyé. This was, like all the others, a collection of round, thatched huts, haphazardly arranged round an empty space on the beach. There were brightly painted *pirogues* (dugouts) arranged above the high-water mark, and, again as usual, we were immediately surrounded by a swarm of young children, running beside us, holding out their hands and grinning as they shouted.

We pulled up in the open space and waded out through a pool of children, to a large hut standing slightly by itself. Sarr caused the children to disperse with a few well chosen words. As we approached, a tall black figure in a loin cloth came out of the hut.

Sarr addressed the tall man: *"Jam nga am?* (Are you in peace?) Youssou Kinne Diane?"

"Jam rek, (Only in peace) Sarr M'Baye Diouf," the tall man replied.

"This is my Chief, Monsieur Michel Arnold," said Sarr in French. "I bring him to introduce you."

"I am honoured, Monsieur Michel Arnold," said the tall man, offering a hand.

I shook it, saying: "The honour is mine, Youssou Kinne Diane." Sarr nodded approval.

"My friend Youssou is the leader of the village and also a *marabout,*" explained Sarr. "It is time for lunch, so we will ask him if he will invite us." He looked enquiringly at Youssou.

"Waowwaow," said Youssou. (*Waow* means 'yes' in Wolof and can be reduplicated any number of times for greater emphasis. This also applies to *dedet,* which means 'no').

He indicated we should go into the hut but, before we could go in, a young boy appeared with a ewer of water. Following Sarr's gesture, I held out my hands and the boy poured a little water over them, three times. He then did it to my companions.

The hut was cooler than the beach and had rudimentary furnishings. There was some cloth rolled up in a corner, a plaited straw mat in the middle of the floor and some wooden boxes on one side.

Youssou made a courtly gesture and we sat round the mat. A lady appeared from somewhere, bearing a large enamel bowl. She was tall and moved with great grace. I had noticed this among Wolof women; they swayed slightly as they glided along, very upright and stately. Perhaps this was the legacy of many generations of carrying heavy burdens on their heads. She was dressed in a *faneaux*, the usual sarong, top and head-dress, but their colours were subdued. She was middle aged.

Youssou said: "This is my first wife, called Xadi. She is a very good cook and mother of many children."

Xadi smiled and set the bowl down between us. The smell was spicy and fragrant.

Several other men came in and sat down with us, with wet hands. The women and children stayed outside.

I was introduced, with full names, all round. Then Youssou dipped his fingers in the bowl and began to eat. The others and I followed suit. We used only the fingers of the right hand and I felt very much at ease, having done the same in Iraq, when I was a boy.

"This is *thiébou dienne*," said Sarr. "It is main Wolof dish." In the bowl was a big heap of rice, with a whole fish on it, some eggplant, okra and peanuts and very highly spiced. "The fish is *thiof*," added Youssou. It looked like a small grouper. The mixture was mouth-watering, but we ate slowly, sharing.

Xadi then brought in a smaller bowl and offered it to me. "Drink," said Sarr. "It is good." I took a sip and found the liquid, a dark brown, was bitter but refreshing. I passed the bowl to my right.

"What is it?" I asked.

"It is called *nététou*. It is juice of *nere* tree.

"Very good to drink," I agreed.

It was a pleasant meal. We all chatted amicably and, when it was time to go, I thanked Youssou very much for his hospitality. At Sarr's stern request, I did not offer payment. "Youssou would be much insulted and hurt. You must not pay in a Wolof house."

"Goodbye and many thanks again, Youssou Kinne Diane," I said.

"It has been an honour, Monsieur Michel Arnold," he replied, smiling. If all the Senegalese were going to be like that, I thought, my stay would be a pleasant one and I would not need any French company.

We drove on. The sand was firm and we followed the contours of the beach towards St. Louis.

We came to a narrow strip of beach, with a sand dune on our right. Sarr, who was driving (much to his pleasure – Jean-Claude hardly ever allowed him to drive), pulled up in the lee of the dune. It was getting towards sunset.

"Perhaps this is a good place to sleep?" Sarr gestured at the dune. "Not good to come to St. Louis in the dark and hard to drive."

I was not quite expecting this, but readily agreed. So far, all Sarr's suggestions and actions had been sensible and successful.

Sarr rummaged in the back of the Explorer, and produced two groundsheets and some blankets. He also took out a long bamboo fishing rod, with what looked like a casting reel and line. The hook on the end had some small feathers tied on it.

"Dinner," he said cryptically. "You sit and watch, Chief, and I will get fish."

He then waded up to his knees in the surf and cast the line out, in a long parabola, reeling it in as soon as it hit the water. He did this several times, without success.

"You will never catch anything with feathers," I called to him. "You should have proper bait."

He just waved his right hand and went on casting. After some minutes there was a cry from him and the rod bent sharply. Sarr reeled in furiously and dragged up onto the sand a fair sized fish. I leaped to my feet and ran down to look. It was a small tuna, thrashing about in the surf.

Sarr unhooked it and, after killing it, cleaned it out with a large knife he carried. He then built a fire from some driftwood he found, and impaled the fish vertically, in the middle of it, on a steel spike from the back of the Explorer.

When the fish was cooked, we ate it, with some stale bread and cold coffee from a bottle as we sat side by side and watched the sun sink, like a red-hot cannon ball, into the ocean.

We sat for some time, with the dying embers of the fire at our feet. Sarr told me about Senegal with much pride. He had acquired a great deal of knowledge of the history of his country, was happy to pass it on, and I was fascinated to hear it.

After an hour or so, we wrapped ourselves in our blankets and wished each other "*Ba suba jak jamm*", or goodnight, using our full names. I lay for some time, looking at the stars, very bright in a black sky, thinking of the day's happenings. There was a lot to reflect on and absorb. As I drifted off to sleep, I felt much more hopeful about Africa.

Early the following morning we washed in the surf and packed our belongings into the Explorer. The day was fine, though there was a strong, sandy wind blowing. The Explorer refused to start, but Sarr, after a brief period hidden under the bonnet, fixed whatever it was and we made our way north, towards St. Louis.

"We must get a new car soon, Chief," said Sarr, as I drove on the wet sand. "I can fix but it's more difficult now – this old car is tired."

We reached St. Louis at midday. It was quite a big town, with the main part on an island, some six hundred yards in the middle of the Senegal River, which was separated from the ocean by a long, thin spit of sand. Sarr mentioned that the massive iron bridge, which connected the island to the mainland, had been bought in Germany, dismantled and re-erected here by a past Governor. It was now quite old, though it seemed sturdy enough.

As I drove into the town, I noticed a great change from Dakar. Here, the centre of town was lined with splendid examples of French Colonial architecture; houses straight out of the early nineteenth century. Apparently, St. Louis had been the capital of Senegal until fairly recently, when this distinction had been conferred on Dakar.

The other difference was in the people I saw. Apart from black Africans, mostly Wolof, there were many slim, elegant people, with fine features and hawk-like noses, walking about. They wore blue robes, and there was a distinction in their bearing.

"Who are these strange people?" I asked Sarr.

"Oh, they are Moors, Chief," he replied. "They live mainly in Mauretania, which is just across the river. They are people who came from the East, across the Sahara, many centuries ago. They inhabit a lot of North Africa."

"They may not be like us," he added, "but they are all good Moslems."

He directed me to a hotel, where I stopped. "Now what?" I asked.

"You go in there and take room for the night and go to restaurant. This is place where Monsieur always said is best in town."

"What about you?" I asked. "Why not come in as well?"

Sarr looked embarrassed. "No, I thank you, Chief. It is not... seemly," he said after a pause. "I have place to go. Just tell me what we do tomorrow."

"Come back at eight o'clock and we will decide," I said. "Go in peace, Sarr M'Baye Diouf."

I went inside, with my small bag, and spoke to the man at the desk. He was light brown, tall, elegant and smartly dressed – obviously a Moor. He graciously permitted me to have a room, and called another man to take my bag upstairs. In giving instructions, I noticed that he spoke in what seemed almost to be Arabic.

"Excuse me," I said. "Are you speaking Arabic?"

"Of course," he looked at me curiously. "At least, that is what it used to be. We call our language *Hassaniya*, from the *Beni Hassan* tribe. It is different from Berber. Why do you ask?"

"Well, I speak some Arabic," I replied in that language. He looked puzzled. "I do not fully understand," he said at length. "But I can make out the sense." He smiled. "But perhaps it is best we speak in French. After all, it is a very civilised language and we, the Moors, are aristocrats."

Later on, I went to the restaurant for dinner. There was an enormously fat lady sitting on a tiny stool by the entrance – she looked like an elephant perched on a shooting-stick – who shrilly instructed a small, thin man to show me to a table. "That is my wife," he said proudly. "She runs everything."

"I would like to try a local dish, please," I said to the little man.

He drew himself up to his full five feet and glared at me. "This is a high class restaurant. Here we serve best French European food. We do not serve native food." He stressed the word 'native' though both he and his large wife were obviously Wolof.

The meal was unremarkable. I struck up a conversation with a solitary Frenchman seated at the next table, and invited him to join me for coffee.

"My name is Marc Duval," he said, seating himself. "I am with the Agriculture Ministry. I noticed you yesterday getting out of that Land Rover – it looks just like the one run by a friend of mine."

"I am Mick Arnold, with Shell. Would your friend be Jean-Claude?"

"Yes," he said. "He came here quite often."

"Well, I have taken over from him. He has returned to Paris."

Marc laughed. "Did you inherit anything else from him, or just his car?"

"No, just his car. What else is there?"

"There are some very pretty and, er, cooperative mulatto girls here," he said, grinning. "I think that is why he liked St. Louis."

"Tell me about St. Louis," I said, changing the subject hurriedly. "Have you been here long?"

"Oh, about twelve years now. I think I know it pretty well. It is an interesting town, very French colonial, you know. But the most interesting thing is the mixture of people. You get your usual Wolofs, whom you know. Then there are the Moors, who have drifted down from Mauretania – they are not truly Africans; more Arab."

He paused and drank some coffee. "But the most interesting are the mulattos. They are mostly the descendants of European slave masters on Gorée island, near Dakar, who would amuse themselves with young slave girls. When they became pregnant, they would be sent to St. Louis, then the capital, to get them out of the way. The offspring were neither white nor black, but they became the elite of society and occupied the best houses, and had the best jobs and looked down on everyone else."

"There were very few whites," he added. "But the mulattos are splendid people and extraordinarily handsome. You will see them walking and driving round, wonderfully dressed and elegant, with their noses in the air. Most of my friends are mulattos."

"But the Moors are an interesting lot," he went on. "You should go into Mauretania and have a look. Or you could drive up the river to Richard-Toll and Podor. Interesting old towns, especially Podor. Jean-Claude never bothered – he was too busy here."

We parted soon after and I went to have a shower and sleep: on a bed.

The following morning, I met Sarr, who was waiting outside.

After greetings, I said: "First we have to go to visit the two service stations – after all, that is my job." Sarr grinned, but said nothing. "Then what do you think if we drive up river to Richard -Toll and Podor?"

Sarr looked astonished. "We can go," he said. "There is no road but the sand is good. But why do you want to go there? Monsieur never did."

"If I am going to spend two years here, I want to see everything. Monsieur had other interests."

Accordingly, we visited the two Shell service stations, and found everything to be in order. The owners, both Wolofs, were pleased to see Sarr and welcomed me as the new Inspector. After a brief chat and some sweet, strong tea, we left.

We stopped for some time at a store to buy some food and fill two jerricans with water. I saw some mulattos, exactly as described by Marc, walking about. Sarr looked at them disdainfully. "Not this and not that," he said. "Very mixed up".

We also saw some Moors, walking by. The men seemed always to be in pairs, and walked along holding hands. I noticed also that they had a powerful body odour, which surrounded them. But they were startlingly good-looking.

We then went back over the bridge, and out through the fringes of the town to the river bank. As we left the built-up area, the landscape changed to proper desert, though there was no real sand – as I remembered it from Arabia – but more of a stony plain, with some cultivated areas. The banks of the river were steep and we could see the occasional dugout or small barge sailing along.

I was driving and showed my inexperience by getting us stuck in a patch of soft sand, which suddenly appeared before us. I went into low range and revved the engine, but the wheels were spinning without effect.

"I fix," said Sarr, jumping out. "Always happens."

He unscrewed the lengths of perforated steel which were attached to the sides of the Land Rover, to give traction in sand or mud. They were the metal components of wartime emergency airstrips and were very convenient to handle.

Sarr got a spade, and dug sand out in front of the wheels and jammed the strips down. "Try now," he said, so I climbed back into the car and slowly moved forward. The wheels gripped and soon we were again on a firm surface. Sarr replaced everything and said: "Easy one that time." I thanked him and we drove on.

All around us now there were green plantations of sugar cane, cotton and groundnuts scattered about and little villages of round huts with reed roofs. I had thought that this would be the Sahara, but the river allowed irrigation of a broad band of land on either bank.

We reached Richard-Toll at about midday. The town was small and dusty, with low houses and huts. But in the centre there stood, in a cultivated and irrigated garden, a large colonial house. This was the famous 'folie' of a past Governor, who had given his name to the settlement. Before St. Louis became the main crossing place to Mauretania, Richard-Toll was the principal ferry port for crossing the river, and there were still the traces of a dirt road leading down to a primitive raft ferry.

We had a meal together at a small shack, where a large Wolof lady was dispensing simple food. Afterwards, we were offered a mango, though I could see no fruit trees anywhere. It was served with salt and spices and was strange, but delicious. To drink, there was an acid and mouth-puckering tamarind cordial.

We decided to go on to Podor, though Sarr remained puzzled as to why I wished to go there. Marc, the previous evening, had told me it was interesting, being the capital of the mediaeval Tekror kingdom.

We got to Podor in the late afternoon, having struggled with the soft sand patches on the track. The landscape remained green and cultivated. It seemed that to get to the Sahara proper, we would have to get away from the river, into Mauretania, and drive due east. But I continued to follow the river.

Podor was a further collection of low huts, surrounding an impressive fort and a handsome mosque, made of sun-baked mud bricks. There were few people about, mostly Wolof, though there were some Moors. Dugouts and rafts were crossing the river, back and forth, carrying passengers and goods to and from Mauretania. A rickety raft, carrying two nervous camels and a large number of people, looked precarious, though they reached the other shore safely.

I thought about following the river, which had begun to curve to the south. Sarr said that there was nothing much of interest, just a few villages and small towns. "Besides, we can go to the far side of the river on another road, from Dakar," he said. "I see that you like wild places, Chief," he added. "Monsieur never liked to leave a good road."

There was nowhere to stay in Podor that looked in the least suitable, so we started back towards St. Louis. I had enjoyed my night under the stars on the beach, and felt that this type of spending the night was something that was better than a stuffy and dirty room in a hut.

Before we got to Richard-Toll, the night came, so I drove down to the edge of the river. We stopped and out came the ground-sheets and blankets. We dined on some tins of beans and vegetables, washed down with water, and went to sleep, looking up at a sky full of brilliant stars. The last thing I remembered was the howling of jackals and the soft burbling of the river.

The following morning we swam in the river to wake up. The water was rather muddy and warm, but it served to wash us. We then drove, non-stop, back to St. Louis. I saw Marc at an early lunch in the hotel and told him where I had been.

"Good for you," he said. "Jean-Claude never went anywhere – he preferred the pleasures of the town."

The inland road back to Dakar was quite good and much faster than the beach. We stopped at two main towns, Louga and Tivouane, where we had service stations. The station owners, after introductions from Sarr, were welcoming and polite and said there were no problems with their sales and supplies. They seemed rather surprised to see me. We got back to Dakar just after dark.

Wendy was pleased to see me, as were the children. She had got herself a new *fatou*, since the previous one had been so languid. She had discovered a place in the market in Dakar where unemployed *fatous* would gather every morning, and prospective employers could go and choose the one they found most congenial. But she said that they all seemed very similar, moving with the same unhurried grace and not getting much done.

I, in turn, told her of my adventures in the north. Since she loved to travel, she was sad that she could not accompany me, but with two small children it simply was not possible. However, Nikki was now quite good company for her and even Robin was starting to crawl about.

The following day, I wrote a report for the Sales Manager, but got no acknowledgement, let alone a reply. I was more puzzled than ever about just what I was supposed to be doing. There was virtually no competition, the only other oil company around was CFP, the French company and it seemed to me, after the cut-throat struggle I had with Esso in Chile, that life would be very placid.

That weekend we all went to the beach. Wendy had discovered that the beach at N'Gor, near the hotel, had to be paid for, while a very similar one, a little further along, was free. The main difference was that the French expatriates went to the private one while the other was frequented by Africans and also, surprisingly, by the diplomatic corps.

The children loved the clean, white sand and the warm ocean. The surf was just a white fringe and the sand sloped gently for some way out.

There were some other children there, and we got talking to the parents, who were seated nearby. They turned out to be the family of a senior Brazilian diplomat and another, from Sweden. The husbands were not there.

It was a great pleasure to be able to talk to someone, after the pointed lack of support from the people in the Company. Everyone was very friendly and the children got along well. I was very pleased that Wendy had now made contact with some possible friends and could meet them on the beach as well as, perhaps, entertaining them, although our house was not the sort to which we would wish to invite anybody formally.

I also noticed that, quite a long way up the beach, some men were casting fishing lines far out beyond the surf. One of them pulled out a good size fish and I thought this may be a good thing to do, though Sarr had told me that the best time was either early morning or dusk.

The following week was devoted to taking over and adapting the new Land Rover to bush travel.

"Chief," said Sarr when I asked him to come with me to take delivery from the agent. "We need much change for the car, because we will go to difficult places. This something Shell does not like to pay for."

I was worried. "How can we do it?" I asked. "I have no money to pay myself for things."

Sarr grinned. "Work has to be authorised by Purchasing Department boss," he said. "He is drunken Frenchman who sign everything put before him."

I was puzzled. "How will this help us?" I asked.

Sarr grinned even more broadly. "Well, Chief, my cousin Sarr Dele Diagne is the high clerk in the department. We tell him what we want and he will arrange. He does not like the boss."

We met Sarr Dele at a small café in the afternoon. He and my Sarr looked very much alike and after I had greeted him by his full name and been introduced, sat down with us. My Sarr explained the situation and Sarr Dele said he would be delighted to put one over his drunken boss. "He is a bad man," he said in passable French.

We had worked out what changes we wanted to make and quickly made out a list, which we gave to our friend. The main adaptations were the perforated metal strips fastened to the sides, eight jerricans (two for water and six for petrol), with holders and a long list of spare parts as well as an extra spare wheel.

"You really want to go into big bush, Chief?" asked Sarr. "I see you like to do that, like going to Podor."

I confirmed that I wanted to go everywhere.

"So now we need winch," said Sarr. "Maybe two, one in front

and one behind. So we can pull car out of deep mud or across river. You agree?" I nodded, bemused.

"Oh, you fix," he said to his cousin. "We will leave the car in Shell workshops tomorrow and get it on Friday." Sarr Dele nodded, smiling broadly. "My friends the mechanics will do everything. You do not worry."

We thanked him and I raised my eyebrows at Sarr, who shook his head. I remembered that Wolofs were insulted if you offered payment for favours.

The following day I got a message to go to see Monsieur de Frescheville in the office. I wondered what he wanted me for.

Accordingly I went to his office. He offered me coffee and said, rather diffidently: "I believe you have come from Chile?"

I said that I had.

"So perhaps you speak Spanish?" he said.

I said that we both did. What was this leading to?

"Well," he said, still in an offhand way, "some friends and we have a little circle to practise Spanish once a week, and my wife thought you and Madame Arnold may like to join us next time?"

I was completely taken aback. This was the last thing I expected. I had begun to believe that there was some sort of plot against us in the company and here was a very formal senior Frenchman inviting us to his house.

"We would be delighted, Monsieur," I said. "How very kind of you."

"If you are free on Saturday afternoon, we would be very pleased to see you. And do bring the children," he added. "We have quite a few and two more will be a pleasure."

He gave me the address, which was a large flat in a block in Mermoz, the green and leafy area which I had seen from the taxi on arrival. Wendy was as astonished as I had been when I told her.

On the Friday I went to take delivery of my new Land Rover, to be named Explorer ll, from the Shell workshops. Unknown to me, Sarr had been there every day, working with the Shell mechanics – most of whom were his long-time friends – to make sure that everything was properly done and nothing missed out. He presented the Explorer to me, with a broad grin.

"There you are, Chief," he said. "Everything is done and works well. I did more things, which we forgot. I put cut up inner tube pieces to make the electrics waterproof, because we have to go through rivers, and I extended the exhaust and air intake up to the roof, so water does not get in."

I was delighted. The Explorer was everything I wanted and more. I gave a large banknote to the head mechanic and asked him to have a drink, with his mates, to wish Explorer many happy journeys. Everyone clapped as Sarr and I drove away.

The next day, I packed the family into the Explorer and we went on our first social visit.

The de Freschevilles lived in a huge flat, surrounded by flowering trees and impeccably kept lawns not far from the beach at N'Gor. The other blocks and individual houses were all occupied by Company French staff and made an unhappy contrast with the hovel in which we had been housed. I determined eventually to get a decent place to live for Wendy and the family.

Monsieur de Frescheville met us at the door and ushered us in. A tall, rather angular, harassed-looking lady turned out to be his wife and there were five children, aged about eight downwards. I thought it was no wonder their mother looked harassed.

"Welcome, welcome," she said in English, with a strong French accent. "Please excuse my English, but I had an English nanny when I was little so I know a bit. My husband tries and tries but is not very good."

We congratulated her and introduced Nikki and Robin. Nikki was somewhat apprehensive at first, but soon was put at ease by Madame, and began to mix with the children, somehow managing to communicate. Robin went to sleep.

The de Freschevilles (or Norbert and Jean, as we were to call them after some months), were an interesting couple. Extremely formal, as were all the French we met, in great contrast to the easy and rapid familiarity of the Chileans, they were nevertheless warm and friendly under the carapace of reserve. They were some ten years older than we were and ruled their numerous offspring with rigid discipline. They were, without doubt, the most devout family we had ever met, being strict Roman Catholics and following the rules with no deviation whatever.

Norbert was a stocky, very strong man, who had been in the French Resistance during the war. He had been captured and maltreated by the Nazis, but would never talk about it. He and Jean's marriage plans had been disrupted by the German occupation; thus it took Norbert some eight years of courtship finally to marry.

We sat and had some tea and some biscuits baked by Jean. While not nearly as poor as we were, having five children they nevertheless had to be careful.

After a short time, the other couple of the Spanish discussion circle arrived. These were Paul and Nicole Fernandez; he was a Frenchman of recent Spanish ancestry and spoke fluent Spanish. We were introduced and began to chatter in a mixture of French and Spanish.

Paul and Nicole were somewhat less formal and our age. He was a tall, handsome functionary in the Finance Department, and she a typically elegant, slim and attractive Frenchwoman.

It was a pleasant afternoon. When it was time to go, we thanked everyone and collected the children, who had behaved well throughout. Norbert said we had to do it again next week and we agreed with pleasure. It was notable that the Company was not mentioned during the entire afternoon.

"Well, that is better," I said to Wendy when we were back in the Explorer. "At last we have got to know a couple of French families. It certainly has been an uphill struggle."

She agreed. "I got on very well with Jean," she said. "We might become good friends. Though Norbert was rather formal, I thought. Perhaps he will warm up later."

On subsequent visits the families did grow closer and, eventually, we formed a friendship that was to last for the rest of our lives. Jean became as close as a sister for Wendy. I valued Norbert enormously and greatly enjoyed his marvellous French. His classic pronunciation, choice of words and the balance of his sentences were a delight. He was also a keen philatelist. I had never had much interest in collecting stamps, but his enthusiasm was catching and both Wendy and I became interested.

Meanwhile, I made some short trips in Explorer, to run it in and to satisfy myself (and Sarr) that everything worked, before trying anything more ambitious. We went out to all points of the compass from Dakar, within a radius of some 250 miles, visiting towns and service stations, and generally getting to know the area. I continued to write my reports, which remained unacknowledged.

Another person I met, who proved friendly, was a young Shell engineer, responsible for the maintenance of pumps in my area. Luc Guichard was a bachelor, younger than I, and very French. He was short, very sunburned and sported a large moustache. He was desperate to learn some English and I promised to help him. He had been in West Africa for some years and knew the country well.

"I am not going to go with you on trips," he announced. "We are both people who want to experience things on our own and anyway, we would fight about silly things." He stroked his moustache, as he always did when embarrassed. "But if I can help you in any way, please say so."

Christmas came. We were going to have it on our own, but Luc dropped so many hints that we invited him home for Christmas Day, and explained English habits to him. He was overjoyed.

"I would have been alone," he said. "Now I can be part of a family." He brought us all small gifts and played with the children, who liked him. Wendy had made traditional English food, plus a Christmas pudding, which I think he found strange, but politely ate. It was a very modest Christmas, but we enjoyed it, mainly because we were together.

The de Freschevilles and Fernandez, all very devout, treated Christmas as wholly a religious festival and there was little carousing. But New Year was different.

We were invited to come that evening. It was our first experience of a French New Year. There was excellent food and lots of wine, but the main item, much to my delight and Wendy's dismay, was a large barrel of oysters flown in from France. I ate until I could eat no more, while she managed to choke down just one, then had to admit defeat, and concentrate instead on the selection of other delicacies. Getting to know Norbert and Jean, as well as Paul and Nicole, made a big difference to our lives in

Senegal

Dakar: our one sadness was that we could not offer them much in the way of reciprocal hospitality, as we were too poor. The procession of *fatous* continued. The only time I was able to take Wendy out for the day, we returned to find the current one entertaining a large number of friends in our sitting room, using Wendy's best china and eating up our small store of biscuits. At this point Wendy decided she would manage without any more house *fatous*.

She kept, however, our washing *fatou*, who came twice a week to do the laundry and ironing, and was a much more reliable person. But her greatest value was that she would pick up Robin, no matter how fractious, and fasten him to her back with a wide band of cloth. There he would immediately fall asleep and remain so, lulled by the warmth of her body and the gentle movements as she went about her tasks.

Jean had told Wendy about a good French kindergarten and Nikki settled happily there, prattling in a mixture of French and English, as the fancy took her.

One Sunday, as we were sitting and arranging stamps, there came a knock at the door. Wendy had taken up stamp collecting with enthusiasm, being a virtually cost-free and entertaining hobby. She had developed a number of stamp exchanges with people as far away as Alaska, Buenos Aires and Sweden, and spent much of her spare time soaking off, cataloguing and sorting, which helped pass the long hot evenings alone when I was in the bush.

I opened the door and there stood a tall, elegant and immaculately robed figure, all in white. He wore a colourful cap on his head, which identified him as a Guinean – probably Malinké – and his manner was dignified and stately.

"Are you Monsieur Arnold?" he asked in a deep voice.

I nodded. "May I speak with you for a short time?" he asked. He spoke a correct and mellifluous French.

"What is it about?" I asked. I had been told to be cautious about strangers.

"My name is Diallo Boubakar," he said. "I have come to ask if you have need of a trained servant." I was astonished. Far from thinking he was a servant, I had taken him for a Government functionary or a businessman.

I invited him to come in. He proceeded (Diallo never just walked) to the sitting room, where I made him known to Wendy, who was staring at him in awe.

"Do sit down," I told him hospitably. "Why are you asking me about servants?"

He looked faintly surprised. "If you please, I will stand," he said. "I have been told that you are not satisfied with many *fatous* who have worked for you and Madame," he bowed slightly to Wendy. "I am presently at liberty and would be honoured to offer my services."

We were astonished. I never found out how he had heard of us, or why such a superior and courtly man should wish to work for us, especially in the cramped and unpleasant house we were living in.

Wendy asked him what he had been doing, and he produced some glowing written references, one from a departed High Commissioner, stating that he was an expert manservant, housekeeper and cook. He also told us that he had worked for superior French families both in Conakry, from where he came and also Dakar.

Wendy and I looked at each other; this was simply too good to be true.

"We are very poor," I said to him. Somehow, I found this a natural thing to do. "I am afraid we could not possibly afford the sort of salary you must be accustomed to."

"I know," he said with a smile. "It does not matter. It is more important to be with people you respect than to become rich at their expense." We later found that he was an elder and judge in his tribe, and respected as a teacher and philosopher. "I will be content to receive whatever you can give me and my fortune will rise and fall with yours."

Wendy and I looked at each other again. She asked him some more questions, and we soon were both satisfied that some sort of miracle had occurred. Diallo came to work for us. We never did discover why he wanted to do so or where he had heard of us, but he became a friend and wise councillor, and made a huge difference to our entire stay in Dakar.

I begin my
Shell business career

Wendy and Nikki in our front garden in Santiago, Chile
with its view of snowy Andes

Nikki welcomes me home

I become a Shell marketer

I go fishing

Tony Westcott and I
in cabaret

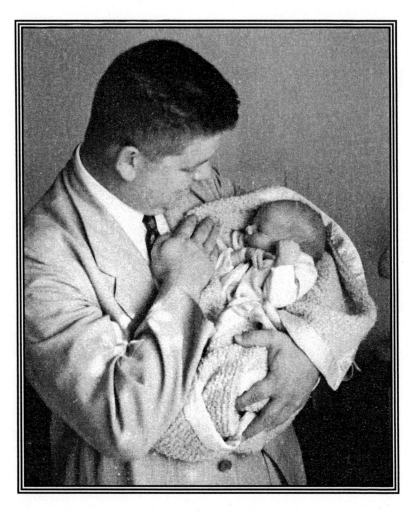

Our son Robin is born
in Santiago, Chile

I show Nikki my Land Rover,
in front of our Dakar house

Diallo, who worked for us
and became our friend

Our African Christmas

An African backroad in the rainy season.
Sarr and I with our Land Rover

The cannibals
I met in the bush

One of many happy days I spent
on the beach with my family

CHAPTER FIVE

Senegal – cannibals with sunglasses

I continued to make short trips within Senegal. But the rainy season (it had been an unusually mild one) was now over and I could comfortably venture further afield. There were some railway lines – such as the one to St. Louis and another, much longer, to Bamako in Soudan – but the trains were slow, unreliable, uncomfortable and very hot. It was not unusual for delays of some days to occur.

There was also a rudimentary local air network, flying small, rickety planes here and there, but I thought these ways of travelling to be very inferior to roaming about in the Explorer. Besides, though my modest expense claims were regularly paid without comment, I did not want to tempt fate by suddenly claiming for tickets.

It was now perfectly obvious to me that Head Office had not the slightest interest in me or my work, and desired nothing more than that I should not bother them. Since my job simply did not exist – the service station maintenance and supplies were done by the Engineering Department, the payments were controlled by the Finance people and there was really no competition – there was nothing left for me to do.

I consulted Sarr. "Look," I said, "the office does not care what we do or where we go, so I am going to drive to the limits of my territory. This means I want to go all the way north, to Fort

Gouraud near the Moroccan frontier, to Portuguese Guinea in the south and the Lower Senegal area and, going east, to Timbuktu."

Sarr stared at me, his eyes popping out. "But, but, Chief..." he stammered, "that is going to places where I have never been. Nobody goes to such places." He paused. "It could be dangerous, you know."

"Nonsense," I said. "If we take food and water and spares and have plenty of time, why not?"

He put his face close to mine. "There are people who eat people," he whispered.

I laughed. "I promise you will be all right," I reassured him. "This is 1959, not 1859."

After some persuasion, he became quite enthusiastic and we sat and planned the first long journey which I decided would be going south, as a contrast to my trip to St. Louis.

Southern Senegal is completely different from the north and the east. The latter tends to be savannah, or stony and sand deserts, first in the Sahel, and then in the Sahara. The south is a lush tropical jungle, reached by passing through a wide band of grassland with eight foot grasses and shrubs as well as a wide selection of trees. Not least among these is the baobub, a freakish tree with a hugely thick trunk (often hollow), sparse branches and strange leaves.

In order to get to the Casamance (as Lower Senegal is called), one has to cross the enclave of the Gambia, a narrow strip of land, on the two sides of the Gambia River, which protrudes, like a finger, from the sea upstream into Senegalese territory, then a British colony marooned in the midst of, at the time, French possessions.

We set off at dawn on a Monday morning, heading out of town and along a reasonable paved road, dodging multicoloured taxis, slow donkeys, ox carts and the occasional camel.

We reached Kaolack at lunchtime and the all pervading smell of roasting peanuts hit us some miles away. I remembered the mountains of nuts we had seen on my previous visit. We had a quick lunch at a roadside stall (fish with rice and peanut sauce), since I did not want us to use up our supplies when there was an alternative.

As we left the town and continued on our way, the road got narrower and the surface deteriorated badly. There was savannah on both sides, with occasional tracks leading off to what I presumed were villages. There were some beautiful flowering trees, notably the *flamboyant*, or 'Flame of the Forest', covered with bright scarlet-yellow flowers.

After about an hour, we came to a road block. There was a diversion, since the rains had washed out a section of road, leaving a mile-long pit. This was being repaired, in a desultory fashion, by a gang of workmen.

The supervisor (or so I assumed him to be, though he was dressed in a filthy singlet and tattered shorts) approached us. His black skin shone through the holes in his clothing, but he had a cheerful grin.

"*Bonjour*, Monsieur," he said in strongly accented French. He then looked at Sarr, whom he recognised as a fellow Wolof tribesman, and spoke to him. Sarr asked some questions and then turned to me.

"We cannot pass this way," he said. "This man says it will take many days to repair the road. He says we should follow the track to the left and if God wills it will bring us out again near the border."

We drove down the track. After some miles, it became very narrow and the tall grasses were brushing both sides of the Explorer. "This is more like it," I thought to myself. "This is Africa."

We suddenly came on a clearing and there was a large troop of baboons sitting around. I stopped and they turned to look at me. Then, quite fearlessly, the bigger ones, the males, approached. Sarr and I hastily shut the windows, in spite of the heat which soon became stifling.

The baboons came closer and began to climb all over the Explorer, banging on the roof, pressing their faces against the windscreen and windows (they had large yellow fangs) and trying to wrench off the windscreen wipers.

I honked the horn, but far from scaring them, it simply made them cross. They howled loudly and thumped the car even harder.

The females continues to sit in the clearing, not paying much attention, and grooming their babies. I began to wonder if we would ever get away.

Then I got an idea. "Sarr," I said, "get in the back and give me the shotgun and a cartridge." Sarr wriggled his way into the kit in the back, and produced the gun and a cartridge. I loaded it and, quickly opening the window a few inches, stuck the barrels out, pointing into the air, and fired.

The noise, in the enclosed space of the car, was deafening. But it worked. The baboons, after a startled instant, fled into the tall grass and the clearing was magically emptied. I started the engine and drove on, as fast as was possible, before the troop decided to come back and investigate.

The track was deeply rutted and would have been impassable during the rainy season. I wondered how trucks managed, since they would be too wide to follow the trail. I stopped, and looked at Sarr.

"I think we are going the wrong way," I said. "Look where the sun is." I took my compass from my pocket and looked at it; the needle pointed north-east.

"Perhaps we should have taken the right fork back before the baboons," said Sarr. "But it looked unused."

I decided to go on. We crawled along at 10 miles per hour, with the Explorer swaying and bouncing. After another few miles, the track broadened and became quite decent. I accelerated and, as we came round a sharp bend, slammed on the brakes. Before us there was a steep downward slope to what seemed to be a rushing torrent of water. I could see the road climbing out on the other side and assumed it to be a ford.

"What do you think?" I asked Sarr.

"We have to try it," he answered. "It will be getting dark soon."

The river was about thirty yards wide, and I could see boulders and sharp rocks in it – it did not look very deep. I put the Explorer into the lowest possible gear and crawled into the water. Sarr had got out and was walking beside the car, stumbling over the rocks; he was up to his thighs in water.

I had got to just beyond halfway, when the Explorer gave a

lurch and I could feel the front wheels drop into a hole, leaving the car at a steep downward angle. Thanks to Sarr's waterproofing, the engine continued to run, but we were firmly stuck – the Explorer would move neither forward nor backward, and was beginning to lean over quite steeply with the force of the water pressing against the side.

I clambered out of the car into the river leaving the engine running. It was quite hard to open the door against the pressure of the water, but with Sarr's help, I managed. We then considered the situation. The hole was obviously not a very large one, though quite deep. I thought once we got the wheels out, I would be able to crawl the Explorer out of the river.

"The front winch," I said. "Yes," agreed Sarr. "Get in again, Chief, and I will fix."

I climbed back and revved the engine, while Sarr freed the winch drum and began to pull out the steel cable across the river. He attached it to a stout tree growing on the far bank beside the road. I engaged the clutch and continued to race the engine, as the cable tautened and slowly began to drag the Explorer out of the hole. After a short time, we were on the opposite bank, the cable was stowed and we were ready to go on.

We were to cross many such rivers, but, after this episode Sarr (or I, since I insisted in sharing all tasks with him) would walk in front of the Explorer, to make sure no sudden pits or hidden boulders would cause us to come to grief. We used both the front and rear winches from time to time to pull us out when stuck in sand or deep mud, as well as some deeper rivers, but we always managed somehow.

A few hundred yards along, we came to a small village. It was just a handful of thatched huts, and there were some children playing, who immediately ran up to us, chattering loudly. Then some adults emerged from the huts and an old man, with a hoe over his shoulder, appeared from the tall grass.

Sarr greeted him in Wolof, but he just looked puzzled. "He must be a Peul," said Sarr. "They have their own language. He does not understand me."

"Yes, I do," said the old man in French. He looked at me. "Good day, Monsieur. A car here is a rare sight. Why do you come?"

He was dressed in a scrappy loincloth and kept scratching his head. One of his eyes was a milky white, and when he smiled, I could see an almost complete lack of teeth.

"Greetings," I said. "I am with an oil company and we were on our way from Dakar to the Casamance, but we were diverted and lost our way. Where are we?"

"I can not describe it, because you would not understand. But I can tell you how to go to regain the road," said the old man, squatting down. He thought for a moment. "But now the sun has left his house so you must not try to continue. You are welcome to share our pot tonight."

I was fascinated by his colourful speech. "We are most grateful," I said and complimented him on his French.

He grinned toothlessly. "I was in a school for a while, many, many seasons ago and I was taught by a priest." He scratched some more. "But his god was a weak, feeble thing so I never thought about him. Here we are not god people – we believe that all round us there is power which will help if we are not bad people."

"Do you wish a hut?" he asked. "Now is not cold at night, but we can make space for you and your man."

I looked at Sarr, who slightly shook his head. "No, I thank you, grandfather," I said. "We will sleep, as usual, under the stars."

The old man nodded. "It is well. But come later and share our pot." I looked around and saw that the villagers, some twenty of them, had clustered round. The men were lithe and strong-looking while the women, of all ages, were handsome and, in some cases very beautiful. Both sexes wore a loincloth and nothing more. The children were naked.

The old man spoke to the assembled villagers, who mostly smiled and nodded, though some of the younger men looked doubtful. But they all turned and followed him round towards the back of the village, where a wisp of smoke was rising against the twilit sky. All round there were jungle sounds: the twittering of roosting birds, and occasional rustling and far-away howls of monkeys.

"Why did you not want us to have a hut?" I asked Sarr.

"Well, Chief," he said. "There people are not Wolof. They are savages and therefore very dirty. There will be many fleas and insects in the huts." I began to realise that there was every bit as much chauvinism among African tribes as there was between the French and the Africans.

We brought out our sleeping mats and a jerrican of water and had a drink. We also topped up the Explorer with petrol from another of the jerricans. "We ought to give them some food," I said. "They have been very welcoming."

Sarr shrugged his shoulders. "They will be happy with anything you give them, Chief, if you want to."

I took some tins of sardines, a tin of processed meat and a packet of cigarettes from our store. We then walked round to the back of the village, where the smoke was rising.

There was quite a large fire burning, of some aromatic wood, which smelled vaguely of incense. In the middle, there was a small pile of stones, arranged so that a large black iron pot could be comfortably seated above the flames. Most of the villagers were squatting or sitting around the fire, and two older women were stirring the pot with long pieces of wood.

As we approached, the old man stood up and made signs that a place should be made for us beside him. "Come, sit and share our pot," he said, spreading his arms.

"These are for you and the village, grandfather," I said, giving him the provisions. "Do you have means to open the containers?"

"I regret," he said. "Our food does not come in such a way."

Sarr opened the tins and everything was emptied into a large wooden bowl, which was passed round the circle. All the villagers passed the bowl round and nodded and smiled.

Smaller bowls were produced, and we were handed one each. A woman at the cauldron stretched out her hand and I gave her mine. She dipped it into the iron pot and handed it back. There was a liquid in it, with bits floating round. The smell was of vegetables.

The old man said: "We grow some millet and peanuts and sorghum. Sometimes there are small fish in the stream. Of course, there are always lizards and snails, but meat is very difficult to find." He sighed. "Some seasons past, a Peul from Casamance shot a white man with a gun. The French came and took away all guns from black people – now only white people have guns. Without guns, the animals are hard to get and now there are fewer than when I was a green man."

I tasted the soup. It was not very appetizing, but not wholly unpleasant. There were peppers added which gave the vegetable taste a boost and I did not wish to examine closely the ingredients floating about.

After we had eaten and drunk some water flavoured with what tasted like aniseed, I handed cigarettes around. Everyone nodded and took one and soon we were all puffing cigarette smoke into the night sky.

The old man looked at me. "Do you wish a woman?" he enquired.

"No, I thank you, grandfather." I was caught unprepared. I did not wish to offend him, but what could I say? "It is against my religion on travelling days," I finally said. "But I am envious. Your women are very beautiful."

He nodded and did not seem offended. I noticed the offer was not made to Sarr. I thought this was really an extreme of hospitality.

We rolled ourselves into our blankets, and spent a peaceful night, though there were some mosquitoes and the jungle noises persisted unabated.

In the morning, we washed perfunctorily in a little water from a jerrican and ate some biscuits. A young boy came and presented us with a green mango, which, though somewhat unripe, was refreshing. Sarr sprinkled it with salt, which enhanced the taste.

The old man came to us. "I shall send my grandson with you to show you the way back to the road. He knows the way well. Go in peace." Some of the villagers had come out and stood around us, grinning and chattering. A group of the younger women made provocative gestures and giggled together.

A boy of about fifteen came and the old man said: "Here he is. Just follow his directions and all will be well."

I thanked him again and bowed to the villagers. We then

climbed into the Explorer and the boy pointed us onto a footpath disappearing into the tall grass. I drove slowly along it and after some hundreds of yards the path got wider, the grasses more sparse and we came out into small, cultivated patches of land, with green plants growing. They were irrigated by a system of hollowed out logs arranged as small aqueducts, and led up to the river bank, where they were obviously filled by hand from the stream. We threaded our way past these plantations and followed another path leading into grass. There were trees dotted about; mainly misshapen baobabs and acacias, with an occasional flowering tree with scarlet and yellow blossoms.

The grass got thinner and lower and suddenly we entered a savannah, a plain of baked earth, low grasses and clumps of trees. It was a relief to be able to see for some distance, toward a low range of hills. The compass told me we were travelling south.

I was able to accelerate, though the earth was very bumpy and, after a pause for a flat tyre – which Sarr changed quickly and expertly – we soon reached the hills.

Here we found a fairly broad track which followed the hills to left and right. The boy made a sign for me to stop, which I did. He then pointed to the track on the right, going west and made gestures that we should follow it straight to the road. He then made a sign that he would leave us here and go back to the village. I gave him a packet of cigarettes and got a broad grin in exchange, after which he went loping back the way we had come.

The track was reasonable and we made good time and reached the main road after a couple of hours. I was astonished to note that the detour, which had taken us twenty four hours to cover, amounted to no more than a hundred miles.

We turned left on the main road, which was of hard-packed earth, and drove on to the frontier with Gambia, which we reached after another hour. The frontier consisted of a rickety pole across the road, with a small, open hut beside it. Here sat, in a friendly way, representatives of both the Senegalese and Gambian governments. There was one of each: a slightly sloppy-looking soldier in French military uniform, with a dirty *képi* on his head and a decrepit looking rifle, who was obviously the

Senegalese and a smart corporal, with spotless khaki shirt and shorts, as well as polished boots, clutching an old Lee-Enfield rifle.

We drove up and stopped. Both soldiers got unhurriedly to their feet and strolled over to us.

The Senegalese spoke first. "You are leaving Senegal for a long time?" he asked, in broken French. "Or do you just cross to go to Casamance?"

"Just crossing," I said. "We are bound for Ziguinchor."

"Then speak to my friend," he said and sauntered back to the hut. The Gambian said, also in poor French. "You have passports?" We produced them and handed them over. He looked at mine and, stepping back, saluted smartly.

"You are very welcome, sir," he said in English. "You must stop in Bathurst and eat some good English food. These Frenchies only eat frogs and things."

I assured him we would, and he raised the pole and waved us on, saluting smartly as we passed. He had taken no notice of Sarr at all.

We drove on for half an hour and reached the ferry crossing of the Gambia river. The river was turgid, muddy and wide and reminded me of the Tigris in Baghdad. The far bank was several hundred yards away, and we could see the ferry, a large raft, on the other side. On our side there were two trucks waiting, with a bedraggled official collecting fares and a small kiosk at which a lady was selling brightly coloured soft drinks and paper twists of roasted peanuts.

The official came over to us, moving languidly, at what I thought of as an 'African pace'. It was relaxed and prudent in the heat, and I found myself slowing down and emulating what was obviously a sensible idea. There seemed to be no such thing as hurry in West Africa.

The fare was cheap. I asked how long it would be before we could cross, and the official scratched his head and said: "Well, it depends, Master. If he come back quick, you cross quick. If he slow, you wait." He spoke English, with some French words mixed in. "Maybe one hour, maybe two, maybe three. He come when he want."

Well, we were not in a hurry. We pulled the Explorer into the inadequate shade of a tree and strolled over to the lady in the kiosk. Sarr spoke to her in Wolof and she grinned and replied. Sarr said: "She says that we will wait at least three hours and the best thing is to buy much drink and peanuts and sleep." This is what the truck drivers were doing, lying in the shade of their vehicles.

More out of courtesy than craving, we bought a bottle each of a virulent, bright green drink and some peanuts. We then retired to the shade of the Explorer and sat down. The drink was rather nasty, and I surreptitiously emptied my bottle on the ground. Sarr managed to drink his.

I got a blanket and went to sleep. It was hot and there were insects buzzing about, but I had become used to napping when I could on my journeys and only woke when Sarr shook my shoulder.

It was dusk, and the ferry had arrived. Up close it looked dangerous and unreliable. It was a large, plain wooden raft, with a little shelter on one corner, which housed an engine. This contraption pulled the raft along on a slimy chain which stretched across the river, and was fastened to stout steel poles on each bank.

There was an argument going on between the ferryman, a thickset, middle aged man in a loincloth and a greasy, naval-looking cap, and the truck drivers. They were anxious to get across and spend the night in the fleshpots of Bathurst, while the ferryman felt he had done quite enough for one day. We joined the discussion and by dint of a discreet bribe, to which the truck drivers refused to contribute, I managed to get him to agree to the crossing.

The vehicles were manoeuvred gingerly onto the raft, with the Explorer at the front, and chocks of wood placed beneath the wheels. The raft was perceptibly lower in the water, with a freeboard of only a few inches. I was grateful that there was no wind and that the water was completely smooth. The current was slow and easy.

The engine in the little cabin was started and began to emit regular puffs of black smoke into the sky. It made the sort of putt-putt noise I associated with cinema cartoons. But the ferryman engaged the primitive gear and the chain slack was taken up as we began to move across the river.

The banks were muddy, and apart from the ferry area, were steep. The river was lined with mangroves, whose gnarled roots formed arches, like claws, reaching down to the water.

"Plenty of crocodiles in this river," said Sarr. "Many village people get eaten when they come to get water. Many snakes, too and other things."

I shuddered and was glad that I had not thought of having a swim. I put my hand into the water and found it to be very warm. My hand smelled disagreeable when I withdrew it and I had to wash it in some fresh water from a jerrican.

We followed the road, with quite a broad earth surface, in the direction of Bathurst (now called Banjul). I wanted to keep ahead of the trucks, which threw up a dense cloud of dust and, since it was now almost dark, made visibility very poor.

Bathurst was reached over a bridge and causeway over sand bars. It stands on Banjul Island, in the mouth of the river Gambia. As I drove in, I immediately felt quite a different atmosphere from the Senegalese towns to which I had grown accustomed. The streets were busy, there were some street lamps and the houses were a different shape. Many were British colonial architecture, very different from their French counterparts, being somehow more familiar, and much less fussy and ornate.

We found the main street, and pulled up at a medium sized building with a sign which pronounced it to be a hotel.

"I am going in," I said to Sarr. "What do you want to do?"

"I will go to see a friend," he said. "Monsieur stopped here once and I got to know some people. There are many Wolofs here," he added, "but only in the town. I will come back tomorrow morning."

I went into the hotel and he drove off. The lobby was a place frozen in time. It was turn of the century British colonial, with a slowly rotating ceiling fan, a uniformed person behind the reception desk and wicker chairs and sofas scattered round. There were several very English-looking people sitting on them, drinking what looked like whisky and soda. The men were dressed formally in white, while the few ladies were in flowered chiffon dresses and hats. It was very hot.

I asked the desk clerk, in English, if I might have a room for the night.

"Certainly, Master," he replied, with a smile. "Do you have luggage?"

"No, just this small bag."

He raised his eyebrows, but said nothing. When I had signed in, he snapped his fingers and a young boy came up to show me to my room. I felt a lot of eyes on me and was rather ashamed of my appearance, in my stained and dusty khakis and dirty shoes.

The room was small, neat and practical. There was a ceiling fan which served to stir the hot, humid air without making it appreciably cooler. But there was a good shower of what was slightly brackish water.

I made myself as presentable as I could – which was not very – and went down to dinner. The restaurant was, like my room, neat and unpretentious in what must have been regarded locally as good taste. I was shown to a small table, again feeling curious eyes on me from the few other occupied tables. There were no African guests.

I could not believe the menu. After uniquely French or native food for so many months, certain words sprang out at me: roast beef, Yorkshire pudding, roast potatoes or potato chips, fried fish, and so on. On the table were bottles of ketchup and Worcester sauce. There was no hint of anything un-English.

A waiter came up. "Have you chosen, Master?" he enquired.

"Since I am in the Gambia for the first time, I wonder if there is anything Gambian I could have?" I asked. "All the food on the menu is English."

The waiter looked at me in horror and astonishment. "You mean... native... food?" he gasped.

I nodded. "Oh no, Master," he finally said. "This is a superior establishment. No one who comes here would eat such... native... food." He managed to load the word with a strong feeling of disgust and disapproval.

I gave up and had some roast beef with Yorkshire pudding

and roast potatoes, followed by an uninspired piece of cake. But a drink of good English beer cheered me up.

The following morning, after a delicious full English breakfast, with all the trimmings, I joined Sarr, who was waiting patiently in the Explorer.

"Good morning, Chief," he said, with a broad smile. "Have you had a good English night?"

"Yes, thank you. But when I tried to get some Gambian food, they did not have any."

"Well," he said. "If you want to look around this morning, I can take you to a place where you can eat some. Also," he added, "when Monsieur came here once, he said that whisky is much cheaper than in Dakar, and he bought some."

"That is interesting," I said. "I will go to the store and have a look."

"It is not good to take alcohol," said Sarr, "but I understand Europeans like it."

We had a good morning. I visited the two service stations and found everything to be in order. The owners were surprised to see the Explorer. "You have come by road, Master?" said one. "The French gentleman usually came by airplane – he said the road was dirty. It was difficult to speak with him, because he knew no English."

The little planes which linked the principal towns in West Africa were mostly ramshackle Herons and Dakotas and were hot, uncomfortable and undependable. I did use them occasionally later on, but much preferred my journeys by road with Sarr and the Explorer.

I went to the one main store in town, and bought six bottles of whisky, which were indeed much cheaper than in Dakar. I also got some bacon and two tins of rice pudding for the children, which were not available at home. Sarr showed me a secret compartment in the Explorer, under the driver's seat, where any contraband could be safely stowed, wrapped in some sacking. "They will ask at the border, but only because of rules. Everybody brings whisky and they do not care if you give them a little sweetener," he said.

After a morning spent exploring the James Fort, 20 miles up

river, he directed me to a small restaurant on the outskirts of town, for a late lunch. I insisted he come in with me and also asked him to choose our meal.

He knew the proprietor, who, in spite of being a Mandingo, spoke both Wolof and English. He was a tall, willowy man with a handsome, aquiline face, and was dressed in white, with a bright blue cummerbund.

After some polite conversation, in both languages, Sarr explained that I wanted to eat Gambian food and left it up to his acquaintance, whose name was Denba. We had a cold mango juice and, before long, Denba brought us the meal. He explained that it consisted mainly of *chew I kong*, a delicious catfish stew with limes and peanuts. "We bring the fish from up river," said Damba, "because water here is salt for many miles up and catfish likes his water sweet." I was also introduced to *fufu*, which I was to eat many times all over West Africa. This was a thick dough, made of yams and formed into dumplings before cooking. It was a common adjunct to the many stews which formed the main part of menus in this part of the world.

I said to Sarr that we ought to sleep early as I wanted to start early the next day. We were going to try to get to Ziguinchor, the main town of Lower Senegal, the Casamance. It was quite a long way and I did not trust Sarr's description of the road as 'passable', Besides, I had plans not to keep to the main road but to explore the rain forest a little.

He drove me back to the hotel and I asked him to be there at six in the morning.

He arrived punctually, and we set off, initially going up river and to the south. We had refilled our jerricans with fuel and water and I had got some tins of corned beef and a large tin of biscuits to supplement our supplies. Sarr had some dried fish wrapped in a cloth, which gave out an unusual aroma in the back of the Explorer.

The road was passable and at the beginning we made good time. The Gambia southern frontier was not far away and we got there by mid morning. It was a very informal crossing, and with small sweeteners all round, we got through easily and quickly. There was a little traffic, mostly of overloaded trucks and some passenger mini-buses overflowing with passengers and produce.

The road, of a reddish clay, wound its way through the dense rain forest, which encroached on both sides. Even above the noise of the engine, we could hear occasional shrieks and screams, which Sarr said were monkeys. It was quite hot and there was a lot of dust.

We passed through swampy areas with mangroves, and through wet, slippery wetlands, where the Explorer skidded and slid about, making Sarr, who was driving, decrease his speed almost to walking pace.

"I have been thinking," I said to him. "You remember when we were at that village, the old man said they could not get any meat because they were not allowed to have guns?"

Sarr looked at me suspiciously. "Yes?" he said.

"Well, if we stop and shoot something and take it to a village, they would be grateful, wouldn't they?"

Sarr nodded. "But it is dangerous," he said. "There are many things in these forests. Monsieur would never go into them; he only shot birds and gazelles in Senegal – never in Casamance in the thick forest."

"Why dangerous?" I asked. "This shotgun is good and I noticed anyway that he left me a box of solid ball, for big animals." I had had no experience of hunting, beyond some partridge shooting in Baghdad.

Sarr looked worried. "But there are big things here," he said. "There are no lions in the forest, or elephants, but plenty of leopards and *phacochères*, or wild pig – very dangerous. And the worst is the buffalo. He is big and very clever and he can smell you a long way."

"I am sure we can deal with all that," I said airily, "you are always exaggerating."

I noticed that, a little way ahead, there was a track off the main road, which disappeared into the forest. I asked Sarr to stop and we had a look.

"If there is a track," I said, "it must go somewhere."

Sarr looked doubtful. "There are no tyre marks and it is very narrow. Maybe it goes to a village…"

Now that the engine was turned off and we were out of the

Explorer, I noticed that there were clouds of coloured birds swirling about in the trees which made a great din, squawking and whistling. There were also distant screams and yells, which I supposed to be the monkeys. The traffic on the road frightened the animals so it was unusual to see anything, except possibly intrepid troops of baboons, from the car.

I could also hear, far in the distance, the rumble and throb of drums. Throughout West Africa there was very seldom a place where the sound of drumming was absent. But after a while, rather like people who live in houses near a train line, the mind automatically shut out the sound and one only noticed it from time to time.

"I would like to explore a bit," I said to Sarr.

"Well, Chief, I suppose if you want to," said Sarr resignedly. "But I do not know what we will find."

I took the wheel and we gingerly entered the track. It was very winding and we almost immediately lost sight of the road. The trees were quite thick and the surface was rough, but dry. We drove for about an hour without seeing anything other than rain forest, occasional clearings and some small streams which were easy to ford, though they made the ground very slippery.

I stopped in a small clearing and we got out, to stretch our legs and have a meal. After a drink from the jerricans, some biscuits and a tin of corned beef, together with a small, chewy and pungent piece of Sarr's dried fish, we sat and relaxed for a while.

Suddenly there was a loud shrieking and a great crowd of small monkeys went racing through the trees beside us and disappeared almost immediately. Sarr jumped to his feet. "Leopard," he hissed. "There must be a leopard nearby. They like to eat monkeys."

I also jumped to my feet and got the gun out of the Explorer. I loaded it with ball in the choke barrel and heavy shot in the half-choke. We stood for a while in silence, but nothing happened.

After a few minutes I decided we should go on and so we started off again. The track wound its way deeper into the forest, and we saw some more monkeys as well as a very large snake, a python, which slowly wriggled its way across the track, causing me to stop and wait while it disappeared into the undergrowth.

It seemed wholly unconcerned with us.

Rounding a sharp corner, we suddenly came upon a man. He was walking along the track and stopped when he saw us, looking surprised. Some distance behind him was a woman, with a large parcel on her head.

I stopped. "Floup or maybe Fulani," whispered Sarr. "Savages!" The man was a medium sized, middle aged person of a dark brown colour, not black. He wore a rag tied around his head and another round his loins. He had a clay pipe clenched in his teeth and was carrying a bow. A quiver of rather primitive looking arrows was slung over his back. His eyes were rather red and he had decorative scars on his arms and chest.

The woman, plump and somewhat younger, wore only a loincloth. She also had stopped some distance away.

"Jam nga am?" I said. "Are you in peace?"

The man stared at me blankly. I nodded at him. There was no reaction. Then I had an idea, and offered him a cigarette. He took one and stuffed it into his pipe; I lit it for him, having one myself. He seemed to relax somewhat and lowered his bow.

I pointed up the track and made enquiring signs, raising my eyebrows. He nodded and pointed in the same direction. Then he made encouraging movements with his hands, as though we should go on.

There seemed little point in continuing the non-conversation, so I gave him the packet of cigarettes and we climbed back into the Explorer. I thought he smiled, but I was not sure.

"I told you," said Sarr. "Savages."

"Everyone lives in their own way," I said sternly. "They are people like us."

"Not like me," muttered Sarr.

We drove on. "There must be a village soon," I said. "We will stop and I will try to shoot something." I took the gun and, followed by Sarr, went into a small path, obviously an animal trail, into the forest. After a few hundred yards, we came to a small stream and could see many different animal tracks in the mud on the bank. I was not then able to tell the different spoor, but we retreated to a large bush and hid. "Do not make a sound," I warned Sarr. "We will see what comes."

"Much better you shoot birds," he whispered. "Maybe something big comes."

We sat there for what seemed long time. There were flies and mosquitoes in abundance, and no other sign of life, except the ever-present birds, which made colourful flashes in the forest canopy.

Suddenly there was a rustle and a small deer, I do not know what kind, though it was slightly larger than a gazelle, came out of the undergrowth on the other side of the stream. It paused at the water's edge and sniffed the air, then lowered its head and began to drink. I shot it with the heavy shot and it dropped.

We manhandled it back to the Explorer and managed to get it up on the roof rack. Sarr was delighted and said if we did not come to a village before nightfall, he would prepare the carcass and we would have a splendid meal.

But after another hour or so, when dusk was falling, the forest began to thin and we came to a very large clearing, with about two dozen round, thatched huts and a big open space all around them. There were people milling about and they came towards us as I stopped and turned off the engine. I looked at Sarr, but he looked horrified and his eyes were popping. "These are Papal people – they should not be here," he whispered hoarsely. "They eat people!"

"Nonsense," I said briskly. "Don't be such a coward."

I got out of the Explorer and looked at the crowd assembled round the car. There was an older man standing slightly ahead of the others. His skin was a shiny, glistening black and he was stocky and muscular. He wore an embroidered loincloth, like a sporran, with bands of feathers round his upper arms and his shins, and he was leaning on a long, wicked-looking spear.

There was silence. Even the children, clustered round their mothers, were quiet. The other men were also dressed in loin cloths and feathers, while the women wore a short sarong in bright cloths, from waist to ankles. Everyone was the same wonderful shining ebony black.

The older men came closer; I could feel Sarr move behind me.

"You are French!" said the man, in broken, accented French.

"No," I said. "I am English. That is different." The man looked at me. Now close, I could see that his eyes were bloodshot to a bright scarlet and that his front teeth were sharpened to points.

"Ah," said the man. "Like in Gambia, yes?"

"Yes," I replied. "I come to see all this country and to know the people. I wish to be a friend." I thought the time was right. "See, I bring a small gift for you," I indicated the deer on the roof. "This is for you and your people, in friendship."

"Your man is not friend," the man said, pointing to Sarr. "He is Wolof."

I could hear Sarr take a deep breath. "My friend," I said, stressing the word, "is my friend. Wolof or not, he is a good man. And what are you?" I asked, to change the subject.

"We are Papal," the man said. Sarr gave a whimper. I was interested; the Papal, mostly in Portuguese Guinea, were the notorious cannibals of West Africa, though it was said that since eating their last white man, some decades ago, the French and Portuguese authorities sent out a harsh, punitive expedition to teach them a lesson. Since then, there were no more reports of white men lost, though rumours persisted that Africans were not altogether safe.

There was quite a long pause. The man then seemed to make up his mind, and turned to address his people in a strange, guttural tongue. His speech was punctuated by long "Ahhhs" and "Hohohos" from the semicircle. He then turned to me and said: "We see a friend. We accept your gift. You are welcome."

I gave a sigh of relief. I do not suppose we were in any real danger, but it was a great release of tension.

The man gestured at a group of young men and pointed to the deer. They promptly swarmed all over the Explorer and removed it, taking it away behind the huts.

The man turned out to be called Djemba. He was the village *marabout*. It seemed that in most tribes there were three principal personalities: the Chief of the clan, the *marabout*, who was the tribe's guide, priest, philosopher and judge and, finally, the *griot*.

This last was the musician, jester and, most importantly, the historian of the tribe. Most of the languages were not written, so the *griot* was the repository of the tribe's history, which he would chant, on demand, from an amazing memory. I was told that some *griots* remembered stories, similar to Norse sagas, which spanned centuries and told of triumphs, heroes and disasters. But is was common, round an evening cooking fire, to sit and listen to a *griot* in full flow. Sadly, I could not understand his singing, though sometimes bits would be translated for me. The role of *griot* was hereditary, and the knowledge and skills were passed down, from father to son, for generations.

Djemba, as the *marabout*, was the keeper of the tribe's morals and discipline. He led the tribe in prayers and invocations to whatever power they worshipped, gave judgments on disputes and advised the chief on any plans for the tribe. There was a curious accommodation with the Moslem religion, which was widespread, so that there was no conflict but rather a synthesis of the control and discipline to preserve tribal unity. It seemed to work well.

"You may sleep here tonight," said Djemba. "And we will eat together. The women will prepare a feast." He took us to a hut, which had its normal inhabitants summarily evicted, and we took in a jerrican of water and some blankets. It was hot during the day, but could get quite cold at night.

As night fell, and the forest noises intensified, the drumming started. It was quite close and I decided to investigate.

I saw that a large cooking fire had been lit, and there was a group of women busy around it, their silhouettes elegant against the light. A little distance away, squatting on the ground and all alone, was a person I took to be the *griot*. He was a small, wizened man, much bedecked in feathers and with a feather head-dress on his brow. He was playing, with great concentration, a *sabar* drum, weaving a complicated rhythm which I was unable to follow with his eyes screwed tight shut, in a sort of ecstasy.

"He is talking to the ancestors," said a quiet voice beside me. "The *griots* can talk to other spirits. We each have four, you know. One passes to another body, one dies, one goes into the air, but one goes to ancestors place where he lives."

Djemba paused. He had come silently up beside me. I also noticed that Sarr was also close by, almost touching me.

Throughout our stay with the Papal, he was never more than a couple of feet away from me.

"The drum is a very special thing," said Djemba. "It is many things. It can rejoice and weep, it can talk love and threaten, it can calm and arouse. It is a great art. I am called after a drum. My name, Djemba, is another kind of drum. His name," he said, pointing at the drummer, "is Sabar Dia, or drum spirit."

"But come," he said, "we will sit near the fire and drink." We strolled over to the cooking fire, with Sarr sticking to me like a burr. There was a complicated structure built over the flames, of some iron rods and green wood. There was also a row of calabash containers and small wooden cups.

The smell of roasting venison, impaled on wooden spits, was delicious. We sat down, and gradually people joined us in a big circle round the fire. I was struck by the good behaviour of the children, who were quiet and did not make any fuss or run around, sitting solemnly with the adults.

A young girl brought a calabash and three small cups. Djemba took them and poured some liquid into them then offered one to me. He gestured at Sarr to pick one up.

"We drink," said Djemba, "it is good. We make from palm tree blood and leave for one season to ripen."

I took a large mouthful and nearly choked. The drink was a fiery, fermented spirit which burned its way down my throat and took my breath away. Everyone laughed and, when Djemba had drunk, also helped themselves. Sarr was very quiet, sitting slightly behind me. I wondered what he would do – he was a Moslem, and would not knowingly drink alcohol. After we left, the following day, he told me he had pretended to drink, so as not to offend, but surreptitiously poured the liquor on the ground in the darkness.

Another girl brought us some food on a small palm leaf. It looked like nothing I had ever seen, but Djemba said: "Eat this. People like it very much."

I noticed everyone watching as I took a mouthful. It had a curious, rubbery texture, with a slightly sour, pungent taste and was very highly spiced with some sort of pepper.

"What is it?" I asked.

Djemba smiled. "It is jungle snail. Very easy to catch but hard to find."

The venison was now ready and a girl brought us large palm leaves with the roast. But I noticed there was also other meat, which looked like rabbit.

"What is this other meat?" I asked.

"Is forest rat," he said. "Very good, much fat."

The meal went on and on. As more and more drink was consumed, the party got merrier and merrier, and everyone seemed very relaxed (except Sarr).

"Chief is away hunting," said Djemba. "He goes often with young men to teach them. I am leader if he is not here. Also," he patted his chest proudly, "I am the only one to speak French. I learn when I spent one year in Ziguinchor as a young man. Old *marabout* tell me I should learn, to help my people."

I took the bull by the horns. "Tell me," I said casually. "I heard that the Papal tribe is very famous and has great warriors. Is it true that you eat some people?"

Sarr, behind me, choked. Djemba looked at me sharply. "Who say such things?" he asked.

"Oh, I just heard here and there," I said airily. Had I gone too far?

"It is true and not true," said Djemba. "In old, old days the warriors eat brave enemy. Now we only eat, sometimes, parts of a very great man or warrior, not to lose his power and courage and strength. His three parts – I do not know the name..." He pointed at his liver, his heart and his head. "Inside parts," he said.

"But now nearly always only inside the tribe," he added.

"So you only do it to receive the qualities of the dead man?" I asked.

"Of course," said Djemba. "We do not want to eat your friend." He pointed at Sarr, who was trembling and rolling his eyes. Djemba burst out laughing, as did one or two other men who were listening, whom Djemba enlightened with a quick phrase in his language.

"Why do you have red eyes and teeth with points?" I asked. I thought everyone was relaxed so it was an opportunity to find out.

Djemba pondered for a moment. "It is our way," he finally said. "We have to look so to frighten enemy even now when enemy is not many. So we rub a special leaf in the eyes which makes them red and we chip with stone our teeth so we look like wild beast." He grinned, showing his teeth. "It worked," he added simply.

The women and children had departed and some of the men, now very drunk, were dancing to the drum. They weaved their bodies in sinuous patterns and the flickering light of the cooking fire, reflected on glistening, ebony skin, was very beautiful. All this, with my head slightly spinning from too much drink and the continuing noises from the forest, persuaded me that this was a good time to retire.

I thanked Djemba and said I had a long trip the next day, so I would go to sleep. We stood up and he put his hand on my shoulder. "It was good," he said. He glanced at Sarr, who was trying to make himself inconspicuous, and added: "Do not fear. We will not harm you."

I slept well, wrapped in my own blankets. I only woke once and went to relieve myself; I was not surprised that Sarr also came out and stood embarrassingly close to me.

In the morning, when I awoke, the sun was already up. I washed my face in jerrican water and started to suck my tooth-stick. This was a twig from a bush which Africans use to clean their teeth. It produces a slight soapy substance, which tastes vaguely minty, and frays into a sort of brush as one chews on it. Even the most elegant *fatous* in Dakar, while shopping or gossiping, mumbled their tooth-sticks.

After a light breakfast of some cold meat and biscuits from my tin, I asked Djemba if I could take a photograph of some Papal warriors in their finery. He looked doubtful, but said he would find out. After a short while, he returned and said as a special favour, three would dress up for me. He said that he had found out in Ziguinchor that photographs did not steal your souls, and had educated the tribe to understand this.

"It is important to be modern," he said. "One year ago I sent my young nephew to Ziguinchor to learn French and become modern. He came back a little while ago and brought new cloth and many things so we are modern." He scratched his chin. "He will be a good *marabout* some day."

Sarr pulled my sleeve, and when I turned I saw three warriors lined up, waiting for the photograph. They were resplendent in white feather bands round arms and shins, embroidered sporrans and loin cloths, animal skin thongs and, to top it all, an amazing head dress of what looked like a feather duster, fixed vertically on their heads in a band of beads and cloth. They looked very ferocious, with their scarlet eyes and pointed teeth. They leaned on wicked-looking spears. They were also all wearing sunglasses.

I asked Djemba if they would mind taking the sunglasses off. He laughed.

"My nephew brings these black eyes from Ziguinchor," he said. "They are very proud of them and will not allow photograph without them."

But I pleaded, and eventually they removed them, and I had my photograph of my friends the cannibals in all their finery – without the sunglasses.

Djemba showed us another track, leading south, which he said was a shorter way to the main road to Ziguinchor. We said goodbye and the villagers, who had gathered round, made farewell noises.

We drove off along the track. It had been a memorable visit. After some miles, Sarr said, in a rather offhand manner: "Of course, I was not really afraid, Chief. I just wanted to show them that you were very brave so I pretended."

"Right, yes, naturally," I said, grinning. "I could see that. You are really very brave; all Wolofs are."

He grunted. "Wolofs are civilised people. We do not eat people or drink bad drink or even eat big rats. These Papal are savages, savages!"

"Savages in sunglasses," I said.

I drove carefully along. Both our spare tyres were flat, so I kept my fingers crossed that we should not get another puncture. We could repair it, of course, but it took a long time.

The forest became more sparse and I could build up quite a good speed, up to some thirty miles per hour. The surface was bad, but dry, except in some patches where the wetlands intruded. We were pestered by mosquitoes and an extremely painful fly, with what seemed to be a barbed sting, since one did not feel it bite, but when the sting was withdrawn there was a flash of pain, as though a red hot needle was applied to the flesh. Sarr said these were tsetse flies.

After a couple of uneventful hours we reached the main road and turned towards Ziguinchor. The road was acceptably wide and we met the occasional truck or minibus, overloaded as usual, passing us in a cloud of red dust and tooting horns.

Sarr had been brooding silently for some time. He finally turned to me and said: "That Djemba! He is not a real *marabout*. He is a savage." He paused. "A real *marabout* is a holy Moslem man, a learned man who has *baraka*, the grace of Allah (may he be venerated). He has to study long at a big mosque, like in Touba and know many things. He also makes and blesses *gri-gri*. Djemba does not do anything. Savages!" he said again, with great disdain.

"What is *gri-gri*?" I asked.

Sarr fumbled in his shirt and produced two sweat-stained little parcels of leather, hanging round his neck on a leather thong. "This is a *gri-gri*," he said. "It has holy Koran writings inside, blessed by real *marabout*. It protects."

We passed through Bignona, a non-descript small town, with huts and small houses made of sun-dried bricks and some of concrete. We refilled our tank and jerricans with fuel (we had been running low) and also got fresh water for the other jerricans: all this at a ramshackle Shell station with three pumps.

The owner, a tall Mandingo, was pleased to see us. "Nobody from Shell comes here," he said. "They all go straight through on their way to Ziguinchor. Last visit was one year ago."

He insisted we each have a bottle of the usual bright green lemonade, hot and sticky. We drank it, though it tasted like boiled sweets.

After another few hours, on quite a decent road, we arrived on the banks of the wide Casamance river and could see Ziguinchor on the far bank. It seemed to be quite a big town, and we were fortunate to catch the last ferry of the day, a small smelly steamboat, which landed us on the town jetty.

The crossing was made interesting by a pod of dolphins, which played round our prow and by large flocks of great cormorants, which skimmed the water to each side of us. The banks had been cleared of reeds, though not of mangrove and baobab, and we could see glimmering lights in a series of villages up river. To our right, the river widened and we could see the ocean in the distance.

We drove through a small port area, with many quite large ships and *pirogues* and on into the town. The streets were quite wide and had an occasional lamp. It was a typical French colonial town, though with a whiff of Portuguese – the town had only been ceded to colonial France by Portugal some hundred years earlier. It had been a major slave port and had exported hundreds of thousands of slaves, mainly to Brazil.

Sarr was driving and went straight to the hotel at which Jean-Claude stayed when visiting the town. He had usually flown there, but had driven there twice (without detours) according to Sarr.

It was now dark and I asked Sarr to come back at eight in the morning. He said he had a cousin living there with whom he would spend the night.

The hotel was very similar to the one in St. Louis, the same rather shabby colonial furniture and facilities. The décor was French and there were people sitting around and drinking. They were mostly very correctly dressed, the men in jackets and ties and the women in dresses; they were all white.

I registered at the desk and felt curious and disapproving looks behind me. I was somewhat dishevelled and dirty, and badly needed a shower.

The room was spacious and had a ceiling fan. The windows were open and there was the familiar sound of drums. It was hot and humid and there was a cloud of insects round the lamp.

At dinner in the restaurant I now knew better than to ask for local food, and settled for an admittedly delicious grilled fish – I do not know what it was – with African rice and a green, cabbage-like vegetable. Then a piece of cake and coffee.

I slept well in the large bed and woke covered in bites, as the sun rose. After a good breakfast of eggs and bread, I joined Sarr who was, as usual, on time.

He had brought his cousin with him and introduced him as Doudou Diap N'Diaye, and me by my full name. His cousin was, of course, a Wolof and seemed to regard me with some awe. He spoke good French.

"You are welcome to Ziguinchor, Monsieur," said Doudou. "Sarr has been telling me your story. You have stayed with the savage Papal and I am glad Sarr was able to protect you and prevent them from doing you harm."

I turned to stare at Sarr, but he was looking at the sky and shuffling his feet. "Yes, I am grateful to your cousin," I said. "Sarr has courage like a lion and the strength of an elephant."

The irony was lost on Doudou. "They are very dangerous," he said. "They eat people, you know." He shuddered.

I said I wanted to visit the Shell service stations, and Doudou directed us to them. At the second one, I was lucky to run into the Shell supervisor, who lived in Ziguinchor and looked after the stations, their supplies and condition. He was another Wolof, who vaguely remembered Sarr and shook me warmly by the hand.

"You must have taken the place of the previous Inspector," he said. "We did not see much of him and it is good to see you." He greeted Sarr and was introduced to Doudou. Sarr spoke to him rapidly in Wolof and Doudou grinned and nodded. The supervisor, of whose existence I had had no notion, turned to me and said: "So you have been visiting villages, including the savages. Are you interested in our country?"

I admitted that I was. "There is no point in travel if you do not learn about the places you visit," I said, rather sententiously. The three nodded.

"And you are English, like in the Gambia," said the supervisor. "I did not know the French allowed anyone to come to Shell who was not French."

The stations seemed to be in good order and the operators were welcoming and courteous. They were all Wolof, and the introductions took some time.

The supervisor, whose name was Abdali, said: "You must allow me to offer you lunch. Sarr tells me that you eat everything, even things he does not eat, so you must try our Casamance food."

I accepted with alacrity. Native food seemed, in the main, to be rather nicer than local attempts to copy French cuisine. We lunched at a little thatched restaurant in the Wolof area of the town. The proprietor was an old friend and we got special treatment. Everyone was very relaxed, and I was told many Wolof jokes and proverbs, which were just as amusing in French as in their original form.

There was a fish stew, *thiébou dieune*, made with fresh ocean fish and highly spiced. It came with African rice dough and *pain de singe*, or 'monkey bread', a green cake-like substance made of baobab fruit pulp. It had a rather acid, throat-rasping taste and I grimaced when I tasted it.

Abdali noticed. "It is not the best of taste," he admitted, "but you should get used to eating it. We find it is the very best thing if you have any sort of upset stomach – it cures it quickly. I always carry some on the road – it can save much inconvenience."

Sarr nodded, and remarked that he also always had some, in the Explorer.

We finished off with green mangoes, sprinkled with salt and spices.

Abdali said: "The most interesting thing around here is the rice. This is African rice, not like the rice you eat in Europe. It is grown locally, and I will take you to see it."

Accordingly, we all set off in Abdali's large Peugeot pick-up (much softer sprung and more comfortable than the Explorer), and drove about ten miles up river, on a track that followed the bank. We soon came to cultivated fields, fruit and baobab trees and green bushes . There were small villages every two or three miles, and people busy working in the fields. There were also fishermen in *pirogues* and pontoons on the slow flowing river, casting round nets.

"The water is not very fresh here," remarked Abdali. "The tide brings the salt a long way up river and makes everything brackish. So, as you see, the villagers make terraces with very clever channels. In the rainy season the channels are opened and the salt washed away. Then closed again and the rain water accumulates in the terraces. The brush is burned and the ashes put on the growing rice – this is women's work."

"But are these Wolof people?" I asked. "They do not look like it." The men were small and very thin, while the women were corpulent and looked very strong. Their clothes were a mixture of bright sarongs and more rudimentary loin cloths – the upper body was bare, but some of the women had quite long hair, dressed in spectacular style.

Everyone laughed loudly. "No, of course they are not Wolof," said Abdali. "Far from it. Neither are they Diola or Sereer, the main tribes here. These are a very small, specialised rice tribe called the Ehing. For them, rice is much more than food. It is their great spirit and they worship it. There are difficult and elaborate rituals connected with every aspect of seeding, growth, care, harvesting and preparation of this rice. No outsider is permitted to see these ceremonies, which always happen in the dark. And it is all done by the women. They are the strong ones. They own all the land, which passes from mother to daughter. Men are only used for menial tasks and to make children." He paused. "I could not live like that," he said. The others nodded and murmured agreement.

There were many palm plantations and the whole scene was a pleasant one, after the desert of the north and the thick and humid rain forest through which we had come.

We walked down to the river bank, which had been cleared of reeds and had a snack, which Abdali had brought, wrapped in a white cloth. There was some smoked fish, some yam dumplings and mango juice, in a large calabash.

"Where do you go now?" asked Abdali.

"Well, I thought I would go to see Portuguese Guinea, maybe as far as Bissao," I said. He nodded.

"Yes," he said. "I have been once. It is quite different. Hard to understand the people; they are very wild and they only speak their own languages – and Portuguese, of course, in the big towns. At least, they think they are big." He grinned and the others chuckled. "Very savage," added Sarr's cousin.

After another night in the hotel, and a fully replenished Explorer, with mended tyres, Sarr and I set off for Portuguese Guinea, going south. The road, as far as the frontier, not far away, was quite passable and we made good time.

The border itself was not very sophisticated; the same pole across the road, the same rather ragged soldiers and ramshackle huts and a small refreshment kiosk. After showing our passports, we were waved through with no formality, though the soldiers accepted cigarettes as a goodwill gesture.

The countryside was much like the Casamance. It was somewhat more lush, with fairly thick undergrowth closing in on the red mud road, with huge potholes, and trees, some flowering, tangling their branches high above. There were many birds flying about, some quite big and most of them gaudy, in bright primary colours.

We crossed the Rio de Canjambari on another rickety ferry. The water in the river was a swirling torrent, of a rich, red colour. It was quite wide and looked deep and dangerous. The ferry, powered by three men pulling on a rope, was forced to cross at a steep angle, with water washing over the wooden deck. Sarr was very excited. He had never been here before and kept up a running commentary, comparing everything unfavourably with Senegal. After a tricky disembarkation, we passed through a section of wetlands, with ponds and lakes beside the road. There were girls, many quite nude, washing clothes and gambolling in the water, who shouted and waved as we drove past. There were also tracks leading into the forest, and I assumed that there were villages scattered about, not far from the road.

There was no traffic and we saw the occasional gazelle and antelope run across the road. In the trees, occasionally, there would be troops of monkeys and once a band of baboons squatting in a clearing some fifty yards from the road.

"There are many animals here," remarked Sarr. "Not many vehicles pass this way."

The first town we came to was Bissorà. This was rather dull: a collection of low concrete buildings, reed-thatched huts and some small brick shops, selling tawdry domestic items. Beside the road, there was a small, open-sided eating place, with two wooden tables and benches. We stopped and a young woman came out.

"Good day," I said in French. "Can we eat something?"

"Please sit," she replied in atrocious French. "I bring." It seemed there was no choice, so we sat down and waited expectantly.

After a short while, she brought two deep dishes, which contained a stew, some millet bread and two spoons. The stew was not at all bad, though I did wonder at the time what the ingredients might be, since neither Sarr nor I could identify them. We were also given a bottle each of the all-pervasive, warm and colourful lemonade, which seemed to be pan-African.

When we had finished, I called the young woman and paid her with a handful of franc coins, with which she seemed satisfied. She was a beautiful person, with a fine featured face and slim body, well wrapped in a colourful sarong which covered her from shoulder to ankle. She seemed to be alone, which surprised me. Sarr could not identify the tribe, but she was one of the more attractive women I had so far seen in the bush.

It was dusk when we reached Bissao, capital and only real town in the country. We could see the buildings clustered on the side of a fairly broad expanse of water, with the ocean some distance away on our right. As we drove in, the colonial feeling became very strong, and reminiscent of St. Louis, though the buildings were Portuguese, rather than French colonial, with ornate decorations and curved balconies. The streets were largely deserted and the lights in the houses flickered – there was limited electricity and oil lamps and candles seemed to be widely used.

After driving around for a while, we found a sort of boarding house. There were no hotel signs to be seen, but there was a restaurant with what seemed to be some rooms above it. I went in to investigate and found the owner, who was serving his customers in the restaurants.

"Do you let rooms for sleeping?" I enquired in simple French.

"Yes," he answered. "I have three rooms." He spoke in Portuguese Creole, which I found, with surprise, I could understand reasonably well through my knowledge of Spanish.

I went to tell Sarr, but after looking doubtful, he said he would rather spend the night in the Explorer, which he would park at a convenient place. I wished him well, and returned to the restaurant.

I had more *maffé* for supper, washed down with some Portuguese beer. The owner told me he was of the Balanta tribe and not Moslem, so alcohol was freely served. There were no Europeans in the restaurant, though there was a number of paler brown mulattos, who spoke a purer Portuguese.

After supper, I was shown to my room. This was a rather dirty, small place, with a bare mattress on a low wooden platform. There was a chair and an oil lamp. The mattress was not very clean. I enquired about bathrooms, and the owner looked at me in surprise.

"There is toilet outside behind restaurant. You go when you want. If you want wash, is extra. I show."

He led me to a room at the end of the corridor and introduced me to my first 'bucket shower'. This was a bucket, suspended some six feet above a concrete floor which had a hole for the water to run away. There was a short rope attached to the lip of the bucket, which enabled one to tilt it so as to spill the contents on one's head. The bucket was replenished by a young boy, who had a short ladder, and would do so for a small payment.

I had a shower – the water was at ambient temperature, which was fairly hot, and climbed back into my clothes, in which I slept. I woke in the night to hear scurrying noises on the floor but could not be bothered to investigate.

In the morning, after a breakfast of fruit, I climbed back into the Explorer (Sarr was there early), and we set off to look around. He told me he had had an acceptable night in the back of the car and smiled when I told him of my own accommodation.

The town, which was quite large, lay on the Geba estuary, a wide stretch of water where the river emptied into the ocean. There were many ships, some ocean-going, in the port and lots of *pirogues* of various sizes, scuttling about on the water. There was a market, with fresh fish and domestic items – notably lengths of brightly coloured cloth – for sale and everywhere Balanta men and women, tall, graceful and with attractive features.

We found a service station, not Shell, and replenished our tank and jerricans. We also bought some tins of sardines which were on sale. They looked rather old.

I do not remember much about Bissao as by this time I had become somewhat blasé, having seen St. Louis, Dakar, Bathurst and Ziguinchor, all colonial slave ports, and in their own ways rather more interesting. I decided not to linger, but to head for home.

We headed back the way we had come, towards Bissorà, but before we had gone very far, a lorry coming the other way flashed its lights, sounded its horn and made signs that we should stop. Sarr pulled up beside it and saw with pleasure that the driver was a Wolof. After exchanging greetings, they had quite a long conversation, and the lorry drove off. Sarr turned to me.

"Savages," he said with disgust. "He says the rope broke, and the ferry on the Canjambari has floated away to sea and there is no way to cross. He thinks it will be many days before another one will be built. So he says no way to go to Ziguinchor on main road."

"So what do we do?" I asked. "Did he say anything more?"

Sarr nodded. "He said if you do not want to fly back, best way is to go east on the river road along Geba to Xima, then into Casamance to Vélingara and so on. We miss Gambia completely – go round the end."

"But he also say the road is bad, it is a long way and there are many savages in the villages," he added.

I thought it would be very unjust to abandon Sarr to make his way back alone and simply fly back to Dakar, so I told him we would try it. "It will be an adventure," I said. He snorted.

We therefore turned back to Bissao, and after enquiring, found the river bank road to Xima. This road, which ran some fifty yards from the Geba, rapidly deteriorated from a fairly good, graded thoroughfare into a rutted track.

It was fortunate that it was not the rainy season, for the way would have been impassable. But the cost of the dry season was that a *harmattan* began blowing. This was a hot, sandy wind from the Sahara, which was the curse of West Africa during this time of the year. Fortunately, after passing over the rain forest, a lot of the grit it carried had been lost and it was bearable. In the north of Senegal and French Soudan, visibility could be brought down to zero, and a veritable sandstorm, sometimes lasting for the whole day, made any movement impossible.

The river, and therefore the track, was relatively straight and we drove east for several hours. We passed through a number of fishing villages, but did not stop. We noticed that there were more Diola tribes, shorter and more thickset than the elegant Balanta.

We reached Xima towards dusk, after a day of hard driving. Xima seemed to have nothing to recommend a stop, so, after topping up our tank at a rusty pump, we decided to drive straight through and sleep in the bush. I remembered my previous night's lodging only too well.

The road wound on and after some miles we found a clearing and stopped for the night. There was no traffic at all.

The forest was not quite so thick, and just before it became dark, we made our way down to the river. We sat on the bank for a while, smoking and listening to the many sounds. The river flowed quietly by and, apart from the sudden shriek of a monkey or, perhaps, a parrot, there was peace.

Then Sarr jumped up and shouted for me to do the same. He pointed to the tangled roots of a mangrove tree and I looked, just in time to see the tail of a large crocodile slide into the water.

After that, we returned to the Explorer and, after a dinner of sardines, stale buns and mangoes, rolled ourselves in blankets and went to sleep. It was quite humid, and the blankets were more for protection from biting insects than warmth.

Early in the morning, we washed cautiously in the river and started our day's journey. We felt we should now head for the Casamance and so, since the broad estuary ended here and became a much narrower and fast flowing river, we followed it when it turned slightly northwards. The track got even more restricted and was full of quite deep potholes, further reducing our speed.

We had a very rudimentary map with us, full of areas marked 'unsurveyed' and so we stopped anyone we saw on the road, which was seldom, and asked in sign language, if we were headed for Bafatà, our next destination.

The *harmattan* was still blowing, so we decided to go back to my system of shooting some game and offering it to a village in exchange for a hut for the night. After an inadequate lunch, I saw quite a wide track go off to the left, away from the river. I drove down it for about a mile and stopped. I had noticed several animal trails leading into the forest.

"We will walk down this trail," I said to Sarr. "It looks well used and perhaps leads to a stream. We could see something there – animals come to streams in the evening to drink."

Sarr looked doubtful, but agreed. "I am sure if you shoot something we will find a village not far away," he said. "I noticed some palm groves and a small cultivated field."

As usual, I had my cartridge belt, with cartridges of various shot sizes. The shotgun was loaded, as always, with solid ball in one side and heavy shot in the other barrel. I could easily reload if we came across small deer or birds.

We followed the trail for some distance, seeing nothing. Just as I was getting discouraged and thinking of turning back, we came across a swampy, muddy patch of ground, full of animal tracks. These were a great mixture, ranging from the dainty hoof prints of gazelle, through the pointy spoor of *phacochère*, or wart-hog and, to my surprise, the deep and clear indentations made by, I thought, an African buffalo. Sarr agreed.

I checked the wind, but fortunately it was blowing into my face – forest animals, especially the rainforest buffalo, have a keen sense of smell, but weak hearing and eyesight. I whispered to Sarr to be very quiet and we walked slowly and cautiously forward.

The muddy track wound quite sharply and we moved slowly and cautiously. As we came round a thick tree there, before us was a clearing. A wide stream passed through it and the water had formed a pool between some rocks. There was a baobab on one side.

Standing beside the pool, dripping with mud, was a buffalo bull. He had obviously just emerged from the muddy water, where he had been having a wallow. He was, as far as I could see under the mud, a reddish-brown, with a heavy, muscular body and great curving horns, with a large boss between them. I heard Sarr give a gulp. *"Nagu àllwi,"* he whispered hoarsely. "Buffalo!" We had both stopped. The bull raised and turned his head and stared at me. He gave a loud grunt and pawed the ground. "Shoot, shoot, Chief," Sarr said. "He can run fast and will kill us." The bull stared and I could see he was feeling aggressive and challenged. I was a novice; I had never hunted game as big as this. The bull pawed the ground again and seemed to be gathering itself for a charge.

He was still standing slightly sideways, pointing to my left. I aimed just behind his left shoulder and fired the solid ball. The cartridge had a cardboard spiral which imparted spin to the heavy, round bullet, but it was still far from accurate. However, the bull was only some fifteen yards away, and I hit him squarely at my aiming point. He gave a great bellow and I fired the other barrel, with heavy shot, at the same spot.

He bellowed again, turned and rushed, like a demented bulldozer, into the undergrowth.

Sarr said: "Oh well hit, Chief, well hit. Now we must run to the car. *Nagu* is very strong and very clever. He will come back and wait for us and kill us. Come, come now." He was pulling at my arm and I was greatly tempted. But it was wrong to leave a wounded animal and run away. "No," I said. "He must be tracked and put out of his misery. You come if you want; I am going on."

Sarr looked at me. "You are my friend," he said. It was the first time he had ever called me that. "I go with you."

I reloaded, with ball in both barrels. We looked at the place where the bull had gone, and found a trail of blood. The end was an anticlimax: we found the bull, dead on the ground, about a hundred yards further on. He had been hit in the heart.

Sarr looked at him in wonder. "You killed a *nagu àllwi* with two shotgun shots," he said in an awestruck voice. "To kill buffalo you need heavy rifle. You are indeed brave and a great shot."

"Pure luck," I said. "It was self defence. Anyway, solid ball has a huge striking force." He looked at me with his eyes popping out. "Great hunter," he said reverently. I felt a fool and a fraud.

The bull was much too heavy – more than a quarter of a ton, I thought – for us to get back to the Explorer, so I tore my handkerchief into strips, and tied the pieces to the odd tree to mark the trail from the carcass to the main road. I hoped we could find a village and tell them about it before the many forest predators found the bull.

We went on up the main trail in the Explorer, and, as luck would have it, soon came upon a large village, with many conical huts thatched with river reeds. There were people about, and as I drove in, they came clustering round us.

They were of an unknown tribe, but wore bright sarongs and I noticed the women had elaborate hair arrangements, kept in place by red mud. They looked friendly though curious. Sarr tried Wolof, French and a smattering of Mandingo on them, but they just shook their heads. Then a young man pushed his way to the front, and hesitatingly spoke to Sarr.

"He speaks some little Wolof," said Sarr. "I will tell him to get the buffalo quick." He turned to the young man, and with many gestures and speaking very slowly, he explained the situation. At one point, he indicated me with his arm and, when the young man had translated his words, the assembled villagers gave a great sound of surprise and, it seemed, admiration.

"What did you tell them?" I asked.

"Oh, nothing," he said casually. "Just that you killed a *nagu*." He grinned as the villagers all stared at me. "I told them it was your gift to the village."

"Take some men with you in the car and show them where the bull is," I said. "You can leave me here, but come back soon."

Sarr spoke again and the young man spoke in turn.

A group of men, with knives and some woven rope, climbed

into the Explorer, and Sarr drove off back the way we had come. I sat down and lit a cigarette, trying very hard to be nonchalant, while everyone continued to stare.

Sarr returned after half an hour or so and told me that the men would cut up the carcass into manageable pieces and bring them to the village. "I did not want blood all over the car," he said, rather piously, I thought.

The young man, meanwhile, had gone off into the bush and now returned with a huge older man, in a decorated loin cloth and with a porcupine quill through his nose, as well as another man who was decorated with patterns all over his body, carried a carved staff and wore a head-dress of feathers, little wooden carvings and bits of coloured cloth. He also wore round his neck a series of necklaces, some of small bones, bits of leather, round beads of mud and other bits and pieces.

The young man introduced them to Sarr who, in turn, told me that the big man was the village chief and the other was the *shaman*, who was very powerful.

I asked that the chief should be given my respectful compliments and that he should be told I was not French and that I was just passing through on my way to Senegal.

This was duly translated. But I noticed that, at the end, the young man made a sign for horns and put his hand over his heart.

The chief looked at me in astonishment and put his hands on my shoulders. He looked down at me and said something. But before the young man could translate this to Sarr, the *shaman* stepped forward and said to me, in very good French: "We are told you shot a buffalo with a shotgun and have made it a gift to the village. The chief says you are a great hunter and welcome."

I was surprised and relieved that now I could communicate directly and that the cumbersome double translation could end. I bowed politely and said: "It is kind of the chief. I am very honoured and pleased, Monsieur le Sorcier (I did not know how to address him), to see that you speak such perfect French."

The man smiled. "Please do not call me a 'sorcier'. They are bad and have black thoughts. I am a *shaman* and we have good thoughts. You should not confuse us with the others."

The chief and the *shaman* went away towards one of the huts and I saw that the young man was speaking rapidly to Sarr, and gesturing with his arms. He looked worried.

After a while, he went away as well, and the crowd of villagers dispersed. I asked Sarr what had been going on.

"Chief," he said. "we have been very lucky." We sat down on the ground and he went on. "This tribe is well known in the area because of the *shaman*, who is a very famous man. The young man told me that he was a Master of Fire and extremely powerful with magic. He can heal and make spells and manipulate nature in many ways. He said that *shamans* have to study for a long time and practise great self-discipline – they are not witch-doctors, but can often remove evil spells and influences."

He paused and I lit a cigarette. Then he went on: "They can foretell the future by casting pebbles, bones and nuts on a sand shape. They can see into your soul." He rolled his eyes. "He can see right into your head."

"Nonsense," I said. "These are just stories." Sarr made the sign against the evil eye. "No, Chief. Truly, he can do many things."

"And what is all this nonsense about Master of Fire?" I enquired.

"I was told that there are three disciplines for *shamans*," said Sarr. "They are of Fire and Water and Earth. A *shaman* has to choose one to study and learn. Nobody can know more than one – too much knowledge for one man. He went away as an apprentice to a sacred forest in French Guinea for seven years and returned as a Master. He can control fire," he added, in an awestruck voice.

I was very sceptical. Control fire! Right.

The group of men came down the road, carrying large cuts of fresh meat, all that remained of the buffalo. The young man came back to us and Sarr passed on his message that there was enough meat for the village for several days, that the head would be used for *fetishes* and the hide would be useful too. He also said that we would be given a hut to spend the night – it was now almost dark – and that there would be a feast and dancing in my honour.

He took us to a hut, which was clean and comfortable, with woven grass mats on the floor and a bed of fresh leaves and boughs, and we settled in, and cleaned up as much as we could. The drums started a soft, complicated rhythm. We went outside and found that there was a large fire burning, with meat being roasted on a lattice of green branches above it and a large cauldron, steaming and emitting an appetising smell.

The villagers were assembling and seating themselves in a large circle around the fire, but well away from it. There were some young women busy over the food.

The chief and the *shaman* arrived together. They motioned me to sit between them, with Sarr on the other side of the chief.

The *shaman* turned to me and said: "My name is Bulo-Doduna. You may use this name. What is yours?" I gave him my full name and that of Sarr.

He put both his hands on my arm and looked into my eyes, bringing his face close. After a moment, he nodded his head and said: "Yes... yes... I can tell you that your wife and two children are well, but they want you to return."

I was surprised, but not impressed. Sarr had probably let the information drop or it was just a good guess. Bulo-Doduna smiled. "So you are not convinced?" he asked. "It was not a guess." It was a bit uncanny.

We were brought some goats milk; there must have been a flock somewhere. It was fresh and tasted good, though rather strong.

There was a small group of men with drums some distance away. The constant rumbling and rhythmic thumping had a slightly soporific effect.

Two women approached us, with sizzling meat on large leaves. The smell was appetizing.

The chief motioned me to take some, but I declined politely, indicating that he should have the first portion. Bulo-Doduna said something to the women, who selected some meat and gave it to me, insisting that I take it. The chief, the *shaman* and Sarr were served, and gradually the whole circle was given some.

Bulo-Doduna turned to me. "If you are expecting some buffalo meat, you will be disappointed," he said. "It has to be cooked for at least a day and a night to become good to eat – it is very strong, like the animal."

"So what is this meat?" I asked. I had been unable to identify it: there were some sausage-like pieces and some quite large lumps, rather fatty. These were wrapped in individual small leaves. There was also something which was much like *fufu*, the doughy cassava filler.

"The long bits are snake," said Bulo-Doduna. "It is very good and will protect you from disease. The other pieces are porcupine, to give you energy (he called it 'force'). It is good if you are travelling."

The meal was good and the small leaves gave an additional, not unpleasant taste to the meat.

When everyone had eaten their fill, the chief, and the other men, took some yellowish leaves, and began to chew them. I noticed that Bulo (as I began to call him), was not chewing. I looked at him and raised my eyebrows. He smiled and said: "You can take it or not. It is not good at first so I advise you not to chew. It makes you forget and makes you dream small dreams."

"I have to help a woman," he said and stood up. "You stay and look if you want." He went over to one side of the assembled men, some twenty yards away, and squatted on the ground. A man brought him a large armful of green boughs and leaves and put them before him. Bulo arranged them in a rough pyramid and thrust his right arm deep into the boughs. He closed his eyes and, after a minute or so, a small wisp of smoke arose from the pyramid. I had not seen him use any form of match, lighter or anything else to start his fire, which soon was burning with yellow, jumping flames. He left his arm in the fire for a good five minutes, while the green wood and leaves burned. It was eerie.

He then took his arm out and it looked unscathed. Reaching into a pouch tied to this loincloth, he took out a handful of something which looked like dried grass or herbs and sprinkled it on his fire. As the soft wind blew towards us, I could smell an aromatic, herby quality and realised that he had positioned his fire so that the wind would blow the smoke towards us. Everyone had moved, so that now we formed a semi-circle before him.

Four women led a young girl towards him and he motioned that she should sit in the smoke. The women backed away and she sat, looking frightened, before him.

He stood and taking a burning green bough from his fire, he began a low chant and rubbed the burning wood on her back and breast. She did not react and there was no sign of pain or smarting from the girl. He put his other hand on her head and sang a long sentence. The he put the burning branch back onto the fire and signed her to get up. She did so and bowing her head, went away into a hut. I noticed, to my surprise, that although the fire had now been burning for some time, it had not diminished at all.

Bulo walked over to me. "She had a bad thing inside her and I had to kill it. It is now dead and she will live a long life," he said. "But of course you do not believe."

I did not know what to say, so I asked: "How do you get green wood to burn without any matches or anything?" He smiled and said simply: "Thought."

"I do not do this much," he then said. "But I wish you to comprehend and remember." He pointed to Sarr and beckoned him. Sarr looked terrified and pretended he did not understand. Bulo said to him: "Come!" and Sarr reluctantly rose and came slowly towards us, looking at me imploringly.

"Do not be afraid," said Bulo. "I only wish to show you something." He turned to me. "There is fire in everything," he said. "That is why I chose it more than water or earth. I tell you now that you may not take your vehicle out of the village unless I permit it."

"What do you mean?" I asked. I was worried in case we were being kidnapped.

Bulo laughed. "No, no," he said. "The vehicle does not want to go." He turned to Sarr. "Go on, get in and try to drive out beyond that tree." He pointed to a tree on the fringe of the village. Sarr looked at me and I nodded.

The Explorer started without difficulty and I could see Sarr grinning as he drove towards the tree. Just as he came level with it, his lights went out and the engine died. He tried to restart it, but nothing happened. The car was dead.

We looked under the bonnet, but everything seemed to be in order, except that there was no electricity anywhere. The lights, horn or starter simply would not work.

Bulo, who had been standing beside us, watching with amusement, said: "Push the vehicle back a bit and try again."

With the help of some men, who had gathered round, we did so and the Explorer promptly started, with no difficulty at all. Sarr drove it forward to the tree again, and it stopped dead, like the previous time.

Sarr looked scared and frantically started to look again at the engine; I think he thought he was being challenged but was also very anxious. He looked at everything in great detail. I helped, but we could not find anything amiss – the engine was dead. Bulo just stood there and grinned.

We pushed the Explorer back again and it started immediately. Sarr, thinking to outwit whatever was happening, promptly turned the car round and headed off in the opposite direction. When he reached the edge of the village, the engine died.

He tried the same thing in a number of directions, even in reverse, but the same thing happened.

"Chief," he whispered when I told him to stop trying. "We will remain here forever. They will probably eat us at the end. He is a mighty *shaman*."

Bulo came up to me. "See," he said. "Fire controls everything. If you control fire you control all."

I nodded. "It is true," I said. "I cannot understand it but I have to believe my eyes."

Bulo smiled. "You should not believe any of your senses," he said. "You should have faith."

He went back to his private fire, which was burning well and apparently not consuming any of the boughs or leaves. He squatted beside it and motioned to the group of men, who were drumming quietly. They stopped, and one of them brought Bulo a medium sized drum. It was a hollow piece of log with an animal skin stretched tightly across the top.

Bulo took it and threw a large handful of his herbs on the fire, from which erupted a thick smoke which drifted towards us.

He began to drum slowly, in an intricate rhythm, and made a keening sound, high-pitched and monotonous. The beat gradually accelerated and he closed his eyes. His hands were moving faster and faster; the smoke billowed towards us. It was now quite dark, except for the light from his fire and the main blaze, where the cauldron of buffalo meat was simmering.

Suddenly, two of the younger women stood up and began to weave their bodies sinuously, in time with the drum beat. Then more stood up and began to dance. The men remained sitting. Bulo's hands became a blur and he leaned his head back, the chant getting louder and louder. The women began to take steps and dance in a small circle, their heads raised and their eyes closed. I was entranced. This was truly Africa as I had always imagined it. Sarr, who looked terrified, huddled close to me.

After some time, the women were stamping and twisting their bodies, sweat running freely over their breasts and legs. They waved their arms and their eyes were open, staring blankly at the sky. Then, as the drum beat reached a crescendo, one fell to the ground and lay there, twitching convulsively, her body rippling in regular spasms. Then another, and another, until the three formed the centre of the circle where the others danced.

I lost track of time; the dance and the drumming seemed to go on and on. I was in a daze, the smoke, aromatic and spicy, was swirling round, and I felt dizzy and disoriented. It was hard to focus my eyes and the drumming was filling my head.

I think the recumbent bodies rose slightly from the ground, in a horizontal position, before settling back after a few minutes, but I cannot be sure.

The drumming slowed and stopped. After a few minutes, the women recovered and went off together to the darkness behind the huts. Bulo stood up and took a deep breath. He put the drum on the ground and extended his arms over his fire, uttering a short sentence. The fire died down and went out. The boughs and leaves looked untouched.

I was still somewhat light-headed, when Bulo came over to me and said:" The chief wishes you to have two women for the night."

I grasped at my automatic excuse. "Two women?" I asked. "I

am so disappointed I cannot take advantage of the chief's hospitality. Please thank him and say, with the greatest respect, that it is against my religion to have women when I travel. I have made a vow."

Bulo looked surprised. "If that is your wish," he said.

"But why two?" I asked. "Is it not usual to give only one?"

"The chief said that any man who can kill a buffalo with one shotgun cartridge must be a great hunter and specially honoured," Bulo replied.

We retired to our hut, where I immediately fell asleep, prey to monstrous and magical dreams.

The following morning, we rose early. I wanted to get on the way as soon as possible – we had a long way to go – but I was still worried that the Explorer would not leave the village.

There were some women about, coming out of the forest with water containers on their heads, but the rest of the village was quiet.

"Where do you think we can find Bulo or the young man who translated yesterday?" I asked Sarr.

He shrugged his shoulders. "I do not know," he said. "I expect that Bulo is in the spirit hut. But I am not going there for anything."

The spirit hut, in which Bulo lived, was a little apart from the others. It was the same conical reed construction, but was hung about with fetishes, round, shield-like woven mats with magical patterns, some strips of cloth, brightly dyed with local indigo colour and skeletons of small animals.

I went towards it, while Sarr hung back. "Oh Master Bulo," I shouted. "May we see you?"

After a moment, Bulo came out, rubbing his eyes. "You wish to speak with me?" he asked.

"Yes, please," I said. "I am sorry to disturb you, but we wanted to thank you and the chief for your friendship and hospitality; we must leave you now." He nodded, "By the way," I added casually, "could you please release my car from your magic, so that we may leave the village?"

Bulo grinned. "Magic?" he asked. "No such thing. I am sure there will be no difficulty, if there ever was." He crinkled his eyes. "I will convey your good wishes to the chief; he seldom is awake at this time. You will be heading for Tambacounda, I expect. It is quite a long way and you will have troubles but it will end well." He pointed. "Go in this direction all day, and do not camp near the swamp – stop before it or after it."

He walked to the Explorer with us. He put his hand on my shoulder and smiled. "I hope you are wiser than yesterday. It will end well for you." He then turned to Sarr, and put both hands on his arm. Sarr looked uneasy, but, after a moment, Bulo said to him: "It will also be good for you. You will have what you want before twelve months are over." Sarr looked bewildered and thanked him.

The last sight of the village we had was Bulo standing with his arm raised, in front of the cooking fire. There was no hesitation as the Explorer drove easily out of the village into the bush, following a narrow footpath into the rapidly thinning forest.

It was our intention to drive though eastern Casamance, try to skirt the end of the Gambia and get to the major town of Tambacounda, having passed through the National Park of Niokolo-Koba, the only nature reserve at the time in Senegal.

It would be a challenge to get to Tambacounda, since we would be steering largely by compass, crossing rivers and swamps, and mostly driving through forest and savannah. When we reached our destination, it would be relatively quick to follow the main road to Dakar, some 220 miles away.

The ground was dry and the *harmattan* was not blowing, so we made good time. There were no landmarks we knew and we hoped we were travelling in the right direction. We crossed some streams and rivers (we only had to winch ourselves out once) and passed through a number of small, isolated villages, where we did not stop. In the evening, I was lucky enough to shoot some partridge and these were our dinner, barbecued on a small fire. They were very tough and tasted gamey.

Since we travelled cross-country, we saw no other traffic and very few people.

We had successfully passed through the swamp which Bulo had mentioned. It was slow going and the engine overheated, so we had to stop, in two feet of fetid water, while it cooled. The air was thick with mosquitoes and we wrapped cloths round our heads and hands, but they still got through and bit us mercilessly. We were both taking a daily pill of some kind of anti-malarial compound, but Sarr had been told they were not very effective. There were also little black flies, whose sting was even more painful. It was a great relief when we started again, and the Explorer climbed painfully out of the stinking water and mud onto drier land in the forest.

We spent the night among the trees, on soft beds of green boughs. There were supposed to be many poisonous snakes about, but we did not see any on that day, although on the next day we saw what I thought was a forest cobra slither across the road. It was black, quite small, some three feet long (they grow to eight feet) but deadly. There was also a thin green one which skimmed at high speed across the path in front of us. It may have been a mamba.

Crossing one of the rivers – this time a wide, shallow one – we saw, about a hundred yards upstream where there was a deeper pool, a hippopotamus, placidly grazing on the bottom. Every time it raised its head, it would give a cavernous yawn – the mouth was huge.

At midday the following day, we stopped at a small village. There was a man there, dressed quite properly in a white robe and turban, who turned out to speak fluent Wolof. After interrogating him, Sarr said: "He is from a tribe of Manjaks. They are good people and harmless. He says to go a bit more to the left and we will get to the road of Niokolo-Koba. But on no account to go right."

"Why?" I enquired. "What's to the right?"

"He said that there are some villages of Felup tribe people. They are thieves and robbers and murderers and they will attack travellers. He says keep the gun handy." He paused. "By the way, he says we are now in Casamance."

We exchanged two packets of cigarettes for a basket of mangoes, papayas and guavas, which made a welcome addition to our rather boring diet. Then, not wishing to get involved in tribal hospitality, we drove on, to camp beside a swift brook. The water, however, was brown and undrinkable, though adequate for washing.

I estimated that, barring mishaps, we should get to the main road in another couple of days, and was beginning to feel quite cheerful. I discovered, to my surprise, that Sarr knew the song: "Auprès de ma blonde," and so we sang it, very loudly, and improvising new, somewhat rude, verses.

The mishaps began the following day. We were in grassland, and going at a fairly good pace. I was driving and enjoying the view: there were baobabs, ebony trees, mahogany and calabash scattered about, and great flocks of birds, large, small, coloured and plain everywhere. Beside the path, we saw some large, black and white marabout storks in a group, pecking at the grass with their long, straight bills. It looked as though there was a carcass of something, on which they were feasting.

I drove on, and did not notice that the grass was getting longer and interspersed with reeds, while the ground got softer. The wheels began to spin, so I engaged low range and revved the engine. The Explorer lunged forward and there was a nasty crack, as the front hit something and we stopped.

Sarr and I looked at each other. "Better have a look," I said.

The ground looked muddy and the Explorer was in it up to the axles. We took off our shoes and socks and stepped into it.

It was difficult to see what was wrong. The front of the car had hit a large rock, which had driven the winch back several inches. There seemed to be no damage that would prevent us from continuing, so we got back into the Explorer and I slowly reversed out and back to slightly drier land. The water temperature on the dial was rising rapidly and we stopped to have another look.

The blow on the rock had dented and perforated the radiator and we were losing water rapidly. This was serious. The hole was not large but we had nothing with which to repair it. Chewing gum may have done it, but I did not have any.

"We have to plug it up," I said to Sarr. "How can we do it?"

He scratched his head and shrugged his shoulders. "I do not know, Chief," he said. "Perhaps some clay or something…"

By now the water had run out and the radiator was empty.

There was no point in filling it up again while the hole was there. I pondered.

After some discussion, we came to the conclusion that the best way to improvise was to take a piece of wood and whittle it to a point. Then to heat some wax from a candle (we had a packet) and, having hammered the wooden spike into the hole, pour some melted wax all round it. It probably would not hold for long, but at least could be repeated and enable us to continue.

This we duly did and, since there was no water around, refilled the radiator with our precious drinking water from the jerrican. I started the engine, and the plug held.

It was obvious that we could not go on through the increasingly swampy terrain, so I turned left and tried to drive round the marsh.

It was a tedious business. The air was full of insects, the bog was featureless, it was very hot and humid and there was a fetid stench pervading everything. To cap it all, with turnings and weavings and avoiding some deep mud pits, we realised we had lost our way.

The compass was not much use, since often the direction in which we wished to go was impassable. The swamp seemed endless.

It took us three days to escape onto firm ground, fortunately more or less in the right direction. We were both filthy, tired and despondent. We were also hungry, since we had finished our meagre provisions and there was nothing around that I could shoot.

But the worst problem was water. We had used up the water in our jerricans to keep the radiator filled. The plug had failed twice and every time we repaired it, a lot of water was lost. We felt that the priority was to keep going, so we filtered the swamp water (there were no running streams) through a double handkerchief, which got rid of the visible wriggly things. After that, we boiled it over a fire in a tin basin we had and drank it when it was cool.

It occurred to me that the microbes, which undoubtedly populated the swamp, might be killed by spirits, so we took out the bottles of whisky, concealed under the seat, and drank a half-and-half mixture of this with swamp water. The taste was indescribable, but at least it was a liquid.

Sarr shied away from our mixture initially. "I am a Moslem," he declared. "I cannot drink alcohol. I shall go to Jehenna." "Look," I said, "better a live sinner than a dead saint. Besides, I need you to help with the Explorer." Finally he agreed.

We also came across the bacon, which I had bought in Bathurst and secreted with the whisky. I had forgotten about it and, anyway, it was green and rancid so I threw it away.

When we finally got onto the firm savannah north of the swamp, I drove as fast as I could across the plains. After a day's hard driving we camped under a huge baobab tree and I managed, though feeling slightly muzzy and also rather tight on the whisky mixture (we had still not found any clean water) to shoot some more partridge and a small gazelle which we had to chase in the Explorer. It was a lucky shot.

We feasted on my quarry and slept. The following morning early after checking the radiator, which was more or less holding, we drove on. After a fierce bump, there was a resounding 'crack' and I stopped.

We got out to look and found that one of the rear half-axles on the Explorer had come adrift. There was no way to repair this, and after removing it completely, we fastened a log to the rear side of the car, like a skid, to replace the missing rear wheel, which we also had to remove. This limited our speed to only about ten miles an hour and we limped slowly on. Fortunately, after only about twenty miles, we reached the main road, just east of Niokolo-Koba.

Perhaps 'main road' is too flattering a description. It was a broad red laterite clay track, full of corrugations and potholes; but to us it seemed like a super highway after the previous two weeks. We were still limping along with our improvised crutch, which needed replacing after every twenty miles or so, as it wore down through friction with the road. We drove with front wheel drive, having disconnected the rear drive shaft.

There was still no water or food and we were getting desperate. As we drove, we kept a sharp lookout for villages, but there were none. I was not feeling at all well, and have only a hazy memory of our escape from the swamp. I do vaguely remember that Sarr, who said he was feeling fine, managed somehow to negotiate the rivers we had to cross, notably the Casamance and the Gambia. I was of no help to him.

In the late afternoon, we saw a cloud of dust approaching down the road and stopped. The cloud resolved itself into a man on a motorcycle, who also stopped beside us. He turned off his engine, as we had done.

The man was an extraordinary sight. He was white, with a pale, freckled face and a huge mop of red hair, as well as a bushy red beard and moustache. His eyes were of a piercing blue, and he was stocky and looked very strong. He was dressed in faded, dirty khaki shirt and shorts, with a pair of boots. He wore no hat. He looked to be in his sixties.

The motorcycle was old but looked serviceable. It was hung about, front, rear and sides, with a variety of bags, sacks and a suitcase on the pillion. There was also a spare tyre hanging at the back.

As the man dismounted, I noticed he had an enormous revolver, in a holster, on his hip.

I got wearily out of the Explorer. He looked at me. "Bong giourr, Missiew," he said, with what sounded like an Irish accent.

I took a chance. "It is a pleasure to see you," I said, in English.

A broad smile spread over his wrinkled face. "Well from the sound of it you are English," he said. " I suppose it is that little bit better than the French." He put out his hand, and I shook it. He looked at me suspiciously. "Have you been drinking, at all, young man?" he asked. "Not something to do in this heat when you are driving."

With an effort, I focussed my eyes and briefly explained the situation to him; he examined our makeshift arrangement with interest. He then produced two water bottles and gave one each to Sarr and me. "Drink, my boy, but not too fast," he said. "Then we will see what can be done."

The water was like nectar. I began to feel better, though I thought I was running a fairly high temperature. Sarr and I drank the bottles empty, and we all sat down, in the shade of the

Explorer, with a sigh of contentment.

"I am Father O'Reilly," said the man. "I ride around West Africa and try to save the heathen. I have been doing it for more than thirty years." He patted the revolver. "They seldom give me trouble – you sometimes need strong persuasion to plant the seed of faith."

We sat for a long time. I told him who I was and what I did, and he told me tales of his wanderings throughout the area, converting whole villages. He was very pragmatic about it all. "Sure, the Moslems are a good lot. They believe in one God and have rules of conduct, with sins and virtues not unlike ours. But there are some very primitive tribes, mainly animist, who are cruel and greedy and who do not behave. They are my target. But there is a lot of difficulty with the *shamans* and witch-doctors and sorcerers. The bad ones have to be neutralised, and even the good ones hate to share their power." I thought it would be indiscreet to ask what he meant by 'neutralised'.

As we spoke, I translated bits into French for Sarr, but he mostly just sat, staring fixedly at the revolver.

Father Patrick gave us some smoked meat and some millet bread he had. We ate it ravenously, with some more water.

We found that it had grown dark and decided to spend the night where we had stopped. We made a small fire and Father Patrick produced a kettle, in which he made some sweet tea. It was delicious. He seemed to have an inexhaustible supply of everything in his various bags, sacks and pouches.

Before going to sleep, he got to his knees and said some simple prayers. Awkwardly, I knelt beside him. Sarr had moved a little way off, perhaps so as not to be contaminated by a foreign faith. But I had never seen him pray.

I tossed and turned all night. I had taken a handful of aspirins, the only medication I carried, but they seemed to do no good. At dawn, Sarr and Father Patrick prepared breakfast, chatting amicably in Wolof which the Father spoke fluently. I only had some more tea.

Sarr had explained to the Father our problem with the radiator, which was beginning to leak again. Father Patrick thought for a moment and said: "Do you not have a tyre repairing kit? You must have." Both our spare tyres were flat.

I nodded. Father Patrick said: "Well, why do you not use a repair patch to block the hole? A small patch of rubber with the adhesive you have will be much better than your makeshift arrangement."

Of course. Why had we not thought of it? Sarr immediately prepared and applied a patch – only losing a little water – and coated the whole with a liberal amount of adhesive. It seemed to work.

Father Patrick said: "I will do my good deed then." He got on his motorcycle. "I will go back to Niokolo-Koba, which is only about fifteen miles away, and warn them that you are coming. There is a small ranger station on the road, and they can look after you. From there, it is only about sixty miles to Tambacounda, and you can sort everything out there."

We thanked him and he turned the motorcycle round and disappeared back in the direction from which he had come in a cloud of dust. We made sure our skid was firmly attached and followed, at a very much more sedate pace.

It took us three hours to get to Niokolo-Koba. The countryside was changing all the time. Behind us, in the far distance, there were some quite high hills, which became the major highlands of Fouta Djalon. This was a plateau, more than 3000 feet high, which was a sort of Shangri-La, cool, green and restful. It was the home of the Fula tribe, a civilised and friendly people; it was always a regret that I had not managed to visit it.

All round us there were patches of forest, with some striking scarlet *flamboyant* trees, baobabs with enormous trunks, and many other species. There were patches of savannah and some gently rolling hills.

We finally reached a little group of huts, which was the home of the wardens of the National Reserve. As we drove slowly into the small compound, dragging our crutch, which was disintegrating, we saw Father Patrick talking to a tall man, who was wearing a smart khaki uniform and a red hat. They walked towards us.

"There you are," said Father Patrick. "You certainly take your time."

I was feeling weak and it was difficult to stand; I could not concentrate. "Listen, Father," I said, in English. "I am not well, but my friend Sarr is very capable, and will cope. He has my full authority to do anything he wants." I paused and leaned on the Explorer. "Please thank this gentleman for receiving us and if there was a bedroll in some shade where I could rest, I would be very grateful."

I must have staggered, because I felt an arm supporting me and leading me into a hut, shady and slightly cooler than the heat in the sun, where I lay down on a mattress and went to sleep.I half-woke once or twice when I felt an arm lift me up and hold a glass of water to my lips, which I emptied greedily.

I must have slept for some eighteen hours, because it was morning when I woke. Sarr was sitting beside me, watching me. When he saw my eyes open, he gave me some more water, with some aspirins and grinned broadly. The water was strongly laced with whisky, which he believed to be a sovereign cure for infidels.

"Chief," he said, maintaining a broad grin. "I have wonderful news."

"What is your wonderful news?" I croaked.

"The Explorer is much happier," he said. "It is cured."

"What on earth do you mean," I asked. This was all beyond me.

"I found that M'Baye Doudou, the top man here, had a broken Land Rover which had been driven hard into a tree," he said. The front was destroyed and they had to get a new one." He paused and grinned even more broadly. "But the back was undamaged. So, with some help, I replaced our broken half-shaft and put our wheel back on. Everything is reconnected. Now we can drive as usual."

He then put on a worried expression. "But I had to give them all our money, yours and mine." He paused again. "And also two bottles of whisky from the four we have left."

"The red-haired man said it was all right," he added. "You said so."

I was too tired and weak to do more than nod. "It is fine," I muttered. "Get some food and water and drive me back to Dakar as fast as you can. There is no need to stop anywhere, not even Tambacounda. Just drive and sleep when you get too tired."

It was about 350 miles back to Dakar, but the road was not too bad and, if the radiator held together, we should do it in a couple of days. We were low on petrol, but the ranger gave us enough to reach Tambacounda where Sarr could fill up at the Shell station. He got some fruit and bread, and filled our water jerrican.

I have a vague recollection of slumping down in the Explorer seat, and Sarr tying me to it with a piece of rope. Then everything becomes a blur. There was endless diving, stopping, dark and light. Lying beside the Explorer at night on a blanket and being tied into the seat again in the morning. Eating occasional mouthfuls of food and drinking water. It seems that the radiator hole opened again and we lost all the water from the radiator, which had to be replaced from our jerrican, after repair with an adhesive patch. So the drinks of water I was given were strongly laced with whisky, to make it go further and as medication. This, combined with regular aspirins, made my head swim and I alternated between a waking sleep and, I think, unconsciousness.

After what seemed like years, the Explorer stopped. I looked blearily out of the window, and saw, with astonishment, that we were outside the house in Dakar. With Sarr's help, I stumbled in. I remember vaguely staggering down the corridor, bouncing from wall to wall; Wendy's horrified face; and the bedroom, where I collapsed on the bed as everything went black.

CHAPTER SIX

Senegal - Journey to Timbuktu

It was some ten days before I was again aware of my surroundings. I emerged from my crisis as weak as a kitten and hardly able to lift my hand. The first thing I remember was Wendy's concerned face, a cooling, damp cloth on my brow and, behind her, Diallo hovering anxiously.

There had been brief flashes of wakefulness; periods of intense cold, with goose pimples and shivering, when Wendy piled blankets on me to give the illusion of warmth; sudden hot episodes, with sweat starting all over my body as I threw off all coverings; a raging thirst but inability to eat; a strange man visiting sporadically, and listening to my chest.

Wendy later told me how horrified she had been when I arrived that evening, staggering from wall to wall in the corridor and stinking of whisky. My eyes, she said, were scarlet and I was incoherent. At first, she was cross, thinking that I was drunk. My clothes were filthy and I was unshaven, I was days late returning from the trip and she had been desperately worried. But as soon as she touched me, she realised I had a high fever, and was very ill.

She somehow managed to get Shell to call a doctor, who quickly diagnosed malaria, with some complications. He was very caring and had much experience, and after my ten days of delirium – Wendy said I babbled incoherently and, at one stage, the doctor thought I was going to die – managed to restore me to a stable and improving state.

While I was still in a weak condition and staying in the house, Nikki, quite inexplicably, also developed malaria, though the doctor was able to cure her fairly quickly.

But this was a hard time for Wendy, with an invalid and a sick child to care for, to say nothing of Robin, who was mobile and required attention. But Diallo was a great support, recruiting an extra *fatou* to help with the cleaning, shopping, cooking and with Robin. It was a good team and, as always, Wendy pulled the family through.

Luc who had never forgotten his Christmas with us, came to call, and said: "Well, you are a great mixture of hero and idiot." I told him I did not know what he was talking about. I could, by now, walk around but was still rather wobbly on my feet.

He grinned. "Sarr has been shooting his mouth off all over the place. The whole company now has a detailed account of what you have been up to, though I wonder if it really was as colourful as we are told."

"What on earth has he been saying?" I asked. Luc took a sip of his cold *sirop*. This was a French concentrated syrup of fruit, much diluted with water. There were no other soft drinks to be had.

"Oh, nothing," he said airily. "Just that you saved his life by shooting a charging buffalo with your shotgun, that you saved him from an attack by cannibals, that you outwitted a witch doctor and that sort of thing." He grinned broadly. "Quite a hero," he added, "though if any of it is true and you did try for a buffalo with a shotgun, you must be mad."

"It is all vastly exaggerated," I said crossly. "Just wait till I get my hands on him."

The doctor had told me that there was no question of my going off on trips for at least a month and that I should occupy myself locally. There was no reaction from the office, though our friends the de Freschevilles were concerned and invited us to their flat quite often. There was the beach, of course but life was somewhat monotonous. Money continued to be a problem and we had to be very careful how we spent the small amount available. Diallo was, as always, most helpful and took over the domestic side completely.

Sarr came to visit and to show me a completely refurbished Explorer, now as good as new, which he left at the house. I tackled him about his wild tales of our journey south. "How can you tell such lies to everybody?" I asked. "You know we never did anything as dangerous as you said. You have made us look stupid."

"Well, Chief," he said, rather shamefacedly, "it was a big adventure. Monsieur never did anything like that." He shuffled his feet. "Anyway," he added. "Stories should be exciting or people get bored. I did not tell any lies, just made everything a bit bigger."

I had only once been able to take Wendy outside the Dakar area. I had driven her out roughly in the Kaolack direction. My destination, which I thought was impressive, was a little way into the bush, a huge mosque being built with amateur labour, devout Moslems who gave their labour free. Wendy had been very excited, not only to see the mosque, but by the whole excursion, the villages through which we passed, the baobabs and the colourful dress of the people. "It is wonderful to be out of the town for once", she had said. But this was the occasion when, on returning home, we had found the current *fatou* entertaining numerous friends to tea.

With Diallo in charge, however, we felt we could safely leave the house during the day from time to time.

We went on an unforgettable and haunting visit to Gorée Island, just off the coast of Dakar. This entailed a short trip in a little ferry and we could see a small, light-brown settlement on the island as we approached. There was a sizeable fort, quite a number of two storey houses and a collection of bungalows and huts. The buildings were all of mud bricks, some were painted and looked very old. There were some trees and, notably, some *flamboyants* in flower.

Gorée was probably the main slave holding warehouse and shipping site on the west coast of Africa and a pivotal point in the Europe – Africa – America trade route. We heard that more than 20 million slaves had been shipped west during the fifteenth to nineteenth centuries. These represented about a third of the total collected and gathered from the interior – the death rate was very high.

We saw the Slave House, where many were kept. There were eight foot square cells, which accommodated up to thirty men, similar quarters for women and narrow cells for children, who were packed like sardines in a can. All wore chains round their necks and legs and the men carried a sixteen pound iron ball, attached to their chain. It was impossible to flee, though apparently a large number threw themselves into the sea, where the weights made them sink, to be eaten by the myriad sharks which clustered round the island, attracted by such easy prey, rather than have a life of slavery.

Young girls were segregated and specially prized, and were frequently used by the slave traders, who lived on the upper floor, in luxurious, airy rooms. Any resulting children assured the girl of freedom, and the *signores*, as they were called, became the aristocracy of St. Louis, then the capital.

There was a terribly oppressive air about the place, even though the sun was shining and the sea looked blue. Wendy, particularly sensitive to what she called 'vibes', was unhappy and distressed. When we saw the sloping corridor which led to the 'Gate of no return', and thence to a small, palm wood wharf where the slaves were loaded onto ships, we decided we had had enough.

I noticed a little old Wolof standing by the wall, with a sad, seamed face and crinkly grey hair. I smiled at him, but he looked through me.

We walked around – the island was tiny, just a few hundred yards long. We saw the fort, with its huge ramparts in clay and cannon still standing at the parapets, guarding the anchorage. There were narrow alleys with houses, but no shops. Just a few stands selling warm drinks and peanuts.

As we left on the little boat to return to Dakar, I looked back. There were some small children playing in the dust under a brilliant *flamboyant* tree They were laughing and running about. I remember thinking that such a huge tragedy was beyond imagining. Both Wendy and I were very unhappy and disturbed by our visit.

Later that week Diallo told us that a wrestling tournament

was to be held in town, and urged us to go to it, leaving the children with him. Senegalese wrestling was one of the favourite sports in Dakar. There were national and international tournaments and weekly impromptu challenges and fights. These took place on an enormous open area, of earth and sand, within the town. There were no seats and no marked out fighting space – simply a vast, bare field. We took our place on the edge of this and looked around.

There were many spectators: drum bands, all playing independently; gatherings of fans of particular fighters; children rushing around; and small groups of gorgeous *fatous*, slim and elegant in their best finery, with coloured wraps and tall swathed turban head-dresses in pastel chiffon. They stood together, swaying in time to the rhythm of the drums, casting casual glances at the wrestlers.

Within the boundaries of the field were the fighters. These were impressive individuals, strutting and preening, to a rhythm of their own. There were the more famous and popular ones, each with his own court of drummers, flag carriers and a sort of jester, in fancy clothes and headgear who capered acrobatically before them as they swaggered along. I noticed that one of these fighter groups was waving the Union Jack and discovered that he was the champion of Gambia, come to challenge his Senegalese neighbours.

The fighters themselves were large men, dressed in loincloths and hung about with many *gri-gri*, or religious and superstitious charms.

After a great deal of posturing and bravado, kicking of dust in the air and gesturing and with the drums continually beating powerful rhythms in the background, pairs of fighters would square off, in what looked a haphazard fashion, and begin to fight.

The object appeared to be to get your opponent to touch the ground with anything but his feet or hands. The fighters prowled round each other, on all fours, rhythmically lifting alternate arms. Then they would pounce, grapple and try to throw each other. There was much more bluster than action and the audience remained very cool. The ladies stood gossiping and meditatively chewing their tooth-sticks.

We felt happy to be there as part of the crowd, sharing such a colourful spectacle.

Another interesting excursion was to an exhibition of drumming. This took place in an open sort of theatre, with a stage and seats. We found places somewhat back from the platform, and settled down. We seemed to be the only non-Africans present. The seats filled up, with people glancing at us curiously; many smiled.

Before long, a man came onto the stage. He was wearing Wolof robes and carried a *sabar* drum, about two feet long called a *mben-mben*. The *sabar* family of Senegalese drums ranged from the small hand drum, through a whole spectrum of sizes and functions – dancing, accompaniment, part of a group and sending messages – to large bass talking drums which could be heard for miles.

The man on the stage looked around, and began to drum softly with both hands, holding the instrument under one arm. As he did so, the audience became quiet and attentive; apparently he was a well known performer.

The drumming slowly accelerated in tempo and got louder. After a few minutes, he was drumming so fast that his hands became a blur. He then started moving round the stage and, as the drumming grew to a frenzy, he knelt and finally rolled on the stage, mostly on his back, writhing and twisting his body. During all these manoeuvres, amazingly, the rhythm did not waver or hesitate for a second. It was constantly changing and of a subtlety that our untrained and unaccustomed ears could not appreciate; it was obviously a very special performance. The audience was rapt, and applauded loudly, stamping their feet, when the performer finally stopped, exhausted and with his body pouring with sweat.

There were other performers, with different types of drums, and a female singer who was accompanied by a man playing a *xalam mi*, a sort of Senegalese lute, with five strings, played with the thumbs.

Wendy was fascinated and enjoyed the costumes of people from different areas who strolled about enjoying the warm evening air almost as much as the evening's entertainment.

One day, Norbert said, during one of our many visits to his flat: "By the way, would you be interested in seeing the annual ceremony at the monument in the Central Square?"

"Yes, of course," we said. "What is it?"

"It is very colourful," he replied. "The chiefs come there in all their robes, the Governor comes, escorted by his *spahis* and so on."

At one of Norbert and Jean's teatimes, apart from getting to know Paul and Nicole Fernandez, who were part of our Spanish practice meetings, we had met another Shell executive and his wife.

He was a Frenchman of Egyptian extraction who was delighted to hear that I had been educated in Egypt. He, himself, spoke little Arabic, having been brought up in France, but it did establish a sort of bond between us.

He and his wife (a charming French lady), were childless and lived in a pleasant flat in one of the grand modern blocks lining the Central Square. It had a large balcony overlooking the square and was on the sixth floor. He invited us and the de Freschevilles to eat lunch and to view the ceremony.

On the appointed day, we presented ourselves and found that Norbert and Jean had already arrived. We went out onto the balcony and saw a large crowd was gathering about a monument on one side of the square. There was a French army band playing, rather badly but loudly, and a constant stream of limousines was disgorging the chiefs.

These, accompanied by their courtiers were easy to identify. Depending on tribe, they wore ceremonial robes of various colours and assorted splendour. I am sure they were not traditional – those would have been much simpler – but had been invented to outshine the competition. Many were in rich purple, sky-blue or emerald green plush and satin, with capes and turbans, everything lavishly decorated and embroidered in gold thread. They must have been unbearably hot. A courtier or two would hold a parasol over their heads to shield them from the fierce sun.

When they reached the monument, they formed a semi-circle

round it and waited.

There was a loud blast of trumpets, and a squadron of *spahis* trotted into the square. They were magnificent. Mounted on splendid horses, with decorated saddles and bridles and carrying long lances, they rode, in a column of threes, towards the monument. They were, it seemed, mostly Wolofs, led by French officers. They were dressed in marvellous uniforms of white or scarlet, with embroidered jackets, cloaks, tall matching hats, lances and shining swords. They formed ranks behind the chiefs and waited, the horses moving restlessly.

Finally, with another blast of trumpets, the Governor arrived in a large black limousine, flanked by motorcycle outriders. He climbed out and walked up to the monument, largely ignoring the assembled dignitaries. He was handed a large wreath, which he placed carefully at the base of the column and took a few steps back, pausing for a minute or so.

He then turned and walked slowly back to his limousine, nodding to various chiefs and shaking hands with one or two. The limousine departed to a loud blaring from the band, followed by the *spahis*, as escort, and the crowd gradually dispersed.

Seeing them had reawakened the interest Wendy had always had in riding. We found out that there was a military riding school, where the *spahis* were trained and the French officers indulged themselves with minor equestrian competitions and leisure riding in a large compound on the edge of the city.

Through our friend at the Brazilian embassy, whose wife also rode, we arranged that Wendy should be able to go there from time to time and ride the military horses, provided she accepted the French military riding disciplines. When she came back, after her first visit, she was stiff and sore, but ecstatic.

"You can't imagine what they made me do," she said, after a comforting cup of coffee. "I had to canter about without using the stirrups and to take low jumps with my arms folded. Besides, the horses are all stallions and very strong." She sighed. "But the teaching officer said he was pleased with me and said I could come back and ride whenever I wished." I was immensely proud of her, remembering my own unfortunate, and unique, experience in an attempt to go 'cubbing' in Sussex, when I fell off and the old mare I was on ran away. Wendy was very happy to be able to ride again.

I had now recovered sufficiently to be able to travel, though the doctor cautioned me to take it slowly at first. He also gave me the unpleasant news that I was to abstain from all alcohol for a minimum of twelve months. "The malaria seems to have affected your liver, which is much swollen and must be gently treated. But I am glad to say that the type of malaria you had, thankfully, is not the recurring sort but a one-off attack. However, you must not donate blood in the future."

Sarr laughed a lot when he heard of my forced abstinence. "You see, Chief," he chortled, "Islam knows what is right and here is Allah showing you the true path." I glared at him, but he was unabashed.

We went on a number of short trips in the newly refurbished and re-equipped Explorer. Sarr had doubled the storage capacity for petrol and water and also fitted containers in the back full off the most amazing number of spare parts. These would almost enable us to build a new car from scratch, although he assured me that everything was necessary, especially if I planned any more hare-brained trips into the bush or jungle. "If you prepare for things, they never happen," he said wisely.

We were still very hard up and hated the house. I wrote numerous notes to the Personnel Manager, complaining about the accommodation but received no answer. I tried to see him once, but was fobbed off by a secretary who said he could not be disturbed. Wendy suffered more than I as she was house-bound at night when I travelled, and so spent the long hours, when the children were asleep, working, in the heat, on her stamp collection. Her enthusiasm for the theatre was frustrated (since neither company Africans nor most of the French wanted to associate with us) and she disliked being idle. Diallo did his best to make her life easy, but living in Dakar was not much fun. Nikki continued at her school, prattling in perfect French to Diallo and the laundry *fatou*, but refusing to speak the lamguage to us.

"Why should I?" she asked reasonably. "You both speak English!"

Robin was now relatively, though precariously, mobile, and spent much happy time on the beach, toddling in and out of the sea.

Remembering Sarr's prowess with a fishing line on our trip to St. Louis, I decided to try to supplement our somewhat meagre diet by catching some fresh fish. Accordingly, provided with a rod, casting reel and some 'spoons', to attract the fish, I joined a line of Sunday fishermen on the sandy beach near N'Gor. I was a little way away from where the family and other bathers were lounging, as I cast into the ocean, beyond the surf, wading in up to my waist. The beach sloped gently and it was not really deep for about a hundred yards from the edge.

The system, which I covertly copied from the experts round me, was to cast out as far as possible, then immediately to reel in slowly so that the 'spoon', twirling and flashing in the water, enticed a fish to go for it.

I was astonished when, on my third cast, the rod was almost snatched from my hands and bent almost double as I gripped it hard. I began to reel in, tightening the brake, in short bursts. I was convinced I had at least a whale on the other end, the pull was so strong.

Fortunately, the fish tired before I did and I managed to pull it up onto the sand. It was a bonito of about three pounds, though I would have sworn it weighed a ton. I was immensely proud and bore it off in triumph to show the family, who were impressed. I preened myself as a great fisherman and said nonchalantly that I would go and get some more.

After an hour's fruitless casting, I gave up for the day. The bronzed Frenchmen round me were pulling in fish, many of substantial size, without too much difficulty. I determined to try again the following Sunday. But my disappointment was tempered by a wonderful and dramatic sight. About two hundred yards from shore. I saw a huge manta ray – wingspan I judged of about ten feet – leap gracefully out of the water and crash back after clearing the surface. A beautiful and graceful creature, it was blackish on top and white underneath. I subsequently found out from Luc that the really big ones could have a wingspan of 22 feet or so. On another occasion some months later, I saw one in the water. It 'flew' over me as I looked for seashells on the bottom, gently moving its wings and questing with the two long lobes projecting from the front.

My catch, as prepared by Diallo that evening, made a delicious dinner and I determined to try to supplement our diet, with what was great fun, whenever I could.

I went fishing in this way on every possible Sunday. My luck varied: sometimes nothing at all, on other occasions a basket full of wonderful silver and golden fish, bonitos, groupers, mullet, beautiful *dorades* and other species. Diallo never failed to make the meals exciting and different, and fresh fish was good for the children, besides saving expense.

But an incident I witnessed gave me pause. I was fishing as usual, one of a long line of fishermen along the beach. We were all in up to our waists as we cast as far as we could beyond the surf.

Suddenly the man two up from me gave a loud yell and we saw him throw his rod into the air and bend over sharply, clutching his leg. He continued making a loud noise, half scream and half sob. The friend beside him threw his own rod onto the beach and went to him. We could see the water turning pink round the stricken man and some of us reeled in quickly and went back to the beach to help if we could.

By now the wounded man and his friend were slowly hobbling onto the sand. We could see he was bleeding profusely from his thigh. The friend sat him on the sand and, tearing a strip of cloth from a towel, rapidly tied a tourniquet above the wound.

As I went closer, I could see that a fist-sized piece of flesh had been sliced, as though with a sharp knife, from the man's thigh. The bleeding had slowed and I marvelled at the clean crescent shape of the cut.

The friend looked up at us. "Barracuda," he said briefly. The group nodded. "I told him to be careful. But he insisted on taking his keys with him." He pointed to a silver chain hanging from the top of the wounded man's trunks, with a key ring on the end.

"Barracuda are attracted by shiny, flashing objects and strike at a tremendous speed. You can't get away."

Everyone nodded wisely, and a couple of the men helped him to get his friend into his car, which he drove off to hospital.

We looked at each other. No one said anything, but when we started fishing again, none of us went in deeper than our knees. I went back to the family and, although I continued to fish on Sundays, was careful not to have anything shiny about me and never went in up to my waist again.

It was not long after this episode that we met the missionaries.

I was driving the Explorer one morning, with Sarr, through the centre of Dakar. We intended to go out to M'Bour, a small town about fifty miles away, to check on the station there.

As we were passing through the main square, I noticed a crowd of Africans clustered round a small, rather shabby car, stopped beside the pavement. Near it there was a tall, young and very blond man and beside him a young woman, also blonde, with a little girl, looking very hot in a shiny nylon dress. They were, inexplicably, dressed in cold weather clothes, he in a full suit and she in a long, woollen dress and shawl. Some of the crowd were shouting and waving their fists.

I stopped and got out, as did Sarr. I shouldered my way through the crowd and found a one-legged woman squatting on the pavement with a small boy, who was writhing round in what looked like agony. The young couple looked bewildered and frightened and were not saying anything.

"Find out what is going on," I said to Sarr, and addressed myself to the young man.

"What has happened here?" I asked him in French.

He stared at me uncomprehendingly. After a short moment, he pointed at his chest and said: "Americano, Americano."

"Who are you? What is the problem?" I asked in English.

Relief flooded his face. "You speak English," he said. "I guess I was getting kind of desperate."

"Yes, I do. But what is going on?" I insisted.

"Well, you see," he started hesitatingly, "we were just driving along when there was a bump and a scream and people gathered round and they looked angry, but I don't know why. Then this woman..." he pointed at the one-legged beggar woman, "she sort of indicated I had hit the little boy, but I swear I didn't. I would have seen him."

Sarr sidled up to me. "She says he hit the boy, but it is a lie. These are the old tricks," he muttered.

It all became clear. In Dakar, at the time, there was a plague of beggars who trained young children to hurl themselves at the sides of slow moving vehicles and then to pretend to be gravely injured. The driver, preferring not to have crowd trouble, would usually part with some money, when the child would be miraculously cured and the beggar, many of whom were maimed, would leave rapidly. Sadly, there was also a whole class of beggars who intentionally mutilated themselves and their babies, so as to make their seeking for alms more effective.

"Get rid of them," I said to Sarr. "Tell them we know all about their methods and threaten to call a gendarme. But give the woman this." I handed him some small coins. "Tell her not to do it again; it is dangerous."

"Who are you and what are you doing here, for Heavens' sake?" I asked the young man.

He grinned broadly. "You got that right." He looked at the girl. "See, hon, it shows." They both chuckled. He turned back to me.

"That's why we are here, sir," he said. "For Heavens' sake. We are missionaries from South Carolina and we have been Sent" (he somehow imbued certain words with a special meaning) "to bring Light to the Unbelievers, who live in Darkness." He looked fondly at his wife and daughter. "We were Called. We have never been outside South Carolina before," he added naively.

"But where are you going?" I asked.

"Well, we are replacing a couple of Good People who were Sent before us and settled near Tumba... Temba... Tom... something like that. I got it written down."

"Do you mean Tambacounda, near the border with French Soudan?" I asked. "It is quite a way from here. But there is a train," I added helpfully.

"No, it is a village a little ways from the T place," he said. "Anyway, we were given a little money for an automobile, so we bought this one." He pointed proudly at the battered little Peugeot. It was a small pick-up, with a canvas covering at the back and looked unreliable.

"I know, I know," he said. "It is not great to look at but the Lord will Provide. He always does," he added.

"Listen," I said. There was a new crowd gradually gathering. "Why don't you all come home with me and we can talk about this. By the way, I am Mick Arnold and this is my friend, Sarr M'Baye."

The young man put out his hand. "We are the Goodyears," he said. "I am Billy-Joe, and this is my wife Charity and this," he looked fondly at the little girl, who seemed to be very hot and tired, "is Connie-May."

We shook hands and I nodded at the family. "Hop into your car and follow me," I said.

When we got home, I asked Sarr to keep an eye on the little Peugeot, which was stuffed with all manner of household things and unprotected with its canvas cover, and led my guests into the house.

Wendy, as always, rose nobly to the occasion. She soon had the Goodyears seated, with cold drinks and Connie-May introduced to Nikki, who eyed her with curiosity, but took her into her bedroom to play.

It was very hot. I was dressed in my usual outfit of very abbreviated khaki shorts and shirt while Wendy wore a thin cotton frock. I persuaded Billy-Joe to take off his coat and tie while Charity removed her shawl.

It turned out that the family had been chosen by the church in their little town to go to Africa to replace another couple, who had previously gone there. Billy-Joe told us that word had come back after about a year that there had been a fire in their hut, caused by an overturned oil lamp, and that both had been badly burned. Their wounds had become infected and they had died, alone in the bush.

He said this in a very matter-of-fact way and did not seem disturbed by it. "It was the will of the Lord," he said. "There must have been a good reason. Anyway, when we were Chosen, we were proud and pleased to go. After all, we owe Africa a great debt and an apology that can never satisfy. In South Carolina we treated Africans very badly a hundred years ago."

Charity took up the story. "So we were given quite a lot of dollars and the address where we had to go. We also got some bibles, and seeds and farm tools and things so we could live off the land."

"But you can't speak any French, which will make things difficult. Do you know what crops will grow here? Do you realise what you are getting into? Have you not travelled before?"

"Well, I guess we have never been outside the States," she said doubtfully. "But the Pastor said that the Lord would look after us and Provide and that we should put all our Trust in him." She glanced at her husband, who smiled at her. I looked at Wendy and raised my eyebrows; she looked horrified.

I told them a little about the bush, and Wendy mentioned prickly heat, the advantage of wearing cotton and the total lack of doctors in the interior. I also spoke of snakes, poisonous thorns, endemic dysentery, malaria and other fevers. Nothing seemed to make an impression. We begged them to reconsider and go home, but they would not hear of it.

We gave them lunch, simple but filling, which they wolfed down. Wendy also gave Connie-May some dresses of Nikki's – she could not bear to see her so overheated in her nylon clothes.

Billy-Joe was reluctant, but I obliged him to accept some tins of beans and sardines as well as giving him a jerrican of water and a large container of disinfectant; he had very few supplies.

He thanked me, but said: "I guess we will stop at a supermarket and get some stuff when we get to the T Place." I assured him that there were no shops, let alone supermarkets where he was going, but only sometimes the odd tin or dried meat or fish.

He grinned and said: "It will be OK. Bless you for all your help and charity. Please don't worry about us. We want to spread Light where there is Darkness and we are happy to go. Prayer will solve everything. See how the Lord sent you to help us."

I asked Sarr to start them off on the right road for Tambacounda and we said goodbye. Connie-May had not uttered a word since I met them and Nikki said she did not like to speak.

The last we saw of them was as the battered little Peugeot disappeared down the street on its way to Tambacounda, some

300 miles away. We never heard of, or from them again, but we marvelled at what a mixture of absolute faith and total naiveté could do.

I was still a little weak from my malaria and could see no merit in retracing my steps, in the Explorer, to places I had been and roads I knew. Thus, apart from towns within about a fifty mile radius, I succumbed to air travel and made several flights, in local small aircraft, to Ziguinchor and St. Louis. On one of the St. Louis trips I went on, to Nouakchott and Fort Gouraud, almost on the Algerian border. This was an old French military outpost, with fortified barracks and a small settlement round it. There was a strong rumour that huge iron deposits had been found nearby and, if true, these would change the face of Mauritania.

But I was determined to make one last, long journey. This was to Timbuktu, the fabled end of the world. It was, strictly speaking, sort of in my official territory and I thought it would be tragic (and remiss of me) not to visit it. Sarr, as always, thought I was mad but agreed it might be an adventure. "Let us just make sure we have enough spares and water this time," he said. "Though I cannot think why you will not fly, or even take the train as far as Bamako."

We had developed a comfortable friendship and I always encouraged him to speak freely to me. He was a courteous and sensible person. My attitude seemed to puzzle him, since he was used to the patronising and superior ways of the French expatriates, not least my predecessor Jean-Claude, who spoke of him slightingly as a *bougnoul* and a menial, which had made me angry.

So early one Monday morning we set off. The Explorer was happy, full of petrol and our stores were at maximum. I estimated the round trip, which was not far off 3000 miles, would take two to three weeks, if all went well. After all, most of the distance was on a reasonably well travelled road which, in the dry season, would enable us to keep up an acceptable average speed. I did not plan any detours.

We drove through familiar country to Kaolack and on towards Tambacounda. The road was not too bad, though the inevitable corrugations on the surface virtually forced one to maintain a respectable speed, if the car was not to be shaken to pieces.

But just the other side of Kaolack Sarr, who was driving, suddenly pulled to the edge of the road and stopped. He jumped out of the car and fastened down the rear window, as well as sliding shut the side windows, which we always kept open to provide ventilation in the heat.

He hurried back into his seat and said urgently: "Slide your window shut, quickly." I did so, rather puzzled. "What is wrong?" I asked. "We will stifle in here."

"Just look to the left, Chief," he said. "Up at the sky over there."

I looked. The sky was blue and cloudless. It looked normal. Then, on looking more closely I discerned a dark cloud, which spread almost from horizon to horizon; a band, rapidly moving in our direction. There was also a growing, shrill humming and buzzing in the air.

Sarr said: "it is *njéeréer bi*. Locusts. They will be everywhere." We drove on slowly and watched the swarm approach. Soon they were upon us. I had thought they would pass over us but, as Sarr had said, they were everywhere, in their tens or hundreds of millions. The sky was dark and it was difficult to see well enough to drive. They covered the road, smashed into the windscreen, making great stains on it, crawled on the bonnet and all this in the midst of a loud whirring, stridulent noise, so loud we had to shout to make ourselves heard. Eventually, I asked Sarr to stop and we sat in the heat, all windows tightly shut, to wait for the swarm to pass. This took nearly two hours.

"They have come from the north," Sarr explained. "This happens every few years and it is very bad. They eat everything. They are bad when they are 'hoppers' (Sarr called them *larves*) and they march across the land and eat everything green. But when they are fully winged they fly huge distances and devour every leaf, grass, stalk and branch. The people starve that year."

Gradually, the swarm passed, the light got better and Sarr got out and washed the windscreen. There were locusts everywhere, but they looked dead. We drove on, the tyres crunching.

There was a small village about a mile away, and we stopped

there for refreshment. There were many people, carrying large, flat baskets and collecting the locusts, which were plentiful everywhere.

"Why are they collecting them?" I asked Sarr.

He looked at me in astonishment. "Why, to eat of course, Chief. They are delicious. If you wait half an hour, we can have some."

There were many little straw huts along the road, selling peanuts (this was the heart of the peanut country), warm sticky drinks and some more substantial food. Fires had been lit behind the huts, from where there came the steady thud – thud – thud, heard in all villages in West Africa, of women rhythmically pounding millet in large mortars, with five foot pestles, two or three taking turns with the pestles.

Other women were preparing large, flat iron platters, on tripods over the fires, onto which they threw the locusts as they were brought in the baskets. There was a smell of roasting, not unpleasant, in the hot breeze. Thankfully, the *harmattan* was not blowing.

Sarr led me to one of the fires. There was a Wolof lady tending the roasting. She was a large, cheerful person and Sarr soon charmed her into accepting us as her guests. He said quite a lot, while pointing to me, and this aroused peals of laughter from the lady, and one or two others within earshot.

"What are you saying?" I asked. "Are they your usual lies?"

Sarr grinned and tried to look innocent. "Why, Chief," he said. "I never lie." He paused. "Sometimes I kind of exaggerate a little, but that is only to make the listeners happy." He paused again. "I just told them that you have a very happy wife and many children."

I looked suspiciously at him. "What has that to do with anything?" I asked. "Why did you tell them that? Besides, there are only two children."

"So far," said Sarr, grinning. "Actually, eating locusts makes a man strong. There are so many in a swarm, you see. It makes him able to... you know... do things many times."

Soon, the locusts were ready to eat. I was handed several on a large leaf. Observing the others, I took off the heads and wings and ate the bodies, rather as one would eat shrimps. They were delicious, tasting meaty and wholesome.

Sarr told me that they were very good as a food supplement. When there were too many to eat, villagers would roast them until they were crisp and brittle, then pound them into powder. This kept for a long time and was sprinkled on other food as a high protein supplement.

We thanked the lady and I gave her a packet of cigarettes since she would accept no payment. As we parted, she made a couple of comments to me, to much hilarity among the onlookers. I assumed the comments were lewd, since Sarr refused to translate them, saying he did not know the French equivalents.

We spent the night beside the road. There was no traffic at night and we were undisturbed, though it was rather colder in the savannah than I remembered from the southern jungle.

As we passed through various villages, we stopped for a moment to stretch our legs. I asked Sarr to enquire from the villagers if they had heard anything about the Goodyears or knew where they may have settled, but no-one knew anything. They had disappeared. On the other hand, in one of the villages, Sarr turned to me and said: "This man says he knows nothing of Americans but there is a mad Turk living in a big house not far away. He thinks he is some sort of Arab, but not a Muslim."

I thought this was interesting. What on earth was 'some sort of Arab' doing in the middle of the African bush? I determined to find out.

After getting directions, we set off down a side road a few miles ahead. The road was, surprisingly a good one and with an even better surface than the main highway. We drove some fifteen miles and came upon an astonishing sight.

In an ordered and well cultivated garden, with shady flowering trees, palms and baobabs there was a brick-built, two storey house, with balconies and a wide veranda running along the front. Some distance away there were many sheds, and some reed-thatched huts, like in the villages. The big house had large windows and looked comfortable. I could hear the whine of a generator. There were some large trucks parked beside the sheds, and people carrying sacks to and fro.

I stopped in front of the house and got out. As I approached the veranda, a man came out of the front door. He was of late middle age, dressed casually in a cool, white robe. He had light brown skin and greying hair and the unmistakable aquiline nose and thin lips of the Eastern Mediterranean.

"Welcome," he said in French. "What can I do for you?" The French was good, but I thought I detected a Lebanese accent.

"Peace be upon you," I said in Arabic. He looked startled, but recovered quickly. "And on you be peace," he replied, in the Lebanese dialect of Arabic.

"You are far from home," I said. "Why are you here?"

He smiled. "Come in, come in," he said, with a welcoming gesture of his arm. "My house is your house." Sarr hung back, looking uncomfortable, so I asked him to have a look round.

The inside of the house was cool and pleasant. There were ceiling fans turning and the furniture, very much in the Arab taste, ornate and comfortable, made a pleasant change from my normal surroundings in the towns and villages. It was obvious that the man had been there for some time and liked his comforts.

I told him who I was and what I was doing. He knew Shell well, but said he avoided going into Dakar, which he visited once a year. He said his name was Aziz al Doula and that he was a Christian Lebanese. "I have now been here for nearly thirty years," he said with a rueful grin, "so I suppose it is my home now."

It turned out that he was the principal trader in peanuts in the whole area. The villages within a fairly big radius would bring their crop to him, and he would pay them a fair price. Then he would ship the peanuts, in his large trucks, to Dakar for export. "It is a good trade," he said. "There is really no competition and everyone profits. From time to time the odd Frenchman tries to settle nearby and take my trade away, but they soon tire of the isolation and conditions and go away."

"But is it not so with you?" I was curious how he could have lived there, alone, for so many years. "Are you not lonely and perhaps homesick?"

He shook his head. "We are Phoenicians," he said. "We are the greatest traders in the world and you will find us everywhere. As for being homesick, I go home to Beirut every five years or so and deposit money and buy land. When I am tired of all this, I shall go home a rich man and enjoy my ease."

He called and a very attractive girl came in, carrying a tray with a pitcher of cold lemonade and some nuts on it, which she placed on the low table between us. She was dressed in European clothes, a smart print dress and sandals. She had the fine features of the Moors, though I could not determine her tribe. She smiled at Aziz as she passed and he gave her an affectionate pat on the rump.

"I am not lonely," he said. "I always have five companions, like this one, and a very good cook. We get on very well together and are used to each other. Of course, I have to find new ones every few years, but the others continue to live here and look after the children. We are all very happy."

The Arabic he spoke had been a bit rusty (as was mine), but soon became easier and I found it a great pleasure to speak it again.

He insisted I stay to dinner and spend the night. The meal was a splendid one, very Arab, with barbecued lamb, fresh vegetables and ripe mangoes. To drink, there was a bottle of Ksara wine, which he had brought from Lebanon and saved for special occasions. The meal was served with elegance, in a pleasant dining room, by three of the 'companions', all equally attractive. I felt much honoured, but he said that it was wonderful to speak Arabic again and to a man who had lived in the Middle East. He disliked Egypt and thought the Eastern Arabs uncouth and primitive. But Lebanon, as far as he was concerned, was paradise on earth.

I told him about my short overnight stay in Beirut, during our escape from Poland, and he laughed at my description of the nightclub.

I asked what was happening to Sarr, but he said the women would look after him.

After dinner, with both of us smoking excellent cigars, he took me to a room behind the salon and said: "Now I will show you something you have never seen before." He drew a hanging carpet aside and revealed a huge steel door with a combination lock. It was the size of a large cupboard.

He fiddled with the combination and turned a handle. The door swung ponderously open and revealed a large steel cavity, with numerous shelves. It was lit by a bulb, which had come on automatically. I was looking into a vast safe.

He stood back and said: "Look. This is why I live here."

On the floor there were stacked bundles and bundles of franc notes, of small denominations. Aziz pointed to them and said: "This is what I pay for the peanuts." He then indicated the shelves. I had to look twice – it was hard to believe. On the shelves, neatly stacked, were many bars of gold and boxes of gold coins. I could not begin to imagine the value.

Aziz laughed. "Yes, it has that effect on people. You see, I do not trust banks or long term paper money. With the gold price fixed at 35 dollars an ounce it is safe. So whenever I go to Dakar, I take all my gains and buy gold which I bring here. Then, when I go home on a visit, I exchange it all in a Dakar bank for a dollar draft to take with me to Beirut. Much safer that way. This is about four years' worth."

I just stood and goggled. A huge gold hoard in the middle of nowhere. I turned to my host. "But don't you worry about being robbed? Most people would kill you for just a small part of this."

Aziz shook his head. "Not all that many people know about it. Anyway, I paid the top local sorcerer to put a very public spell on this house, so that anyone who harms me or tries to take anything away will die in horrible agony." He chuckled. "It works very well." He paused. "He renews it every year."

I spent a very comfortable night, after a hot shower, in a soft bed with clean sheets. I dreamed of a house built of gold bricks and guarded by a dragon with the grinning face of Aziz.

In the morning, after a delicious breakfast on the veranda, with freshly ground coffee, Aziz looked at me quizzically. "Are you in a great hurry to go?" he asked. "If you can spare an hour or so, I would like to introduce you to my neighbour. You may find him interesting."

I was puzzled and looked questioningly at him. "I did not

realise you had a neighbour," I said. "Who is he?"

Aziz looked mysterious and said: "Ask your man to wait and I will drive you there." Sarr was hanging round and I asked him to check the Explorer and make sure we had enough water. He nodded and said he had had a pleasant night.

Aziz and I went off in a large and comfortable Peugeot saloon, further up the road. We drove for only about ten minutes, as the road became narrower and more and more overgrown. There were tall grasses on both sides and clumps of trees and baobabs, here and there.

The road, now little more than a track, stopped. Aziz said we should get out and we walked some fifty yards into the bush, along a path. There was a concrete shack there, with a thatched conical roof, and some bedraggled flower beds round it. Aziz went up to the door and hammered on it. "Come out, Pierre," he called. "I have a visitor for you."

After a moment, a pale, bearded face peered out. Then the man came out and revealed himself as a painfully thin, rather bedraggled white man dressed in a dirty singlet and a sort of brown sarong. His feet were dirty and his hair, slightly grey, as was his beard, long and unkempt.

But he had piercing black eyes and I noticed many coloured dabs of paint on his hands.

"This is my friend, Monsieur Mick," said Aziz. He turned to me. And this is my friend and neighbour, the Count of Saint-Seine." I grinned at him; he was obviously pulling my leg. The bedraggled man looked at me. "Yes, it is true. For my sins I was born a Count." He smiled. "My father's fault, you know…"

"I am sorry, Monsieur le Comte," I said apologetically. "I thought Aziz was making a joke."

"I am afraid not," said the Count. "But why not just call me Pierre? This is not a place which encourages formality."

It turned out that Pierre had lived in the shack almost as long as Aziz occupied his comfortable house down the road. They were old friends and spent much time together, mostly playing chess. Pierre was a painter and, when we went into his hut, there was a multitude of paintings everywhere, competing for space with a bed, a table with three chairs and a cupboard.

There was a sort of annexe to the single large room, in which there was a kerosene stove and a very beautiful brown girl, bare breasted, cooking something in a pot.

"This is Malami," said Pierre. "She keeps me warm at night and also cooks." Malami grinned. "She is my main model." We were now speaking French; I noticed that Pierre still had an exquisite Parisian accent. Looking round, I perceived that, indeed, there were many paintings of the girl, and many others, in various poses and states of undress. None looked in the least self-conscious.

Malami brought us some fresh mango juice and Pierre told me that he had determined to be a painter and had thus had much trouble with his father, the old Count. It was unacceptable that he should let the family down, so he decided – as he put it – to 'do a Gauguin' and lose himself in Africa.

"It has been wonderful," he said. "I have complete freedom and can do and live as I like. The family send me a small monthly sum on condition I stay away, and it suits me very well."

After some persuasion, he agreed to sell me one of his paintings, of two girls' heads, for a very modest sum and after some more chat, we returned to Aziz' house.

I told him I had had a fascinating and exciting time, and thanked him very much for his hospitality. "And also the bonus of meeting le Comte." I shook my head. "Whoever would have thought to find such interesting people in the middle of the African bush."

Aziz laughed and with the usual Lebanese courtesy, thanked me for coming. "Do drop in whenever you are passing. My house is yours." We shook hands and we drove away, back towards the main road. I found out later that day that he had arranged for a box of fresh mangoes, some tomatoes and two melons to be put into the Explorer when neither Sarr nor I were looking.

On the main road again, we made good time and reached Tambacounda in good order, apart from one puncture. I did not remember the town from my last visit, since I was then full of malaria and high fever. But Sarr knew the place and drove us straight to the Shell station, where we replenished our fuel and fixed the tyre.

In the morning we took the road towards Kayes. We crossed into French Soudan (now called Mali, after the great mediaeval empire there in the Middle Ages). We had been following the railway, which ran parallel to the road all the way to Bamako. We passed a train, which was standing, wheezing, in the middle of nowhere (presumably having one of its regular breakdowns). It was amazingly crowded, with people sitting on the roof with baskets of produce and goods, sweltering in the sunshine. They also occupied the spaces between carriages, crouching on the buffers and clinging on to any protuberance on the carriages. But they seemed in good spirits and, when I honked the horn, waved cheerfully back.

We passed through Kayes, a somewhat nondescript town. It was quite large, with streets and houses, having been the original capital of the vast province of the Soudan. But since Bamako had become the capital, it was in decline – though it remained a major stop on the railway and a produce-gathering centre for a large area round it. It is also a port on the Senegal river, which runs westward to St. Louis on the Atlantic coast.

After Kayes, the countryside was typical Sahel: not at all the sandy wastes of the Sahara proper, but gravelly and rocky plains, with quite a lot of greenery and trees, mainly acacia and baobab.

We took the road to Bamako, left the Senegal river and followed the railway tracks across the plains. There were occasional glimpses of small herds of antelope and gazelle, and sometimes troops of monkeys, but all at some distance. Obviously, the animals kept well away from the noisy trains. There were many villages beside the railway line, but the only difference from the ones with which I was familiar, was in that new tribes we encountered wore different robes and were taller and even more languid than their brothers more to the west.

It took us two days of hard driving to get to Bamako. This was a large bustling town – or as bustling as the endemic languor of the inhabitants permitted. There were many buildings, some shops and hotels and a sprinkling of expatriate French. As the capital of French Soudan and the administrative centre of the region, there was a mixture of tribes and styles in the street and also of languages. It was also the main office of

Shell, subsidiary to the Head Office in Dakar, which looked after French Soudan and neighbouring Upper Volta. I kept well away from this. I did not want Dakar being asked what I was doing there, somewhat outside my official territory, though this was rather vague.

The town was close to the terminus of the railway. From now on we would no longer have the friendly reassurance of the gleaming tracks beside us.

We had finally reached the Niger river. This, the third longest river in Africa – some 2,600 miles – perversely flowed from west to east, unlike all the others. It rose in the south west, in French Guinea and described a huge arc northwards, with Timbuktu as its northernmost point, before plunging south to the delta in Nigeria, on the Gulf of Guinea.

It was a huge and impressive waterway, which changed and affected the landscape for hundreds of miles around it. The seasonal change in the water flow meant that in the dry season – which this was – the main river courses were not very wide and ran in well defined channels. But during the rainy season, the river flooded, creating marshes and swampland for many miles on each side and an enormous lake, some 150 miles long, in the Central Niger valley, where we were heading. The water was shallow throughout, and the busy river transport was all in *pinasses*, large flat bottomed boats and the ubiquitous *pirogues*, long, dugout canoes.

The port of Bamako, together with the railway station, seemed to be the centres of activity, though there were many markets and many rather battered cars, camels, donkeys and horses wandering about.

We spent the night in reasonable hotels. Mine was owned and run by a French lady of dubious ancestry, but provided an adequate bedroom and a good dinner of fresh fish and green vegetables. Sarr told me he had found a modest lodging with a Wolof couple, where he was comfortable. I had noticed he was always slightly uneasy when mixing with other tribes, not least the Fulani and occasional Moor.

I was anxious to get on the road again, so we spent no time looking round and visiting the many mosques and ancient houses. Early the next day, we checked in at one of the three Shell stations, and filled our tank and jerricans up to the brim. The owner told us that he was receiving regular supplies by rail and transhipping many drums to *pinasses* on their journey down river toward Mopti, Timbuktu and on.

After Bamako the road became rather more difficult, with constant corrugations and with occasional mounds of sand blown onto the surface.

As we drove, the landscape began to change. We were not very close to the river, but the greenery increased, and we lost the arid, rocky character of the Sahel. There were cultivated fields and trees, and the earth began to have that rich, alluvial look, which I remembered from the Nile delta when I was a boy in Egypt.

We passed through a number of villages. The cinder block houses of Bamako now gave way to mud brick huts, mostly with one room, and a thatched roof. As we drove further from the river, the soil became arid again, and the groves of mango trees, the acacias and the flowering *flamboyant* became more rare. Here the baobab again was king, with its massive trunk and widespread, though often leafless, branches.

At Ségou, a minor town, the mixture of people became pronounced. Here were the Bambara, a handsome race with very black skin, contrasting with a sprinkling of Touareg, who had become urbanised. The streets were narrow and dusty and there was a multitude of donkey carts and women, walking very erect, with baskets of produce on their heads and the inevitable baby strapped to their back with a swathe of coloured cloth. There was nothing much to see except more examples of Soudanese architecture, the characteristic mud buildings with numerous wooden beams projecting from the walls.

Another night on the road, this time a disturbed one as overloaded trucks rumbled past and a group of *bachés*, crammed with singing people, drove by. These were local transport, a sort of pick-up conversion which seemed able to absorb an unlimited number of passengers.

We reached Djenné in the late afternoon. It was visible from many miles away, thanks to the huge mud mosque. When we drove into the town, we were accosted by a Fulani man, who spoke comprehensible though somewhat fractured French. He was anxious to be our guide, and after haggling for a few minutes, I asked him to show us round.

Amadou, as he called himself, was very proud of his town. He had experience as a guide and quickly fell into his professional patter of information.

"Listen," I interrupted. "We do not have much time. We are on our way to Timbuktu and want really to see just the mosque and the river bank." The town stood on the Bani river, where it joins the mighty Niger.

"But there is much to see, Monsieur," implored Amadou. "At least two full days. You must not hurry."

I declined his importunities and said: "You will be well paid. You must be glad we wish to see your town."

As he directed us to the main square, on one side of which stood the Grand Mosque, Amadou chattered to us. "This is the oldest town in West Africa south of the big desert," he said. "An American professor told me that last year. And the mosque is not only the biggest mosque in the world but also the biggest mud building there is."

"What professor?" I asked.

Amadou said: "He was a very big professor with a beard. He was from America," he repeated.

We drove into the square, which was crowded with colourful market stalls and with crowds of people milling around. We stopped and got out.

Before us stood a gigantic mud building, bigger than several football fields, with innumerable towers, turrets and crenellations. It was three storeys high and was overwhelming. The colour of the mud was pale brown and the surface was smooth, though with many regular lines of palm wood beams sticking out. I was staggered to find something so huge and in such good repair in a small, lost town in the middle of Africa. Sarr stood and looked, with his eyes bulging, saying nothing.

Amadou looked satisfied. He must have experienced the same reaction from his past clients.

"It is very old," he said. "Probably several hundred years. You come at a good time to see it. It is now dry season; in the rains it becomes a bit spoiled and many people have to put special new mud on the walls." He nodded. "And yes, they have to stand on the wood sticking out to do it. The whole town helps."

I suggested to Sarr that he should go into the mosque to pray and he did so, with some trepidation. I continued to chat with Amadou as we walked round the market.

There was everything on the stalls, which were attended by large, vociferous ladies in multicoloured sarongs and swathes of material on their heads. There were no young women selling: the ones I saw were pacing slowly in small, elegant groups, gossiping and giggling. There were children everywhere, in multitudes, mostly naked and cheerful, not the insistent beggars who pestered everyone in the big cities.

"So you are going to Timbuktu," said Amadou. "It is certainly worth a visit, but is not as beautiful as Djenné. I suppose there are one or two things to see there," he said grudgingly. "But it is good that you do not come in the rains. Then it is impossible to go anywhere – just water and mud and swamp for miles and miles. And the rivers become huge and angry, too."

I decided there was nothing I wanted to buy in the market – we could get some fresh provisions in the morning – and asked where we should dine and sleep.

By now Sarr had rejoined us. He looked slightly stunned. "What a place, what a place," he muttered. "Allah is indeed great and merciful for such a place to grow in the desert."

Amadou grinned. "Yes, it is good. There were some missionaries, Catholics, who tried to live here but they left. Nearly everybody is Moslem. It is the only true religion."

It was very hot and I was not prepared to argue, so I asked again where we should have dinner.

Amadou took us to a small restaurant, which proved quite good. We spent the night in a small guest house, run by a Fulani couple, who spoke a few words of French. Amadou had arranged everything and I saw some money go into his pocket, so I assumed he took all his clients there. He departed and said he would see us in the morning. The rooms we had were small, primitive and hot, but clean and tidy.

Amadou arrived early, soon after dawn, as arranged. We went back to the market, which was already busy, with the stall holders arriving and arranging their wares. We bought some smoked fish, some fruit and some tins of sardines, which tended to be our diet on the road. There was also fresh bread, in thick round loaves.

We had a brief look at the riverside. It was not remarkable: the usual throng of *pirogues* and other boats, many carrying cargo and produce to other villages up and down the river. There was a strong smell everywhere, and hundreds of woven baskets, full of many varieties of fish, some quite big, still flopping about in the bright sunshine.

Finally, we went to the Shell station (there was only a small one) and filled up. I remained incognito – I did not want the office in Bamako enquiring what I was doing in the Soudan.

Amadou made it clear that parting from us would break his heart and plaintively begged us to stay longer. "You will go to Mopti and on but you waste your time. Stay here and I will show you many wonderful and secret sights and rituals, in hidden villages and..." he lowered his voice,"...the Dogon country." This was a highly individual tribe to the south, who lived in the foothills and mountains near the great escarpment. They had special ways and customs, unlike the surrounding tribes, and their dwellings, mostly built into the slopes of the hills, were different from the others. Their dress, and especially their tall, carved wooden masks were all in red, white and black, and they kept apart as much as they could. It was certainly a temptation to make the detour, but I decided against it.

I therefore declined politely and gave him a large tip over and above the agreed sum for his guidance. His unhappiness quickly vanished.

"Go safely, Inshallah and have good fortune. You are about 250 miles from Timbuktu, but as far as Mopti the road is not bad. After that, I do not know; perhaps there is no road. Everyone goes there on the river."

He waved as we drove off. I thought we had been lucky to find him. Sarr said grudgingly: "I suppose he was all right. For a Fulani," he added.

The road was reasonable, but the surroundings changed. We could see hills, rising to mountains in the far, blue distance, on our right while we were surrounded by lots of cultivated land, mostly in smallish plots. There were highly irrigated rice fields, and green areas of sorghum, millet and cereals. Rather disorganised orchards abounded and flowering trees as well as groves of palms were scattered everywhere.

We were now driving into the flood plain of the Niger, which was largely inundated in the rainy season; thus there was little permanent about it. The villages were straw and thatch huts, which were erected yearly and the tracks disappearing into the fields looked temporary.

There were birds in abundance. I wished I had had the sense to learn about the different species, for my knowledge was rudimentary at best. But I recognised black storks (I was familiar with the white ones which roosted on the country roofs of Poland) and innumerable varieties of finches and other small birds, some coloured. Amadou had mentioned that on top of each of the three towers of the Grand Mosque in Djenné there was an ostrich egg, fastened there for good luck and the fertility of the faithful.

We were approaching Mopti, a major, though relatively recent town on the main watercourse of the Niger. As we got nearer, the ground became waterlogged and the dry laterite clay of the corrugated track became slippery and greasy.

Mopti turned out to be a sizeable town. It was the jumping-off point for major river traffic to Timbuktu and on and its activities were centred on the port. This is where we went to look. It was dusk, so we spent a little time looking at the bustle of *pinasses* and *pirogues* coming and going. There were hundreds of them.

But it was also our first sight of the main river itself. This was hugely impressive, very wide, and remarkably shallow – hence only boats which were virtually flat-bottomed could use it. There were a myriad islands dotted about, some with huts on them, and there were also occasional deep pools, which had a different colour and where the water swirled in small whirlpools. We hoped we might come back in the morning and see the fishermen set off.

I was fortunate to see, in the main street, a small sign, in French, which had the name 'Pension Flaubert' painted on it in rough letters. I stopped and went in, to find an elderly French lady at a small desk in the hall.

"Good evening, Madame," I said politely. "Am I right in thinking that you may have a room for me for tonight?"

The lady, who had a lined, kind face, burned dark brown by the relentless sun, smiled and said: "Certainly, Monsieur. You are very welcome to Mopti."

It felt odd to be exchanging formal French greetings in a small African town, in the middle of a relatively unvisited area.

I told the lady my name and she introduced herself as Madame Flaubert. "My husband and I have lived in Mopti for more than forty years now," she said. "We were some of the first French people to settle – and now, I think, there are only two or three families remaining." She paused and sighed. "My husband organised the river transport and became a trader, but now there are trucks and airplanes and so on, nobody bothers locally very much, except the natives."

I went out to get my grip and ask Sarr what he wanted to do, since there was room for him as well. But in his usual way, he decided to find his own lodging and said he would return early the following morning. "They seem quite civilised here," he said. "I am sure I will be all right."

Madame Flaubert said she could provide dinner for me, which I accepted gladly. I was very tired and wanted to eat and get to bed early. But then Monsieur Flaubert came in, and disrupted all my plans.

He was a grizzled, lean Frenchman, very much the colonial type, in immaculately pressed khaki shorts and bush shirt. His face was bright red; he had the sort of complexion which did not tan, but sort of fried, and the bright colour was set off by a large white moustache.

He shook hands with me enthusiastically and proved to have a powerful grip. "Ah, Monsieur," he said. "What a pleasure to have you as a guest. Sit down, sit down, and have an aperitif. You must tell me all about yourself." He was obviously starved of company.

Madame produced some Pernod and, to my delight, some ice cubes. I could hear a generator thumping away, and there was electricity, so they must have had a refrigerator, probably one of a handful in thousands of square miles.

After a meticulous cross-examination, which Monsieur Flaubert conducted with subtlety and while refilling my glass assiduously with the fiery liquor, he finally said: "How very interesting. It is a pleasure to see that there is still a spirit of adventure among the young." He paused and took a gulp. "But then the British have always been great explorers. I suppose it is because the island is so crowded they have been looking for other places to live."

I was beginning to feel rather light headed; Pernod on an empty stomach is a dangerous brew. Fortunately, Madame reappeared to say that dinner was served and ushered me into an adjoining room with a small table laid for a meal. Monsieur promptly followed me and sat down opposite.

"Now," he said, lighting a foul-smelling pipe. "What do you wish to know about Africa?"

"I am amazed to find so much greenery and cultivation in what I thought was a desert," I said. "I suppose it is the river."

Monsieur nodded and was about to explain when Madame arrived with the soup. This was strange but appetizing once my taste buds had recovered from their surprise. It was a sort of hot fruit soup, made largely of mango but with a tang of coconut – the surprise was that it was both salty and peppery.

Monsieur puffed at his pipe and enveloped my head in a cloud of rather strong smoke – his pipe was full of a locally grown tobacco, which he said he had cured himself. It did not smell as though it had been completely cured.

"You are right," he said. "The river is the lifeblood of this whole area; without it, everything would be desert, as in the north. It is really the boundary of the Sahara and it serves as a high road, it provides food and water and it enables us to grow a big variety of crops. They built a large dam about fifteen years ago and now there are enormous rice fields." He puffed some more and blew the smoke at me.

Madame reappeared with the main dish. This was a large

plate on which reposed what looked like a giant goldfish, grilled whole. It had golden scales all over it and nasty looking teeth, but proved delicious to eat. There were also vegetables, including couscous, and a spicy peanut sauce.

"The tribes are interesting," continued Monsieur. "They all seem to have their own occupations. The Bambara are farmers, the Bozo are fishermen (you can see their huts on the islands in the river), and the others are herders." He paused. "And then there are the Touareg, mainly herders but also traders – they are rather strange (a sort of Berber) – and they travel a lot and keep to themselves."

He looked at the fish on my plate. "There are lots of fish in the river. There are huge catfish and Nile perch, which is known as *capitaine*. These can be more than five feet long. Then there are the smaller sorts. The best to eat are like the one you have and tilapia and, of course, the *capitaine*. Sometimes the natives kill a manatee and eat it, but I do not like the taste. Also why kill such a creature when there is so much else to eat – good beef, goat and sheep. One might as well kill the hippos which you will see down river towards Timbuktu."

I had now finished eating and was toying with some fruit.

"So you want to go to Timbuktu," said Monsieur. Madame had produced coffee and had joined us at the table. "Anyone would be crazy to try to drive there; the normal way is to make a leisurely three day trip on the river. The *pinasse*, with a sail and a good wind, is a very comfortable way to go."

"No," I said. "It is the dry season and I am determined to drive." Monsieur sighed.

"The road, if you can call it that, cuts across to Gao, a long way away. But what we call the 'braided waterways' of this inland delta mean that the tracks have to be remade after every rainy season and the flooding, and you have to navigate by stars or compass. I wish you good luck." Madame nodded. "But you are crazy," she said.

In the morning, having thanked and paid the Flauberts (Monsieur assured me he was no relation to the famous author), Sarr and I looked round the town and returned to the port. This was now a bustling place, with water-craft coming and going, departing fishermen, merchandise being loaded and unloaded and a strong smell of fish everywhere. The people, a great mixture of tribes, were colourful and seemed cheerful.

We also had a look at the mosques and a couple of forts, which were of the typical Soudanese mud and palm trunk construction. Mopti was mainly a major trading centre and as such, was not particularly interestingly furnished with ancient buildings and architecture.

We replenished our supplies, taking on fuel from drums through hand-operated pumps, and set off to the north east.

At first we followed a good track, in the direction of Gao. But, having passed through a number of villages with memorable names, like Kona and Bobo, we struck off to our left, following rather imprecise directions from a villager we found, who had rudiments of Wolof – unusual so far east.

We had been very lucky with the Explorer, which gave us no trouble, apart from some minor things like flat tyres and, on one occasion, a faulty spark plug. These were soon repaired.

The going was rough, but relatively uneventful. We had frequently to cross dry watercourses which would be small rivers in the flood season. There were few people about, other than occasional clumps of reed huts for the farmers of the area.

It took us three days to get to the bank of the main river opposite Timbuktu. The last twenty miles or so were along the river bank, and we saw hippos, crocodiles and a large water snake. There were some fishermen scattered about, in small communities – they were Bozos.

We could see Timbuktu across the river, which was about a mile wide at this point. There was a village on this side, with some *pinasses* and *pirogues* coming and going, and ferrying people and produce across to the town.

We locked the Explorer carefully and managed to explain to a man who was standing and watching us, that we would pay him if he kept an eye on it until our return. This was done entirely by gesture and a sort of miming, but he appeared to understand, and nodded vigorously. I tried to secure the arrangement by giving him half of a banknote, which I had torn across, and indicating he should have the other half on our return. Sarr was somewhat sceptical, and offered to stay with the car, but I thought he deserved to come with me and told him I was sure it would be all right.

We crossed on a *pinasse* with a sail, and were soon disembarking in Timbuktu. Timbuktu! I was very excited. Here was a place which symbolised the back of beyond, the middle of nowhere, and here I was, standing on the outskirts. I clapped Sarr on the back, but he just looked at me. "Just another town, like everywhere," he said morosely. "Not worth the journey."

It was dusk. The day had been very hot – in excess of 120 degrees Fahrenheit in the Explorer – but the nights, as we found on our journey, were quite cool, if not cold. There were trees around, and some of the streets were lined with bushes, but underfoot, the ground was of fine white sand, very different from the Sahel. We were now on the edge of the Sahara, the great sand ocean.

We found a small hotel, and, as usual, Sarr decided to find his own lodging. I was content to eat a simple supper and sleep. It had been a long drive. The hotel was run by a couple of indeterminate ancestry, who were taciturn and did not like to talk.

In the morning, Sarr arrived and we walked into the town. There was a large mosque, much like the one in Djenné, and a series of smaller ones. In its time, Timbuktu had been a major centre of Moslem learning, with libraries, hundreds of scholars teaching in *madrassas*, or religious schools, and savants from many countries visiting to study. There were ancient buildings and some fortified structures. But the whole character of the town was subtly different from the others we had visited on the way.

It was a desert town. It reminded me very much of the provincial towns in Iraq, during my boyhood; the same sand, the same brilliant, searing heat, the same uniformly brown, mud brick houses. It felt much more Middle Eastern than African and I felt at home.

But there were still women pounding millet and men, in groups, making mud bricks. The fishermen on the boats were black and the whole tempo of the town was muted and languorous. We found a small post office in the central square, but there was no one in it. Sadly, it did not occur to me to send postcards (there were some poor quality ones on display) to anyone.

Of greatest interest to me were the Touareg. These 'blue men', as they were called by the French, were very like Arabs. Their robes of blue (both men and women) and the men's blue turbans and veils made them look sinister and mysterious. The women wore much silver jewellery and some of the men had ornate swords and daggers.

I had told my host that I wished to see the Touareg in their encampment and he duly produced an elderly man, all in blue, who spoke Arabic. He was known as the Hajji, and told me that, as a young man, he had gone on a pilgrimage to Mecca and, on the way back, had been seduced by the bright lights of Cairo and had decided to stay there.

However, after some ten years in Egypt he was missing the clear open world of the Sahara and his people. He had therefore returned to his family and reverted to the life of his youth. The tribe was impressed to have a Hajji among them and he had become the learned guide, interpreter and elder.

"It is a great pleasure to me to speak Arabic again, Hajji" I told him. "Especially the Arabic of Egypt. I was educated there, you know."

He opened his eyes in astonishment. "Oh *khawaja*," he said. "It is truly wondrous to speak to someone from a far country in the language of the Prophet, blessings upon Him."

He added that it would be an honour to introduce me to his tribal group, which was encamped, for a month or two, just outside the town. Sarr said that he preferred not to come, and that he would try to go fishing.

Hajji brought two donkeys and we rode out to the camp. It looked much like the Bedouin camps of southern Iraq, which I had visited with my uncle, Dr. Max, as a boy during the war. The striped, woven walls and roofs, the angled poles and the carpeted floors were familiar. A number of camels wandered about, hobbled and trying to find bits of grass and bushes to eat. The fine white sand everywhere, except for a few patches of gravel round a small clump of palms.

Two Touareg on camels came riding up, swaying with the peculiar one-sided gait of the animals, and stopped beside us. They were true Touareg, as I had always imagined them: dark blue robes and turbans, and veils which hid all but their eyes. When one of them adjusted his cloak, I could see that his arm and hand were tinged with the same blue.

Hajji spoke to them in his own language, explaining who I was. He must have been flattering, for they made the gesture of salaam, and nodded their heads. I had been staring with fascination at the accoutrements of the camels: hanging braided woollen strings in many colours, shaped leather saddles with a cross-shaped saddle bow, and ornate swords. Each man carried a long, thin stick with which to encourage his camel. I tore my eyes away and bowed back.

I noticed that some women were busy round a cauldron which was steaming over a fire. Hajji noticed me looking and said: "Come and see. This is a very important thing in Touareg life. These women are making indigo dye for our clothes."

We approached the women who stared at us curiously but went on with their work. They were tall and handsome, of a light brown colour and unveiled. One of the younger ones stared boldly at me.

"They gather the leaves of the plant and boil it in the special pot. When it has been sufficiently simmered, they strain the leaves and some other things out of it and it is then a golden brown." I looked into the cauldron, but the dye was a pale blue. "But it is blue," I said.

Hajji laughed. He said: "It is very young still. It starts like that then goes green, then pale blue, then a darker blue." He pointed to a heap of brown cloth, which looked like a loosely woven wool, and said: "When the dye is ready, they will steep the cloth in it, and it will come out blue. The darker the blue, the more it is valued so the good cloth has to be put into the vat many times – sometimes twenty – and allowed to dry between dips."

He added: "Indigo is the best natural dye in the world. But it stains and after a while our skin gets blue as well. But it is good for keeping the insects off."

The sun was burning and I kept wiping my face, while he seemed unaffected. "You must come into the shade," he said kindly. "We will sit and refresh ourselves."

He ushered me into a tent, where we sat on colourful woollen cushions on the carpet. There were some attractive hangings on the walls.

A young boy came in carrying two glasses of milk. I thanked him and downed mine in a gulp. I realised it had the familiar tang of camel's milk, which I had not drunk for some fifteen years. I found that I still enjoyed it. Then there were small glasses of sweet mint tea, which also aroused nostalgic thoughts.

Some men entered and sat with us. Conversation was difficult, since everything had to be translated by Hajji. They had unfastened their veils and revealed lean, fierce faces with aquiline noses and thin lips. Except for a band round the eyes, the faces were strongly tinged with indigo. I felt somewhat underdressed, wearing my usual kit: colonial French abbreviated khaki shorts, a khaki bush shirt and low boots. The Touareg looked dignified and imposing, squatting in their voluminous, dark blue robes and turbans.

Hajji translated for me. I had asked how they managed to cross the Sahara using only their camels. The men replied that a true Touareg could live indefinitely with just camels and dates. "The camel is a miracle given to us by Allah. He carries us willingly across the sands, he provides us with milk, with meat, with warmth at night. His dried dung lights our fires and his wool gives us cloth, while his hide makes us saddles and many useful objects. Dates can last many months and give sustenance and richness. With a few oases which we have known for centuries, we have water. After all, a journey to Morocco only takes six weeks or so."

Hajji added: "Touareg caravans have crossed the desert for a thousand years. They have brought salt from the north and exchanged it for gold and hides from the south. In the old days there were also slaves."

The afternoon wore on and soon it was dusk. I had been regaled with many glasses of tea and small, sweet cakes. The generosity was overwhelming but I felt it was time to go.

When I said this to Hajji, he shook his head and said: "The men have told me you should stay a while. There is to be a wedding celebration soon and they wish you to be present."

I agreed readily. I wondered what a Touareg wedding would be like.

I was led to another tent, this one much decorated and festooned with coloured cloths and hangings. The men sat at one end on the carpet. The other end was partitioned off with a brightly striped hanging.

After a while, the bride was led in. She was unveiled and wore a dark blue robe with a multicoloured head-dress. She was hung about with silver jewellery and her eyes were thickly outlined with *kohl*. I noticed that her hands, in the Arab tradition, were decorated with complicated patterns in *henna*. She looked solemn and her attendants, also splendidly attired, led her to the top of the central part and sat around her. There was the occasional strident ululation by women, both inside the tent and outside, which normally announces joy or tragedy.

The music started. I had not noticed that in a dark corner there was a group of men who began to play. There was a *djembe* drum, two men playing flutes, a 21 string *kora* harp and calabashes to give additional rhythm. The music was somewhat monotonous, but improved as the seated men began to chant.

After some time, the bridegroom was ushered in. He, also, was splendidly attired in his dark blue robes and turban. At his side there was an ornate sword and dagger. He was not veiled. His friends led him to sit beside the bride – neither took the slightest notice of each other.

After another few minutes, an old man stood up in front of the bridal pair and spoke to them. One of her companions handed the bride a round loaf of bread while the bridegroom took the dagger, in its silver sheath, out of his belt. The pair then exchanged these items, while the old man continued a monotonous tirade. It was quite a solemn moment: the music had stopped, as had all conversation.

It was then that I disgraced myself. I had now been sitting, cross legged, for quite a long time and I got a vicious cramp in one of my calves. I could not help myself; I sprang to my feet and hopped round on one leg, trying the massage the offending limb at the same time. I stumbled over Hajji and fell to the ground.

Everything had frozen and was still. A multitude of puzzled black eyes looked at me. I bowed and smiled shamefacedly, and sat down again, with an aching leg. The ceremony proceeded.

It appeared that the marriage had taken place. There was a buzz of conversation and a line of about ten women came into the tent. They lined themselves up and began to dance. The two women at each end had a curious instrument, like a one-stringed violin, which they sawed at with a sort of bow. It made a nasty noise, like a tortured cat.

The dance, which Hajji told me was called the *takamba*, involved sinuous, serpentine movements of the body and arms, while the dancers sang a song which, to me, was tuneless. The audience, however, seemed appreciative and began to clap their hands in a slow rhythm.

After a while, the partition at the end of the tent was pulled aside and revealed large platters of assorted foods: barbecued kid, fish, millet, rice, couscous and varieties of fruit. There were large wooden bowls of camel milk and some cheeses made from it.

The men formed a large circle round the feast and began to eat. The women made their ululating sound, but did not join us. I noticed that the bridal couple had disappeared and asked Hajji where they were. He grinned and replied: "They have waited a long time. They have their own tent and will not come out of it for a day or two. No one may disturb them."

Then it was time to go. There was a full moon and it was quite light. We rode our donkeys back into town, feeling full, and happy for the young couple. I had thanked the chief of the tribe (he was not called a sheikh) and he had said he was glad I could come. I also gave him, after asking Hajji if I could do so, several high denomination franc notes and asked him to give them to the bridal pair. He accepted them gracefully and thanked me.

As we rode, Hajji said: "The houses and buildings in the town are interesting; they are different from the other towns."

"Why?" I asked. I had noticed they were somehow less African and more Arab in style.

"They were not designed by local people," explained Hajji. "Long ago we brought, in our caravans, Moorish architects and builders from Morocco. This is the same style as in the Moorish buildings in Spain and North Africa – that's why they are different."

On the way to my lodging, he took a roundabout route to show me the elaborate and ornate silver decorations on the doors of some old houses. They glittered in the bright moonlight and were very beautiful.

I said goodbye to him at the door. "I am most grateful to you, Hajji, for everything you have done. You have shown me many wonderful things. I hope your tribe will prosper and your camels multiply."

He grinned. "It was a good thing for you to know, *khawaja*," he said. "It was also a pleasure to converse again in Arabic. Peace be with you and may you wake healthy," he added, using the formal Arab phrase.

I replied in kind: "May you be of the healthy people. Upon you be peace."

He rode away on his donkey, leading the other one. I went to bed and slept soundly.

In the morning, Sarr appeared. We exchanged stories of our activities. He listened to mine and shrugged his shoulders. "Savages," he said, in his usual way. I asked him how his fishing had gone, but he did not want to talk about it, beyond saying sourly that he had caught nothing, his net was always empty, and he had been mercilessly stung by innumerable insects.

I decided it was time to go home. I had satisfied my curiosity about the Niger and I had visited Timbuktu. Now I wanted to hurry back to Wendy and the children; there was so much to tell.

We crossed the river and found the Explorer unscathed, though filthy, with sand everywhere. Our friend the guardian came up to me, grinning, and pointed proudly at the car, nodding his head. I gave him the other half of the banknote and a little more besides and he seemed happy.

We retraced our steps, as far as we could remember. We passed through Mopti, stopping briefly to lunch with the Flauberts, who were interested in my account of the journey. Monsieur puffed his pipe and said: "Well, you were lucky. Me, I prefer to go comfortably by river."

Then on to Djenné, where we tried to find Amadou, but it seemed he was away somewhere. As we took the main road, through Bamako, Kayes and home and I drew up outside the house at dusk, I thought the trip had been very worthwhile though It had taken us twenty two days, longer than I had planned.

Wendy was very happy and relieved to see me home; when I was delayed she had begun to imagine the worst. I felt rather guilty at my self-indulgence, though I was pleased when Diallo said: "Master, a great journey. You are now a true explorer."

We soon settled down to the routine life we were forced to lead. Wendy said that she had seen the de Freschevilles, who had been very kind, and had spent a lot of time at the beach, often with our Brazilian and Swedish friends, and had been riding again. She and the children were deeply suntanned.

The children were a constant delight. Nikki was showing great intelligence and had very much a mind of her own. She was always curious and demanded detailed explanations of everything. She was a pretty and active little girl and made the house seem brighter. Robin, now relatively stable on his legs, remained his usual placid, cheerful self. He seemed to derive great pleasure from the world around him, and gazed with interested wonder at anything new.

When Wendy and I had first met in Cambridge, she had had no interest in children or domesticity, as she was intent on being a famous theatre director. Once she had decided she wanted to marry me instead, however, she had evolved rapidly into an outstanding wife and mother. Her intellect and cultural interest had not been diminished by this, but rather enhanced. She was a fascinating companion and friend as well as a very attractive and feminine woman – in a bikini she made heads turn. Altogether, it was a wonderful family and I was immensely proud. I also felt that they were much more than I deserved.

The news from home seemed all good. My stepfather Ronnie had been enticed out of retirement by BP, who had been asked by the Government to start up and launch the Middle East Association in London. This was to be a meeting place and focus of business interest between Great Britain and the rapidly developing countries of the Middle East. Ronnie had agreed, and found a delightful house in Duke Street, St. James's to be office, centre and place of entertainment and hospitality for meetings. There was a small, but luxurious flat attached, where he and Mother would live.

Mother was ecstatic. The appointment would not only alleviate any financial pressures, but would also enable her to play the *Grande Dame* – after years of being number two behind Aunt Ina in Baghdad – in her own right. She would be meeting and entertaining top British businessmen and diplomats, as well as many elevated personages visiting from the Middle East. There would be domestic staff and a reasonable entertainment budget; a far cry from the slightly straitened circumstances of the commuter belt.

Aunt Ina, meanwhile, after the death of my beloved Uncle Max, having decided to settle in England (her other choices might have been Vienna or Paris), had sunk the modest capital she had managed to salvage from Iraq into a lease on a house in Clarges Street, off Piccadilly. The very genteel and selective bed and breakfast establishment she had set up appeared to be thriving.

Wendy's brother had married his long-standing girl friend and moved to Oundle School to begin his career as a teacher. Wendy's parents were beginning to look for a house on the South Coast, since D was nearing retirement, and M missed her gardening in the flat in Hove. Thus the home front seemed to present no worries.

I wrote a brief report to the Company, not particularly mentioning my trip to Timbuktu, but stressing my activities in Senegal. As usual, there was no response.

Then, soon after my return, Luc came to see me; a visit that was to change our lives. Wendy and I were sitting and chatting.

Diallo was in the kitchen and Robin was happily asleep on *fatou's* back as she washed clothes in the little concrete yard at the back. Nikki was at her school.

"So you have done it again," he said, settling himself down in his usual chair, and having greeted Wendy. "The buzz is that you have been swanning around Timbuktu, surveying hippos and crocs, and all on the Company's time."

"Just doing my no-job," I said. "It was very interesting. I was a sort of ambassador for Shell," I said grandly.

"Yeah, yeah," said Luc. "All for the good of Shell, right?" He stopped for a moment. Then he looked at us.

"Listen," he said. "This is serious; pay attention." He leaned forward and lowered his voice. "As you know, there has been a sort of campaign against you. But if you move quickly, you could improve things for yourself and the family."

"What are you talking about?" I asked. "What should I do?"

"I have heard, confidentially, that two staff people have been suddenly sent back to France – some kind of fraud, I think – and this means there is a chance for you."

"I still don't understand," I said, puzzled. I looked at Wendy; she shook her head.

"But can't you see that this means there will be two spare houses – and one of them is in Bel Air, near the installation and tank farm. One has been grabbed already and they are proposing to give the Bel Air one to a slimy character I don't like, a bachelor, who has been sucking up to Morineau, the Personnel Manager." He looked at me meaningfully. "If you ever want to get out of this hovel, you have to move now and get tough."

Wendy stood up. I had never seen her so cross before. "A bachelor!" she exclaimed loudly. "A bachelor getting a house while we live in this place?" Her voice rose. She glared at me. "How can you just sit there and do nothing? This house is airless and unhealthy and stiflingly hot, there is no green anywhere and there is drumming all night long. I am worried that Robin is not very well, and we are all getting thin and sickly. A bachelor is going to get a house with a garden while a family with small children live here? Go and do something!... NOW!... PLEASE!!"

I thought for a moment. What Luc said was true. I had to do something to get the family out of the slum in which we were living – anything would be better. Give the house to some bachelor when I had been writing constantly to Morineau, asking for different accommodation? It was outrageous! I began to be very angry. Luc leaned back; he could see the effect Wendy's words were having on me. "Go to it," he said. "Go and yell at Morineau."

I jumped to my feet and rushed out of the house, scattering the resident lepers and beggars on the pavement. I jumped into the Explorer and drove furiously to Head Office.

I skidded to a halt outside the main entrance and, leaving the Land Rover, rushed inside, past the startled doorman. I bounded up the stairs to the Personnel Department and rushed through the big room with staff working quietly at their desks. They looked up, startled, as I made my way towards Morineau's office and crashed open the door, pushing past the secretary, who was vainly trying to stop me. By now, I had completely lost my temper, for only the second time in my life.

Morineau was at his desk, speaking with the very man who, Luc had told me, was going to get the last house. The bachelor! As I burst into the room, with the secretary gabbling behind me, Morineau jumped up and stood behind his desk, with his shoulders pressed against the wall. The other man retreated hurriedly to the far end of the room.

I do not remember clearly what I said or what I did. I do remember, however, that I crashed my fist on the desk and yelled that I had had enough, that I was not going to stand any more and that I wanted a proper house for my family. I then turned to the other man and bellowed that if he did not give up his claim to the house, I would kill him.

The man promptly sidled out of the office and Morineau, who had gone rather pale, made placating gestures at me with his hands. After some minutes, I realised the enormity of what I was doing, and my rage began to subside. Morineau sensed this, and gestured me to a seat, while resuming his chair behind the desk.

"No decision has been made about any house," he lied fluently. "In fact, I was just exploring possibilities." He stroked his moustache. "It had not occurred to me that you might wish to have that house – I presume you mean the one in Bel Air – since that would mean changing your job. The house is for an installation worker."

"I don't care," I said loudly. He was not going to get away with it. "I don't have a proper job anyway; you made sure of that. I can't afford to fly my family home, or I would have gone long ago. But unless I get this house, by God I am going to make it hot for all you bastards when I get to London." By then I had thrown all caution to the winds.

Morineau flapped his hands up and down. "Calm yourself, calm yourself," he said. "If you are willing to become Assistant Manager of the installation, you can have the house. But then, there is no question of travelling." He added: "Authorised or not."

"I accept," I said. "But only if it happens immediately. I am not prepared to wait and get fobbed off."

"This week," said Morineau. "You will be told when to move."

I did not thank him. I simply got up and walked out of the office. The staff outside did not seem to have moved since I went in. It was clear they had heard every word and were in a slight state of shock.

When I got home, Luc was still there. I told him and Wendy what had happened and that we would be moving in a day or two and that I was no longer an Inspector. I could see that Diallo was listening in the kitchen. Wendy hugged me.

"Come," said Luc. "Let us take the children and go and look at the house." Nikki was back from school. Wendy was as keen as I to go, so we got into the Explorer and Luc directed us to Bel Air.

The area was a pleasant one, not far from the sea. It was almost next to the Shell installation and depot, where fuels were stored in huge tanks and there were mountains of drums which contained a variety of products. Luc directed us down a little cul-de-sac, a short road lined with flowering trees and with a row of houses down one side. On the corner there was a small block of flats, then some two-storey houses and finally, at the end, where the road stopped, a nice looking bungalow. It stood in its own garden, with a garage and a little extra house at the back, presumably for a servant. There were *flamboyant* trees everywhere, some shrubs and flowers and the garden was enclosed with a wall. Beyond were fields and, some distance away, the ocean.

We stopped and Luc said: "Well, here it is."

Wendy and I and the children got out of the car and gazed about us in wonder. This was more like it – memories of happy times in Chile came flooding back. We all hugged each other, the children not knowing quite why but realising how happy we were, while Luc looked on indulgently. We poked about: the house was empty but locked, so we peered through the windows. There was a cool breeze from the ocean, there were birds singing and it was very quiet.

Wendy sighed. "Oh, yes." She said. "This is the house for us. I can hardly wait to move."

To my surprise, Morineau was as good as his word. The next day, one of his junior clerks appeared with the keys and said we could move when we liked. I was told to see the Installation Manager, who would explain my new job. I was also told to return the Explorer to the Company garage – I was no longer entitled to Company transport – there was a small pick-up which Installation people could use.

We wasted no time, and were quickly ensconced in the bungalow. Diallo was very pleased with his little house at the back and pronounced himself satisfied with the kitchen and the house. "I am happy, Master, that now you can live properly. It will be good for the children," he added.

The bungalow was fairly spacious, cool and with a breeze blowing through the open windows. The furniture was an improvement, particularly the cloth-covered chairs which replaced the hot yellow plastic monstrosities in the old house. Above all, there was a blessed silence – no more noise and shouts and drumming from the compound behind our house, separated only by a concrete wall. The children were particularly delighted with the garden, where they could run about in greenery and fresh air.

Parting with the Explorer – and Sarr – was painful. Naturally, he had heard of the fight I had had with Morineau – the office telegraph was very efficient – and when he had helped us with the move, walked with me a little way outside the gate.

"Chief," he said. "You are a good man and I think you are my friend. I thank you for my time as your driver; it has been a happy time for me, even if you are a bit crazy." He grinned. "I will give our car back and then I will leave Shell. I have saved enough now for a wife and maybe I get a small workshop so I can live. I do not wish to be a driver for a different man."

"You do not need to thank me," I said. I was much moved. "You have not been my driver; you have been my friend and companion and I have learned much from you. I am grateful – we will share many memories." Sarr nodded. "I hope you are doing the right thing in leaving Shell. But if you can have a wife and a business of you own, I think you will be happy."

Sarr nodded again. "It is just as the *shaman* said, you remember? He said I would have what I wish within a year. So all will be well."

He took both my hands. "Be well with your family Monsieur Michel Arnold. Allah guide you and bless you."

I squeezed his hands. "Peace be with you, Sarr M'Bayc Diouf. *Ba souba akjam*, goodbye."

Sarr nodded again, climbed into the Explorer, and drove down the road. I stood and watched him go until he disappeared round the corner. I would miss them both.

I walked round to the Installation, about half a mile away. This was quite large, with a tank farm, storage areas for drums and hoses, a loading rack for tanker lorries and a small, whitewashed office building. There were pipelines criss-crossing the area. The whole was enclosed in a high, chain link fence, with a large gate which stood open. There was no one to be seen, although it was mid morning.

I went to the office building and entered a large, bare room, with two desks and some filing cabinets. At one of the desks there was a Wolof clerk. He was elderly, with grey hair and a lined face. A small man, dressed in a white robe, he was given dignity by gold-rimmed spectacles perched on the end of his nose. He was pecking away at a typewriter, but looked up when I came in.

"Yes, Monsieur?" he said after a moment.

"My name is Arnold," I replied. "I would like to see the Manager, please. I shall be working here."

"Ah, yes, Monsieur Arnold. We heard yesterday that you were coming. I would like to bid you welcome." He stood up.

"*Jam nga am?*" I asked. "Are you in peace?"

He smiled broadly and nodded his head. "*Jam rek*," he said politely. "Only the peace."

We stood for a moment, grinning at each other. Then he came forward and we shook hands. "My name is Hamood Abdulaye, but everyone calls me Ham," he introduced himself. "I am the chief clerk here," he paused, "in fact, the only clerk. I sort of run the place." There was a pause. "Under the direction of the Manager, Monsieur MacMann, of course."

I was astonished. "MacMann?" I said. "Is he French? Or perhaps English?"

"Oh, no," said, "Monsieur MacMann is from Scotland, I think. He is not English. He gets very angry if you say so." Well, I thought, so there is someone from Britain already in the Company. Why had I not heard of him?

Ham pointed to a door. "That is his office," he said, indicating a door. "But be sure to knock and wait before you go in."

I went to the door and knocked. I paused, but since there was no answer, opened it and went in. I had obviously not waited long enough, for I saw a man hurriedly taking his feet off the desk and trying to hide a bottle of what looked like whisky in a drawer.

"What do you want?" the man said, in execrable, broken French.

"My name is Arnold, and I have come to work here and help you," I said in English.

"Och, is that it?" he asked in a strong Scottish accent. "To help me, is it? And who says I need help?"

I noticed that he was slurring his words badly, and was obviously drunk. I was rather surprised, since it was only about eleven in the morning. He was a short, tubby man, of uncertain middle age, with a red face and slicked back black hair. He was dressed in a rather grubby set of white shirt and shorts, with sandals on bare feet.

"I was told to come," I said. "Can you tell me what I am supposed to be doing?"

"Aye, well," he mumbled. "I've no time for that. Go ask Ham and the bloody Corsicans and find out for yourself. I am busy. Leave me alone." He leaned back in his chair, and closed his eyes. I left the room and went back to Ham.

He raised his eyebrows and said: "How was it?"

"I don't understand. Monsieur MacMann is not interested. He told me to ask you and some Corsicans what I should be doing." I paused. "Is he always like that?" I asked.

Ham nodded sadly. "Yes, Monsieur. We try to disturb him as little as possible. The work is not difficult."

"But what about the Corsicans?" I asked. "Who are they, what do they do, why Corsicans?"

"Ah," said Ham. "We have about ten expatriate engineers, mechanics and technicians working here. They seem mostly to come from Corsica. They do not like the Frenchmen – they call them *metros* – and they keep themselves to themselves. They are very stiff, angry people. The other French seem to be scared of them. Then we have labourers; they are all Wolofs and very good men. There is no trouble."

He turned. "Come, you must meet them. They are all having their morning coffee in their room."

He led me to another door and knocked. There was a growl and we went in. It was a large room, with a big window looking over the gate and the main forecourt. There were scattered tables and easy chairs about and a group of men in blue work overalls was scattered round, sitting and drinking coffee from large mugs. As we went in, they turned as one and stared at us,

"What do you want, Ham?" asked one, in heavily accented French. "We are having our break."

Ham indicated me and said: "Excuse me interrupting, but I wanted to present Monsieur Arnold, who has come as Assistant Installation Manager. He wanted to be made known to you."

One of the men, a tall, thin individual with bristly black hair and an olive complexion, stood up and came towards me. "Are you French?" he enquired.

"Or from Scotland?" said another.

"No, I am English," I said. I knew the Corsicans disliked the French, whom they considered foreigners occupying their island, so I added: "No more French than you are."

There was a murmur of agreement, and several of the men began talking to each other. It was not French, but sounded curiously familiar – I later found out that, among themselves, they spoke *Corsu*, a language related to Catalan and Tuscan. I was never able to learn any, since they refused to speak it with outsiders.

"Go away, Ham," said the tall man. "Get back to work." He turned to me. "Sit and have a coffee and we will tell you what we do here." He pointed to a chair. "Not French," he growled. "That is good. They are learning."

He introduced himself as Monsieur Poulani. No forenames were ever used. Even men who had known each other and worked together for years always said Monsieur and the surname. It was an incredibly formal society. The names were very Italianate, and tended to end in –ni. The accent was that of Marseilles, many words ending in g and with r being rolled, as in Scotland. It was altogether a new linguistic experience, which gave a tinge of Marseillais accent to my French, which I have never been able to eliminate.

Monsieur Poulani said, while the others listened and growled approval at intervals, "I will explain. There are certain ways of doing things and making things work. This Installation is not complicated and we have been running it for a long time. We do not accept outside discipline and, since everything works properly, we wish to be left to do it." He took a sip of his coffee. I had been given a mug: the liquid was black, sweet and hot – there was no choice.

He continued: "Monsieur MacMann leaves us alone and does not interfere, so we do not make trouble. You, also, should not intervene – if you have questions, you can always ask and we can discuss and explain. But we take no orders. People who try to change things do not last very long." There was nodding and growling. I was entranced. It was a completely new experience, far removed from anything I had ever known.

"There is no reason why I should do anything to change the

way things are done," I said. "You know everything about this Installation and I know nothing. I do not know why I was sent here – I am a marketer, not a technician. I shall be wholly dependent on your work and good judgement." Flattery worked when faced with high odds against you.

There was a murmur of approval. "Then you are welcome and we shall get on well together," said Monsieur Poulani. "The work is simple: we receive bulk products in tankers at the port, which pump them ashore to our tanks. We control the tanks and load tanker trucks which come to us. The *bougnouls* do the manual work, and Ham keeps the accounts. Monsieur MacMann keeps himself busy in other ways."

"Everything seems under control, then," I said. "I will just watch and try to learn everything." Monsieur Poulani nodded. "But what about Head Office?" I asked.

"They keep well away. Ham sends in the figures and the reports – Monsieur MacMann even told him to sign in his name."

I was amazed. There appeared to be no control whatever of anything outside the main office which was astonishing, given the French penchant for rigid hierarchy and formal discipline.

Then, as though some signal had been given, the men all rose and left the room, scattering around the Installation. Two tanker lorries came in for loading, a number of labourers began rolling drums around and there was activity everywhere. I went and sat near Ham and looked at some files, to understand the operations and quantities.

When I got home that evening, I told Wendy about the amazing way the business was being run and she found it hard to believe. But it was a pleasure to sit down at a proper table, with the children, and have an excellent – though modest – dinner, prepared and served by Diallo.

After dinner, Diallo came and stood before me. "May I speak to you, Master?" he asked.

I hated being called Master, but he insisted. "Of course," I said. "What is it?"

Diallo looked embarrassed. "Well, you see, Master," he said hesitantly, "I am a sort of Elder, a sort of Judge in my own tribe in Guinea. So people come to me for advice and for arbitration of problems. There are some of these people here in Dakar..." He stopped, looking worried. "They still want to come to me," he went on after a moment. "Now I have a small place behind the house, do you mind if they come to see me there?" He paused again. "They will be very quiet and not disturb you in any way."

I looked at Wendy. She was smiling. "Of course not, Diallo," I said. "Of course we don't mind. In fact, we are proud that you are such an important person."

Diallo sighed and smiled. "Thank you," he said. "You will not be troubled." He looked embarrassed. "There is one other thing..."

We wondered what else he would ask.

"May I bring my wife and small son to live in the house with me?"

We told him that we would be delighted to have his family living there, and were in time duly introduced to a tall, gracious lady and small bashful and well-behaved little boy.

From then on, we noticed that there was a number of visitors who quietly made their way to Diallo's little house through our garden. They never made any noise and never came when Diallo was busy with his duties. This fresh evidence of his elevated status made it even more puzzling why he should have chosen us as his employers, and for a very modest wage. His family lived their own quiet life, independently of us.

Diallo built a chicken coop in one corner of the garden, and fed us fresh eggs. He also killed the large puff adder that came to eat the chickens.

Our social life was as it had been throughout. Apart from the de Freschevilles and the Fernandez, we did not meet any French people. Wendy's beach friends, the Brazilians and the Swedes, invited us from time to time to glittering embassy parties. It was strange to move, if only for a few hours, in the elegant and opulent diplomatic world – a stark contrast with our own extremely unpretentious and impoverished existence.

But we did invite them back to the new bungalow and had simple, informal meals, often in the cool shady garden. Diallo, who had apparently been employed at some embassy or other (he was reticent about his past) would don his ceremonial uniform of immaculate black trousers, a white jacket with shining brass buttons on the front. He also wore white gloves. His stately and practiced serving of a party dinner lent it an air of great dignity and ceremonial.

For a month or so, I behaved very cautiously in the installation. The Corsicans regarded me with great suspicion and, while not actively unfriendly, gave me the impression that I was not to be accepted into their society. I therefore spent much of my time with Ham, learning about procedures and accounts and sometimes chatting with the labourers and tank truck drivers, most of whom spoke some French. Of MacMann I saw very little. He kept to his office, arriving late and leaving early – sometimes not coming in at all. On the few occasions I spoke to him, he looked befuddled and rather confused.

One day Ham said to me: "There is a tanker coming in to unload gasoline and aviation fuel." I told him I was interested to see this.

"Go and speak with Poulani," he advised. "See if he will take you along."

I found Poulani near the loading rack. "Tell me, Monsieur," I said. "Will you be supervising the unloading of the tanker?"

He looked me up and down, rather suspiciously. "Yes," he said. "Why?" He was a man of few words.

"Perhaps you would not mind if I came to see how it is done. I would like to learn and perhaps I can help."

He thought for a moment. "Very well," he said. "But you must be careful." He had already told me that the greatest risk in the installation was fire and that there were extremely strict rules of safety. In fact, one of the labourers had been summarily dismissed, the previous week, for carelessly bringing into the installation a box of matches with a packet of cigarettes. All visitors had to leave such things at the gate and the only smoking permitted was in the office, where the matches, lighters and cigarettes were permanently kept.

We went to the port in the pick-up. There was the tanker, moored at the Shell loading dock. Some Corsicans had already connected our pipelines to the ship with hoses and the pumps were going. Poulani led me up the gangplank and to the Captain's cabin – it seemed they were old friends.

The Captain, a short, stocky man with receding grey hair, was Dutch. "Hola, Monsieur Poulani," he said jovially. "Back again, you see. Sit and have some Jenever."

Poulani introduced me and the Captain shook hands. He had a fierce grip and a habit of pushing his face up close. "Ah, an Englishman," he said. "Good." He turned to Poulani, "And how is the Scotsman? As usual, is it?" Poulani nodded.

The drink was fierce, burning its way down my throat. There were some biscuits and some ham. Poulani looked at the papers of the shipment and explained them to me in a surprisingly patient and kind way. The Captain sat there drinking and making the odd sarcastic comment.

When we left, having signed for the product, the Captain gave us each a bottle of Jenever, which I bore proudly home.

Life settled down to a pleasant routine. It was a real pleasure to sit in our bungalow, to have regular hours with time to be with the children and watch them grow. The house was mostly cool and Diallo looked after us. Then there was the beach at weekends, and frequent visits to the de Freschevilles, who had become close friends. But I did rather miss Sarr, the Explorer and adventures in the bush.

The houses in our short street were mainly occupied by people connected with the Installation. On the far corner, there was a block of flats, in which lived most of the Corsicans. Then there was a two-storey house occupied by Poulani and his family. Then two more, very similar; one occupied by MacMann, who lived alone and the other, to my astonishment, by an Englishman, called Jerry.

He was a middle aged efficiency expert, who was spending four months in Dakar, to study the accounting operations. The French management in Head Office seemed very distrustful and I believe he was not able to achieve very much. He lived with his wife and three children, rather older than ours, and a nanny. The nanny was in her early twenties, blonde, very beautiful and with a stunning figure. She had the habit of washing one of Jerry's two cars, every morning at about eleven o'clock.

To do this, she would don a microscopic pair of shorts, with bare feet and a loose, white cotton shirt. She somehow always managed to get the shirt soaking wet from the hose, and it left very little to the imagination. We noticed that a significant number of cars would daily drive slowly by around this time, without stopping, turn opposite our bungalow and drive slowly back. But something must have been said, for she departed after about a month. Jerry himself, and his wife, made it clear that they were not interested in mixing with us, and we did not get to know them at all before they left.

My Corsicans were still somewhat stand-offish, but I did get to know some of them. They all had names like Rossini, Valentini, Gallini and so on. I was baffled as to how I could break the ice.

Then, one day after work, I noticed that, behind the flats, there was a group of them apparently playing some sort of game. I strolled over and stood, some distance away, observing. I made no effort to talk or go any closer.

They were playing *boules*, or, as they called it, *pétanque*. It was played in teams of two, each man using two steel balls the size of coconuts, and a small wooden jack, called the *cochonnet*. The idea was to end up as close as possible to the jack.

I watched for a while, but none of them took any notice of me. They exchanged unintelligible remarks, some angry, some pleased, as they played. They used a large, sandy area as their playing field. The *cochonnet* was usually thrown some fifteen yards away.

For three evenings, I stood and watched silently. No one took any notice, though I was conscious of being covertly watched.

On the fourth day, Poulani and Rossini walked over to me.

Rossini, a big, burly man with a large walrus moustache stained with tobacco – outside the Installation he chain-smoked Gauloise cigarettes – looked at me and said, " Eh, Monsieur. You like to play *pétanque*?"

"Well," I replied. "I don't know how to play and I have never seen it before. But if you permit, I would like very much to try."

Rossini turned to the group and called: "Hey, fellows, he has never seen *pétanque*! Shall we let him play?"

The group looked amazed. "Sure, very well, let him come," they called. "Never played *pétanque*! Imagine!"

We walked over together and Valentini gave me the two steel balls. "Throw them as close to the *cochonnet* as you can," he instructed. I did so, and was not too far away. Rossini then gave me his and said: "Now try to knock the other two away and leave yours the closest." I aimed and threw, as I had seen them do; I missed one and hit the other.

"Now," said Poulani, "the one who tries to place the *boules* close is called a *pointeur*, or aimer, while the one who tries to displace the opponent is known as a *tireur*, or shooter. Which do you want to be?"

I said that I would like to see which I could do better and that they would have to be patient with me while I learned. They all nodded and smiled – a rare occurrence – and two of them shook my hand. "You can play with us," said Valentini. This was an enormous compliment and I expressed my gratitude.

The change in their attitude to me, immediately, was amazing. We became friends, they laughed and joked with me and tried to correct my French accent, which they said was too Parisian. "The southern accent is more honest," they explained. Working with them became a pleasure and we shared jokes, cigarettes, and games of *pétanque*, which we played most afternoons.

As time advanced and Poulani saw how much I enjoyed visiting tanker Captains, he said one day: "Why don't you take the tanker deliveries over? I have a lot of other things to do." I thanked him and said I would be glad to do it.

I tried to see MacMann every day, if I could, but the meetings were very unrewarding. He was simply not interested and just wanted to be left alone. He was usually inebriated.

I enjoyed my tanker activities. The Captains were a great mixture: Greeks, Spaniards, Portuguese, Danes and Swedes. They all had their special habits but were, almost all, pleasant, cynical and efficient men. I would sit with them, chatting, as the pumps thumped below us, and eating and drinking whatever national specialities they had on board. I got into the habit of bringing them a basket of mangoes, or a sack of peanuts, or fresh eggs or vegetables as a gift. They would always reciprocate with a bottle of *retsina* or *akvavit, jenever* or red wine as well as hams, olives, cheeses and so on. All these were a very welcome addition to our diet, since these things, while mostly available in the bigger stores – the French still flew bread and ice-cream and so on in daily from France – were so much beyond our means that we had never had any.

I now had only about eight months to go for my twenty month contract and looked keenly forward to the end of my time in Dakar, which I felt had been largely wasted. But life was immeasurably better in our new abode, and I was enjoying the company of my Corsicans.

The wet season was approaching. This ran roughly from June to September, and thus would just about see me out. It was a time of torrential rains, heat and saturation levels of humidity. It had been almost unbearable in our slum but now, with a slight breeze and shady trees, it was not going to be so bad.

Our first intimation that the season had arrived was one morning, when Diallo came hurrying in and began to close the windows and shutters in all the rooms.

"What are you doing, Diallo?" asked Wendy.

Diallo turned. "Madame," he said. "I have been outside and I see a *tornade* approaching. We must take precautions. You should, perhaps, keep the children in the house until it passes."

A *tornade* was a sudden cataclysmic rainstorm, with thunder, lightning, a high wind and torrents of rain. Fortunately, they seldom lasted more than half an hour or so, but left a trail of huts destroyed, streets awash and general chaos.

Wendy and I went outside to see it. From our vantage point behind the house, we could see a long way. On the horizon, we saw a huge wall, miles and miles wide and several thousand feet high, walking across the land towards us. It was purple-black and there were flashes of lightning within it. There was also a deep rumble of almost continuous thunder.

As the storm-wall approached, there was a great stillness: not a breath of wind, the birds had disappeared and it seemed even the insects were hiding. It was very oppressive.

We watched as the *tornade* got closer and closer and ducked into the house at the last moment. Then all hell broke loose.

The thunder crashed overhead, making the windows and doors vibrate, the wind howled and the house shook. But it was the rain that I shall never forget. It fell in a torrent, a cascade, a continuous stream, as though from some giant bucket. There were no individual drops – only a steady and massive bulk of water. Visibility was down to a few feet. We sat with the children and tried to calm them.

But it was soon over. The birds began to sing again, the thunder receded and the wind dropped to its usual ocean breeze. Diallo opened all the windows again. We looked outside and saw that our street was a river, and that there were deep puddles everywhere.

One Sunday, as I was preparing to go fishing, accompanying the family to the beach – normal rain made no difference to our activities – Diallo suddenly asked if he could borrow my shotgun and some Number 7 shot. I was not using it, but what he was asking was wholly illegal. However, he had my absolute trust, so I said: "Take it. I don't know what you want it for, but please don't do anything to make trouble for us or you!" I added.

Diallo smiled in his usual dignified way. "Have no fear, Master. I will not disgrace you."

That evening he came home, cleaned the gun immaculately and offered us three seagulls he had shot. "They are good to eat," he said. "I try to help. I will prepare them."

Wendy and I looked at each other. Seagulls were not something we wished to have for dinner. They would be tough, oily, fishy and unpleasant.

I returned to my favourite excuse. "How kind and thoughtful, Diallo, to do this for us. Sadly, and much to our sorrow, our religion prohibits us from eating seagulls. But it was a wonderful thought; please prepare them for your friends."

Diallo looked disappointed, but agreed. We were very touched by his gesture.

From time to time after this Diallo would ask to borrow my gun, and to have a couple of days off, and would go hunting for us, returning with game rather than seagulls.

The Installation was running smoothly and I had settled into a comfortable routine. The children's health had improved and Wendy had regained a little weight, and was very happy in her new house.

Poulani accosted me one morning. "Monsieur Arnold," he said formally. "Would you and Madame do us the great honour of dining with us?"

I was thunderstruck. My relations with the Corsicans had improved immeasurably since I joined them in their games of *pétanque* on most afternoons, but this was unheard of. The Corsicans all lived in the greatest possible economy, saving every centime towards their eventual return to their island. They lived on the very cheapest food, never bought new clothes or anything else, and sent their children to schools paid for by the Company. They entertained each other very little. But Diallo had told me that, about once a month, they invited one or two couples from the clan to dinner and then pulled out all the stops. Nothing was too expensive or tasteful – it was for the 'honour of the house'. But they never had been known to entertain any one outside the Corsican group.

"We would be most privileged and honoured to accept, Monsieur Poulani. It is most kind of you and Madame."

I had never met any of the families. I had seen them sometimes, as they went out to shop and returned, but had never spoken to them. None had any servants; the wives did everything. They had mostly been there for many years and knew their way about very well.

A date was fixed, and when I told Wendy, she was as surprised as I and as delighted. Diallo was astonished.

On the appointed evening, dressed up in our modest best finery, we presented ourselves at the Poulani house, about fifty yards up our road. The door was opened by Poulani, in a dark suit and big smile, who ushered us in. The house was fairly sparsely furnished, with many African carvings and masks and well worn armchairs and sofa. We were introduced to Madame Poulani, a black haired, sparkly small woman, who shook hands and immediately excused herself, saying she had to go to the kitchen. We sat and Poulani gave us some French *digestif* to drink. Very soon there arrived Valentini and Rossini with their wives, very properly dressed and speaking to each other in a formal manner. They had known each other for at least twenty years.

The dinner was splendid. Course after course of opulent tastes and sauces, everything imported from France. A marvellous soup, grilled fish, a wine-rich stew of plump chickens, puddings, delcious French cheeses and a constant flow of Corsican wine, red and honest. It was the best meal we could remember for years.

The conversation was interesting. I enquired about Corsica, the food, the countryside, the hunting (all the men were avid hunters) and told them a bit about England and Chile. The evening was a happy one and we returned to our bungalow in high spirits. We subsequently invited the Poulanis to dinner, trying to reciprocate their hospitality, but we were not asked again to any Corsican family. Our own dinner was as good as we could manage, a cold Polish soup, roast guinea fowl thanks to Diallo, assorted tropical fruit. Diallo's presence, in his formal dress, somewhat overawed our guests.

About six weeks before the end of my contract, we decided that Wendy should take the children home early; there seemed no good reason for them to stay and the grandparents were clamouring for them to return. Thus I asked Personnel Department for tickets for them and was rather surprised to receive them without comment. Wendy packed almost everything up and said goodbye to her Swedish and Brazilian friends, who invited us to a small farewell party. She also bid a fond farewell to the de Freschevilles and the Fernandez. We all agreed that we would keep up our friendship even after we left Dakar. On the day, after a sad parting from Diallo, I drove them to the airport in the little Renault and saw them safely on to an Air France plane to Paris and London.

Wendy said: "I am not too worried about leaving you alone. You have Diallo and he will take good care of you – he promised. Just be careful, and do not do anything crazy."

The house seemed empty and I was glad to receive a letter from Wendy, saying that the trip had been all right and that the grandparents were ecstatic. This helped a lot and I settled down again, to an uneventful life. Diallo cosseted me and behaved like a nanny.

Then came the night of utter catastrophe.

I was in bed. It was well past eleven when the telephone rang. I climbed out of bed, rubbing the sleep from my eyes. It was Poulani; he sounded agitated.

"What is wrong?" I asked. "It is almost midnight."

"There is a very big problem at the jetty," he said. "You must come at once."

I hesitated, but he was insistent, so I agreed.

It was raining hard. I took my raincoat and drove down to the jetty in our little Renault. Poulani was standing at the bottom of the gangway, waiting for me. There was an overpowering smell of petrol everywhere.

He came up to me as I got out of the car. "You will never believe this," he said. There were some other Corsicans standing around and a small figure, wearing a naval cap, with them. They all looked very wet.

Poulani went on: "The tanker has a full load of high-octane aviation gasoline and the stupid idiots have been pumping the stuff into the harbour. They connected some hoses, which we left here. We told them to wait till morning, as usual, when we would be here to do everything, but the bastards just went ahead. They started the wrong pumps and most of the cargo was pumped over the side." He was furious. "This is the head idiot; may I present the Captain. Everything is stopped now." He spat on the ground. "By the way," he added," I tried to telephone MacMann, but there was no answer."

The Corsicans thrust the Captain towards me – he looked terrified as they glowered at him.

"I am Capitán Moreno," he gabbled at me in a high-pitched voice. He spoke in broken French, with a Spanish accent. "These men want to kill me." He grasped my arm with both hands and tried to get behind me.

He was a tiny man, and looked to be in his late twenties. He took off his cap and rubbed his soaking hair, which stood on end.

"Calm down, Capitán," I said in Spanish, removing my arm from his grasp. "Tell me what you have done."

"We are a replacement crew," he gabbled nervously. "We have never been here before and this is our first voyage. The old crew and officers and captain were on strike so we had to take over in one day. We don't know the ship very well." He paused, and suddenly realised that he was answering me in Spanish. The Corsicans looked on, puzzled.

"We were told we had to hurry and get back to Marseilles refinery very quickly so we thought we would start straightaway."

"Do you realise how dangerous this is? Do you understand the risk we are running?"

I turned to Poulani. "How long did they pump overboard?" I asked. He shrugged eloquently. "I don't know," he said. The watchman smelled gasoline, so he called me. It must be a four or five hours at least."

I thought furiously. What do I do first? This is a major emergency – I am not an engineer or professional depot manager. I made my decision.

"Listen," I said to my Corsicans. "By now there must be an inch or more of aviation gasoline floating on the surface of the harbour. Since it is a horseshoe shape, very little will get out." I paused for breath. "Monsieur Poulani, get hold of the Chief Engineer and tell him what has happened. Monsieur Rossini, tell the Chief of Police that he must immediately cordon off the harbour and get the Fire Brigade standing by. Monsieur Bellini, tell the watchmen to keep everyone away and also tell them to make sure nobody smokes. We are sitting on a huge bomb. Monsieur Valentini, get the Port Captain and tell him what is going on. I will go and tell MacMann. Let us all meet here in half an hour – get as many of them to come as possible." I turned on the cowering Captain. "You, get aboard and order them to turn off all motors and unprotected lights. No man may use lights or smoke on the peril of death!" I could see him trembling as he scurried up the gangway.

I jumped in the car and drove, as fast as I could, to get MacMann.

There was silence in our street as I skidded to a halt outside his house, though the lights were on in the Corsicans' flats and house. MacMann's residence was silent, though I could see a light on in an upstairs room.

I knocked at the door, waited and knocked again. There was no response. I hammered loudly on it but still nothing happened. I tried the handle; the door was open.

I went in and called MacMann's name loudly several times but nothing happened. I went up the stairs, calling loudly. The door to one of the rooms was ajar and I could see there was a light on. I pushed open the door, and went in.

I looked round me. The room was a bedroom, with a large bed in the middle. There were clothes strewn around and several cases of what looked like gin and whisky, as well as boxes of empty bottles against one of the walls. MacMann was in bed, fast asleep on his back, snoring loudly.

I shook the sleeping man roughly by the shoulder, but he did not stir. It was obvious that he was virtually insensible from drink. He started grumbling and moaning.

Deciding that nothing was to be done, I retreated and drove back to the jetty.

Some cars had arrived. There was a man in a police uniform, and the Port Captain, whom I had met several times. The Corsicans were grouped around them, all talking at once and waving their arms.

Then another car screeched to a halt and a burly man got out. He was dressed in a raincoat over a pair of striped pyjamas, and his short, grizzled hair was standing on end.

Poulani immediately went up to him, beckoning me to follow. He introduced me to the man, who was glaring round him angrily. The man was the Chief Engineer of Shell.

He turned his glare on me and said roughly: "What has happened? Tell me what is going on and what you have done about it."

I told him, as succinctly as I could, the story so far and whom I had notified. Poulani stood by, nodding his head.

When I paused, the Chief Engineer – whom I had never met before – said: "All right. I understand. Where is MacMann?"

"I have just come from his house," I said. "I am afraid he is… indisposed. He can't come."

The Chief Engineer looked piercingly at me. "I understand," he said. "This is the end." I later learned that he had sent the police to the house, where they had found Macmann exactly as I had left him.

He strode to the policeman and the Port Captain and greeted them briefly. Then he turned to me again. "I am taking over. Make sure our equipment is safe." He turned away to speak to the others.

I gathered my Corsicans and told them what had been said. "Why is MacMann not coming?" asked Valentini.

"It is the usual," I replied. They nodded.

After a while, the Chief Engineer told us to go home. "The matter is now in hand and being dealt with. There is nothing more for you to do – do not talk about it to anybody."

I went home and recounted the tale to Diallo, who was waiting up for me, with a cup of coffee. He was aghast at the danger of the gasoline on the surface of the harbour. I did not say anything about my visit to MacMann.

In the event, the Port Captain arranged to equip two tugs, with muffled engines and huge padded booms attached to their prows, to sweep the gasoline slowly and carefully out of the harbour mouth, to disperse in the ocean. The harbour, which had been isolated and cordoned off for the whole of the next day, was reopened. The tanker Captain and his First Mate were arrested, though the tanker sailed away two days layer, with different officers. The potential catastrophe had been narrowly averted.

By the end of the day after the incident, MacMann had disappeared. Some days later, a truck came and took away his belongings. I do not know what happened to him, or where he went.

Also that evening, I received a note from the Chief Engineer. It stated, simply, that I was to be, until further notice, Temporary Installation Manager. The postscript said: "This will not affect, in any way, your terms of employment."

The atmosphere in the Installation improved and even the Corsicans began smiling. I authorised Ham to recruit and train a young assistant; he was greatly overworked and laboured away until all hours. Surprisingly, Personnel Department confirmed my new recruit.

The days passed; I spent much time with Luc, fishing, and frequently visited the de Freschevilles, who had taken me into their family.

Two days before I was due to leave, Diallo came into the room. "There is a gentleman to see you, Master." He paused. "A local gentleman." I was puzzled, but said: "Please show him in."

In a moment, the door opened and there was Sarr. I sprang to my feet. "Welcome, welcome, Sarr M'Baye Diouf. What a wonderful surprise. Sit down and tell me what you have been doing."

Sarr had a huge grin on his face. "It is good to see you too, Monsieur Michel Arnold. It has been a long time."

Diallo left the room, looking doubtful Sarr sat gingerly on the edge of a chair. "Chief," he said. "I came to tell you that the witch doctor was right. He said my wishes would come true and they have." He clapped his hands with glee. "I am now married and I have a small workshop which makes a small profit and I am busy." He paused. "I wished to bring my wife to have the honour of meeting you, but she would not come." He shook his head. "She is very young, you know..." he added apologetically.

"Well," I said. "*Chetetetet*! I am astonished and pleased. I congratulate you with all my heart. You deserve it all."

Diallo entered with a tray. On it were glasses of mango juice and some small biscuits. He had realised at once that Sarr, a Wolof, would not drink alcohol. We thanked him and toasted each other, grinning.

We chatted away, exchanging reminiscences of our adventures. But finally he had to go.

"I wish you joy and strength, Monsieur Michel Arnold. I believe you have brought more to Senegal that you are taking away."

I accompanied him to the door. "*Ba suba ak jam*, farewell Sarr M'Baye Diouf. I wish I had something to give you..." Sarr hurriedly backed away, shaking his head, "... but I have nothing. Be happy and have many sons."

It had been kind of him to come and I was very touched.

The day I left, I handed over the little Renault to its new

owner, a young Wolof recommended by Sarr, who paid me a fair price. Luc came to collect me and take me to the airport.

Diallo had said that he would not stay in Dakar, but return to his tribe in Guinea, where he was an important man.

I thanked him warmly for looking after us. "I still cannot understand why you chose to work for such a low wage – so much less than you could get elsewhere – for us. You have made our stay very much happier than it would have been without you." Diallo smiled and said: "I choose very carefully with whom I spend my life. I have been happy with you and Madame – and with your children. Money is not important if everything else is right."

I picked up the shotgun, which was lying, in its case, on my single suitcase. I handed it to him, and said: "Take this as a token of my friendship. I know it is not lawful, but I wish you to have it." I paused and added mischievously: "You can always shoot some more seagulls." We both laughed.

As I left with Luc, he stood at the door and bowed. He was a wonderful person.

The flight was uneventful, and the following morning I landed in London. Africa had been fascinating and exciting. It had also at times been very uncomfortable (especially for the family.) But there had been unforgettable experiences and the valued friendships of Sarr and Diallo, as well as the de Freschevilles. Now it was time to relax; I had not had a holiday for twenty months and was looking forward to my entitlement of four months' leave.

Wendy had rented a little house for us on the seafront cliffs of Rottingdean, in Sussex. It was a pleasant, undistinguished chalet-bungalow, not far from where her parents lived in Hove. Christmas was rapidly approaching, and I looked forward to our family celebrating together in England.

After a week or so, I wrote a comprehensive report on my sojourn in Dakar, stressing the apparent boycott, the penury in which we had lived and the inability, forced on me, to communicate with London or, indeed, leave. I tried to be as objective as possible, but I resented the undeserved inconveniences heaped on us.

I made an appointment to see Patch, in Shell's London office and went up with my report.

Patch received me kindly, and listened patiently to a short version of my tale of woe. She was surprised at the intensity of Shell Paris paranoia and upset at their refusal to remit my pension contributions for almost two years.

"I don't know exactly what can be done," she said, "but I will give this report to the Regional Co-ordinator (a very senior man) and we will see what we can accomplish."

She gave me my usual cup of coffee. "By the way, your new posting has come through," she said casually but with a big smile. "I suppose you are interested."

"You bet I am," I said enthusiastically. "What is it? Tell me!"

"Panama," she said. "It is an interesting one." Oh, not again, I thought. I don't want any more interesting ones.

"There is no Shell company there; we work through an agent. You will be an ambassador and start up a new company." I quailed, but thought, well, four months to think about it.

"We will send you all the information in good time. Leave me your telephone and address. I will be in touch."

Wendy was most excited when I told her about Panama. This time we did not need to get out the atlas, we remembered passing through the Panama Canal on the way to Chile and recalled the happy Latin American atmosphere of what looked a very civilized town with strong North American overtones.

But it was time to relax, to enjoy the family and grandparents, to visit friends and to think about Christmas. The Channel looked grey in the winter sunshine as we looked out over the cliffs. Africa seemed far away.

Postscript

by Wendy Arnold

Sadly the adventures we had in Panama and thereafter will never now be told, nor the next three volumes planned, written.

Mick hugely enjoyed our time in Panama, exploring its jungles, encountering its Indian tribes in the Darien Gap and on the San Blas Islands, and learning many new songs.

Following this we spent an idyllic five years in the pre-tourist era Arabian Gulf, where Mick introduced me to traditional Arab culture, and showed me all the different countries round the Gulf, and Persia, and was happy in his many friendships from rulers to depot workers.

We then returned to Africa, to Khartoum, taking with us our newly-born daughter Tiffany, and this time being able to meet and get to know local people, as Mick travelled up through the deserts and down to the southern swamps.

Honduras followed, its forests still then intact, glorious with huge flowering giants and orchids.

After this Mick left Shell and worked for the Japanese trading house Itocho, commuting monthly to Tokyo while the family lived in a big rambling Edwardian house in Oxford, acquiring from his Japanese colleagues the affectionate double-edged nickname "yokozuna" indicating a (presumably portly) Sumo champion of champions who has gained victory with style.

He left them for his final job with Charter Oil in the USA, where we lived on the edge of a Florida swamp with alligators on our lawn. Here he became friend and informal advisor to several US Senators and two Presidents.

Retiring at fifty, he had time to enjoy being Fellow of an Oxford College, and watch our grandchildren grow up. Ill health finally overtook him, but he lived to celebrate our Golden Wedding with our children and grandchildren, and to give me, as he had promised, the manuscript for this his second book, on my birthday. And then he died, quietly, and with me, at home.

Our son Robin said of him at his funeral:

> *"He was charming, funny,*
> *absurdly generous, learned,*
> *a great raconteur,*
> *salesman, and a*
> *romantic to the core."*

Michael Arnold's 1st Book
A GAME WITH DICE

The true story of a daring
wartime escape, a Royal
friendship and a strange
new life

Michael Arnold

A Game with Dice

"A tantalising mixture of adventure and excitement"
PETERSFIELD POST

"Captivating… laced with dry wit"
PETERSFIELD HERALD

www.heronhillbooks.com